JUDAISM:
An approach for GCSE

C. M. Pilkington

Hodder & Stoughton

A MEMBER OF THE HODDER HEADLINE GROUP

Acknowledgements

My thanks go to the many people who have helped in the preparation of this book. I am especially grateful to Geoffrey Shisler and Geraldine Auerbach, who have afforded me so many opportunities to learn about Judaism. Geoffrey Shisler has read the entire book to check its accuracy and Geraldine Auerbach has produced an audio tape to accompany the book. Thanks are also due to the teachers and students who have tried out various chapters in their classrooms.

The Publishers would like to thank the following for permission to reproduce material in this volume:

BBC Enterprises Ltd for the extract from *Bright Blue* by Reverend Lionel Blue; The Board of Deputies Community Research Unit for the extract from *British Jewry in the 80's*; Faber and Faber Ltd for the extract 'Prayer Before Birth' from *Collected Poems* by L MacNeice; Elaine Green Ltd for the extract from *Proofs of Affection* by Rosemary Friedman, copyright © Rosemary Friedman 1982; William Heinemann Ltd for the extract from *The Chosen* by Chaim Potok; Hodder & Stoughton Publishers for the extract from *Almonds and Raisins* by Maisie Mosco published by New English Library; Jewish Chronicle Publications for the extract from *The Jewish Yearbook*; The Jewish Publication Society, Philadelphia for the extracts from *On Women and Judaism* by Blu Greenberg (1981) and *This People Israel* by Leo Baeck (1965); Penguin Books Ltd for the extract from *The Jewish War* by Josephus, translated by G A Williamson (Penguin Classics, Revised Edition, 1970), Copyright © G A Williamson, 1959, 1969; Piatkus Books Ltd for the extract from *To Live in Peace* by Rosemary Friedman; Reform Synagogues of Great Britain for the extract from *Forms of Prayer*: Vol. 1, Daily & Sabbath Prayerbook, 1977 © The Reform Synagogues of Great Britain, also for the use of their logo; The Union of Liberal and Progressive Synagogues for the extracts from *Judaism for Today* (1978) and *On Zionism and Israel*, also for the use of their logo.

The majority of Scripture quotations contained herein are from The Revised Standard Version of the bible, copyrighted, 1946, 1952, 1971 by the Division of Christian Education of the National Council of the Churches of Christ in the United States of America, and are used by permission. All rights reserved.

The publishers would like to thank the following for their permission to reproduce copyright photographs in this book:

The Ancient Art and Architecture Collection – p28t. Associated Press – p54. Mervyn Cahal – p34r.; cover. J Allan Cash – p51l. Common Ground, Journal of the Council of Jews and Christians – p13. Genut Audio Visual Productions – pp7b.; 29; 39r.; 42; 64; 65; 68r.; 74; 77; 102; 106l.; 124; 131; 136l. 136r.; 152b.; 154; 155; 160. Ray Goodburn – pp19r.; 19l.; 111l. Hanoch Guthmann – p106r. Sidney Harris – p66. Israel Government Tourist Office – p53l. Jewish Chronicle – p73. Leo Baeck College – p46t. Micha Bar Am/Magnum – p53r. Manchester Jewish Museum – p28b. The Mansell Collection – pp144l.; 146. Mike Abrahams/Network – p107. Picturepoint – p39l. Richard J Plunkett – pp76t.; 76b; 80; 112; 118; 148. Juliette Soester – pp44; 46b.; 68l.; 81; 82; 91; 97t.; 97b.; 113r.; 114; 132; 161. Sotheby's – p58. Tel Aviv Museum of Art – p50. Mel Thompson – pp25; 36; 140r. The Wiener Library – p18. Yeshiva University – p15. Zefa – pp7t.; 34l.; 51b.; 59; 111r.; 113l.; 123; 130; 139; 140l.; 144r.; 152t.; 153.

Every effort has been made to trace and acknowledge ownership of copyright. The publishers will be glad to make suitable arrangements with any copyright holders whom it has not been possible to contact.

To my mother
and in loving memory of my father.
'The Lord bless you and keep you.'

Orders: Please contact Bookpoint Ltd, 39 Milton Park, Abingdon, Oxon OX14 4TD. Telephone: (44) 01235 400414. Fax: (44) 01235 400454. Lines are open from 9 am - 6 pm Monday to Saturday, with a 24-hour message answering service. Email address: orders@bookpoint.co.uk

British Library Cataloguing in Publication Data
A catalogue record for this title is available from The British Library

ISBN 0–340–51951–7

First published in 1991

Impression number	19	18	17	16	15	14	13	12	11	10
Year		2004	2003	2002	2001	2000	1999			

Copyright © 1991

Typeset by Wearset, Boldon, Tyne & Wear
Printed in Great Britain for Hodder & Stoughton Educational, a division of Hodder Headline Plc, 338, Euston Road, London NW1 3BH by Redwood Books, Trowbridge, Wiltshire.

Contents

Introduction

To the Teacher

The three parts of this book represent the main thrusts of the syllabuses of all the GCSE examining groups, namely:

I   the foundations and development of Judaism;
II Jewish life today;
III the importance of the ritual year in Judaism.

The six examining groups have their own particular emphases and orders of approach. This book covers all the common elements. It also touches on the few elements which appear in only one group's syllabus, with suggestions for further work.

The chapter starts with a summary of its main points. Within the chapter is extension material with suggested questions and activities which often make greater demands in terms of language or resources. One resource, an audio tape, *Songs and Prayers of Jewish Life*, has been made specifically to illustrate points made in the book. It comes from Jewish Music Distribution. The address for this, and for other audio and video tape sources mentioned, is given at the end of the book. The extension material is provided for those who want to explore a topic further, but each chapter can be read and the questions answered without it.

Questions of fact and understanding come at the end of each chapter. These should be answerable from the information given in the chapter. It is envisaged that the entire chapter will be covered before the questions are tackled, but the relevant section is indicated after each question to enable the teacher to divide the chapter and its questions if desired. Also at the end of each chapter come questions of evaluation. These relate closely to the chapter, but more to the whole than to one particular section. There is also a suggested assignment for each chapter, designed to encourage progression from fact, through understanding, to evaluation. A short vocabulary section at the end of each chapter helps students to build up their knowledge of the main Hebrew words needed for their study of Judaism. All these words are explained in the word list at the end of the book.

Teachers should find sufficient ideas here to suit the requirements of the different examination groups. The questions can be supplemented by my pack of worksheets, *Understanding Judaism at GCSE* (Hodder and Stoughton, 1989), which concentrates, as the title suggests, on the important GCSE objective of understanding, in its various spheres defined by the National Criteria. The worksheets include quotations from the Bible and the Talmud which are useful for students to keep in their own notes.

Most of the biblical quotations in this book are taken from the Revised Standard Version.

Rather than giving in full all the many biblical passages referred to, I have assumed that the resource of a Bible will be available for students to look up references.

GCSE is still evolving. This is particularly so in the area of criterion referencing, where grade criteria relate to skills which the students are expected to show. The study of religion involves the cognitive skills of investigation, analysis, classification, application, and evaluation. Also vital are the affective skills of empathy and self-understanding. This book seeks to develop these skills in relation to what is distinctive in Judaism.

To the Student

Judaism is a living faith. This book aims to help you explore this faith: the challenges which it presents, the responses to issues of belief and morality which it offers, and the questions of human experience which it raises.

To understand a religion such as this you have to try to get into other people's shoes. Many of the concerns of this book can arise outside Judaism, and outside any religion, but your task is to think about the religious response to these concerns, and specifically the Jewish response. For example, you could express an opinion about the value of the Sabbath as a day of rest without reference to anything religious, but if you are truly thinking about Judaism you will need to consider how observing the Sabbath expresses the Jewish religion. This needs knowledge of the long history and development of Judaism, of the ways in which Jewish people live, and of the meaning of special days in the Jewish Calendar.

This knowledge can be acquired in many different ways, for example, from your teacher, from artefacts, and from visits to Jewish communities or buildings. Knowing something, however, does not necessarily mean that you understand it. There are many areas of understanding which you will need to develop. When studying the Passover meal, for example, understanding should include:

a) symbolism (e.g. the Seder plate) and the meaning of terms (e.g. Haggadah);
b) the Torah and Talmud as sources of religious belief and practice;
c) Jewish beliefs about the role of the people of God;
d) the value of freedom and the means by which freedom may be achieved;
e) ways in which the lifestyle of Jews outside Israel expresses the sense of community and of belonging to a delivered people;
f) fundamental questions about suffering in a world created by God.

Understanding Judaism should enable you to evaluate it, that is, to make your own personal reflections on Jewish beliefs, values, and practices. You may, of course, already have some views about these matters, but the hope is that, as you know and understand more about Judaism, your views will reflect a greater sympathy for other people's standpoints and a greater understanding of your own.

THE JEWISH PEOPLE AND HISTORY

People of God: In Ancient Times

- The Jewish religion began with Abraham, who believed in one God who would make from him a great nation.
- God entered into a covenant (agreement) with Abraham and later with the whole people, represented by Moses at Sinai.
- This covenant was based on God delivering the Children of Israel from slavery in Egypt. They were to live fully by God's Law (the Torah).
- After many years travelling through the wilderness, they settled in the promised land of Canaan.
- At first, leaders called 'judges' ruled the Twelve Tribes of Israel, but then, beginning with Saul, they were ruled by kings.
- King David made Jerusalem the capital, and King Solomon built the first Temple there.
- After Solomon, the kingdom divided into the northern kingdom of Israel and the southern kingdom of Judah.
- Both kingdoms were brought to an end: Israel by Assyria and Judah by Babylon. Many people went into exile.
- A new start was later made in Judah and a second Temple was buiit.
- There were further conflicts, first under the Greeks and then under the Romans, who destroyed the second Temple.
- The focus of Judaism was then the Torah and the hope for the Messiah developed.

A) What Is Judaism?

If you were asked to define Communism, pacifism, vegetarianism, or sexism, you might begin by outlining its main ideas. An 'ism' is a distinctive theory or system. If you try to define any of these 'isms', however, it will all seem very abstract and difficult, possibly even unimportant. For what really matters are people and what they do. Yet, how people think and what they believe will surely affect what they do. If they believe in the superiority of their sex, for instance, they are likely to demonstrate this by treating a member of the opposite sex as less capable or less intelligent. If we are the targets of this particular 'ism', we are likely to view it in very practical terms.

When it comes to the term 'Judaism', we shall be well advised, right from the start, to think in practical terms. Some religions (Christianity, for example) tend to define themselves in terms of beliefs. Judaism does not do this. Indeed, the word 'Judaism' was not widely used until the 1880s, and only then to distinguish it from other 'isms' or religions. Judaism is the religion of the Jews and, as we begin to study it, we must direct our attention straight away to the people. What Jewish people do, based on what they believe, is Judaism. Not all Jews, of course, are religious. Some are Jews by virtue of the fact that they are born Jewish, and they themselves may not hold to specific Jewish beliefs and practices. Our study lies, however, with Judaism, the way of life of the religious Jew. Jews belong to many different nationalities. We shall concentrate on British Jewry and its main institutions and expressions. To begin to understand these, however, we need to delve deep into history.

According to Genesis 11, Abraham left Ur with his father and settled in Haran. There God said: 'Go from your country and your kindred and your father's house to the land that I will show you. And I will make of you a great nation.'

B) When Did It Start?

WORLD HISTORY		JEWISH HISTORY
Ancient World		*Biblical Period*
Egypt united	2000	Abraham
Pyramids		
	1500	Moses – Exodus
Raamses II		Hebrews enter Canaan
	1000	Saul, David, Solomon
Assyrians		Northern Kingdom falls
Babylonians		Temple of Solomon destroyed – Exile
Persians	500	Return
		Second Temple built
		Ezra and Nehemiah
Greeks		
Alexander the Great		
Antiochus IV		Maccabees
Roman Empire		*Age of the Rabbis*
Pompey		
Augustus		Hillel and Shammai
	0	Jesus of Nazareth
Nero		Jerusalem revolt
Vespasian		Ben Zakkai – Yavneh
		Second Temple destroyed
Titus		Masada
Trajan	100	Akiva
Hadrian		Bar Kochba
Antoninus Pius	200	Mishnah
Constantine		
Fall of Rome	500	Talmud

Before the Common Era (BCE).

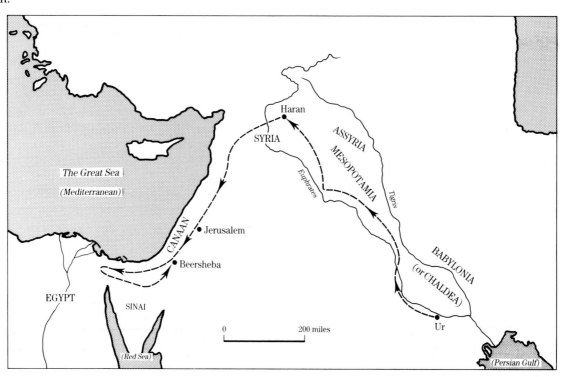

Though the term 'Judaism' is comparatively recent, the Jews are an ancient people, over 3000 years old. Their history is told in the Bible, and the first book, Genesis, traces it back to Abraham. (Read the opening verses of Genesis 12; 15; and 17 for details of God's promises.) Abraham was a nomad from Mesopotamia who obeyed God's command to go to the land of Canaan. You will see from the map on page 2 that this is the country now called Israel. In your studies, you will notice that the country has different names in different periods of its history: Canaan, Israel, Judah, Judea, Palestine, and finally Israel. It is also sometimes referred to as the Holy Land. The name of its people also changes. The word 'Jews' was not used until the sixth century BCE. Before then the Jewish people were called Children of Israel or Israelites and, earlier still, Hebrews (see, for example, Genesis 14:13; Exodus 2:6).

Already it is clear that what the Bible offers us is no ordinary history. Its writers are not simply historians, but also men of faith, believing in a God who communicates his purposes to his people. In answer to the question: 'Who started everything?' the Bible says: 'God'. This introduces us to the first and most important idea of Judaism: God – not many gods, as most people of ancient times believed, but one God.

The story continues with God speaking not only to Abraham but also to his son, Isaac, and to Isaac's son, Jacob. These three men are known collectively as the patriarchs (fathers) and their wives as the matriarchs (mothers). Abraham, in particular, is still called by Jews 'our father Abraham'. The third patriarch, Jacob, is renamed 'Israel' (Genesis 35:10), and this becomes the name of his people and, later, of their land.

C)   The Covenant People

The Book of Genesis tells us that God entered into a covenant with Abraham and later with Isaac (15:18; 17:2,7,19). A covenant is an agreement between two parties. In a covenant, both parties, such as a man and a woman in marriage or two countries in a trading agreement, commit themselves to looking after each other's interests. Throughout the Bible, and throughout later Jewish writings, runs the idea that God made a covenant with the nation of Israel. He rescued them from slavery and made them his people, to have a particular knowledge of him and of what he requires, to have a special relationship with him and to witness to other nations. The clearest expression of this central Jewish belief comes in Exodus 19:4–6.

> You have seen what I did to the Egyptians, and how I bore you on eagles' wings and brought you to myself. Now therefore, if you will obey my voice and keep my covenant, you shall be my own possession among all peoples; for all the earth is mine, and you shall be to me a kingdom of priests and a holy nation.

From the period of the patriarchs, it is with the establishment of this covenant with the whole people of Israel that the entire story is concerned.

D)   In and Out of Egypt

Jacob and his twelve sons migrated to Egypt to escape a famine. Several generations later, the Israelites were enslaved by the Egyptian Pharaoh. From this oppression, a man called Moses felt commanded to deliver his people. The account of Moses' encounter with God is recorded in Exodus 3. You should read the whole chapter, noting especially the assurance that God cares about the sufferings of his people and wants to bring them to the land promised to their fathers, 'a land flowing with milk and honey' (verses 7–8).

The following chapters of the Book of Exodus tell the story of the eventual going out (which is what the word 'exodus' means) from Egypt. The Exodus is the major event in Jewish history and is celebrated annually at Passover. Several weeks after crossing the

Red Sea (or, more accurately, the Sea of Reeds), the Israelites came to Mount Sinai. We are not sure of its exact location, but notice the general area of Sinai on the map. It is here that God revealed himself to Moses, giving him the laws by which the covenant people were to live. All these laws are known by the Hebrew word **Torah**.

God tells Moses his name: 'I AM WHO I AM'. What do you think this might mean? Jews today believe God's name is too holy to be spoken and so they call God **Adonai** (Lord).

Torah means more than the rather cold English word 'Law'. It means 'teaching' or 'direction'. The Torah is seen as God's direction for people's lives. The idea is not that God makes all sorts of demands on people to spoil things for them. Rather, Jews believe, there is one God who has created the world with a purpose, and this purpose is fulfilled when people recognise and obey him.

This depends on another central belief of Judaism: God is not an absent or indifferent God. He has revealed himself. According to the **Talmud** (the collection of Jewish teachings compiled about 500 CE), part of the Torah is not only for Jews. God, the creator of all, is believed to make demands on all. So the Talmud includes the Noahide Code. These are laws given to humanity, as represented by Noah (see Genesis 9:18–19). This Code has seven basic principles, which can loosely be summed up as:

- To have only one God and not to worship idols;
- To lead a moral life and not to commit adultery or incest;
- To behave with fairness and to have law courts;
- To play a useful part in society and not to commit murder;
- To be honest and not to steal;
- To be kind to animals and not to cause them unneccesary pain;
- To have respect for God and not to blaspheme.

Non-Jews who live by these moral and spiritual precepts are called 'the righteous of the nations of the world'. Judaism stresses the freedom and responsibility of each individual for his or her actions. So everyone has the choice of whether to serve God by obeying his laws. Non-Jews are given the basic seven laws and Jews the whole Torah. There are 613 laws in the Torah which, of course, include the basic seven. Clearly, the demands made on Jews are much greater than those made on the rest of humankind, and that is the point of the covenant which they accepted at Sinai. From then on, they were a people under Law.

E)   The Promised Land

Jews refer to Moses as 'our teacher Moses'. It is through him that the people received the Torah. Moses did not live quite long enough, however, to lead the Children of Israel into Canaan. After leaving Sinai, they wandered for 40 years through the wilderness. The Israelites finally entered the land, long since promised them, under the leadership of Moses' successor, Joshua. According to the Book of Joshua, he won some major victories over the then occupants of the land, the Canaanites.

Conquest took time, however, and a succession of leaders, known as 'judges', led the Twelve Tribes of Israel through many crises.

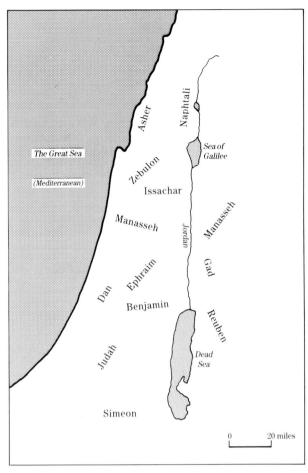

Israel in the time of the judges. Note the names of the Twelve Tribes, each descended from one of Jacob's sons.

In the time of Samuel, the people decided that they wanted a king to unite them, and so a monarchy was established.

The first king was Saul. We are told that Samuel anointed him as king, that is, he poured oil on his head as a sign that he was set apart by God for a special task (1 Samuel 10:1). The king was to be God's representative in ruling his people according to God's laws. Successive kings were all regarded as God's 'anointed', in Hebrew **mashiach**. The most famous king in Israelite history is David, not least because he captured the city of Jerusalem and made it his capital (see 2 Samuel 5:1–10).

Solomon, David's successor, built in Jerusalem a Temple. Until then, the Israelites had only a temporary structure as a sanctuary in which to worship God. After Solomon's death, the kingdom was divided. The tribes of Benjamin and Judah formed the southern kingdom, which they called Judah. The remaining Ten Tribes formed the northern kingdom, Israel.

At the heart of Solomon's Temple was placed the Ark of the Covenant, a box containing two stone tablets on which were engraved the Ten Commandments.

The Books of the Prophets (see Chapter 3) tell us about the history of the two kingdoms with their succession of kings. They also tell us about the rising up, in times of crisis, of prophetic figures who rebuked the people, and often the kings, for failing to uphold the moral and spiritual standards by which, at Sinai, they had agreed to live. There was always the temptation to adopt the ways of other nations, especially when the superpowers, notably Assyria and then Babylonia, threatened. Eventually, Israel fell to the Assyrians in 721 BCE and Judah to the Babylonians in 586 BCE. The promise of the land seemed to be over as its Temple lay in ruins, and many of its people were taken into exile in Babylon.

F)   A New Beginning

When the Persian ruler, Cyrus, defeated the Babylonians in 538 BCE, he allowed any people who had been exiled to return to their native lands. Though some Jews chose to stay in Babylon, others returned to Judah, to start the difficult task of rebuilding the Temple. This was completed by 515 BCE. Foremost amongst those who gave direction in the fifth century BCE were two Jews from Persia: Nehemiah and Ezra. Nehemiah, governor of Judah, supervised the physical rebuilding of Jerusalem, notably the city walls.

Ezra, a scribe (an expert in the Jewish Law), supervised the spiritual rebuilding of the nation. He read the Torah publicly, requiring the people to swear:

> an oath to walk in God's law which was given by Moses the servant of God, and to observe and do all the commandments . . .
>
> (Nehemiah 10:29)

Among these were the commands to keep the Sabbath and not to intermarry with non-Jewish people now living in Judah (Nehemiah 10:29–31). If the Jewish people were not to be exiled again for disobeying God, it was considered important that they maintain the purity of their religion.

Why do you think the escape of thousands of Jews from Iraqi oppression in 1950–1 was called 'Operation Ezra and Nehemiah'?

G) A Challenge from the Greeks

By 323 BCE, the ruling power was no longer Persia but Greece, under Alexander the Great. This powerful ruler tried to unite his subjects under Greek ways and beliefs. This process of Greek influence, called Hellenisation, brought some benefits to the Jewish people of the time, but it also posed a threat. There was the temptation to abandon Jewish tradition and adopt Greek ways.

After Alexander's death, his empire was divided among different rulers. The land of the Jews, by now called Judea, became part of the Seleucid (that is, Syrian–Greek) Kingdom. In 175 BCE, Antiochus IV, the ruler of the Seleucid Kingdom, stepped up attempts to force the Greek religion on the Jews, who had remained faithful to belief in one God. He proclaimed himself a god and urged the Jewish High Priest, who in effect governed Judea, to spread Greek influence among the Jews.

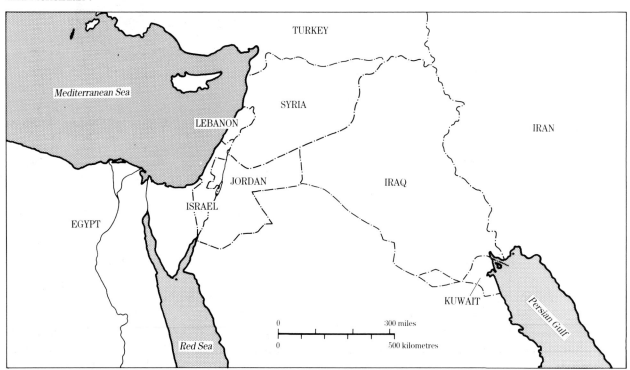

In the following years, Antiochus became quite fierce in his hatred of the Jews, for example, banning circumcision, the study of the Torah, and Sabbath observance. He placed a statue of the god Zeus in the Temple court. Finally in 167 BCE, he ordered that pigs be sacrificed on the high altar. This sparked off a rebellion led by Mattathias, a priest in Modin, a town outside Jerusalem. Mattathias and his five sons launched guerilla attacks on the Greek units. After Mattathias' death, the loyalist Jews were led by his son Judah, nicknamed 'Maccabee'. The name 'Maccabee' means 'hammer' and probably refers to Judah's heroism in 'hammering' the Greek forces.

By 165 BCE, Judah and his men had gained control of Jerusalem. There they restored and rededicated the Temple. After the Maccabean Revolt, the Jews set up their own monarchy, which lasted until the Romans occupied Jerusalem in 63 BCE.

H) Under Roman Rule

Roman rule was to last for the remainder of the country's ancient history. In 37 BCE, the Romans appointed Herod as king of Judea. His extensive elaborations to the Temple in Jerusalem included mounting a huge golden eagle, the symbol of the Roman Empire, on its gate. (Can you think why this would be so offensive to Jews?) There was always the possibility of rebellion, and in 66 CE, one Jewish group led a revolt. These were the Zealots, who were violently opposed to Roman rule.

The war was a long one. The most crushing defeat came in 70 CE with the destruction of Jerusalem and the second Temple. But still small groups held out in the wilderness. The most famous of these made a last stand in the fortress of Masada. All pockets of resistance were destroyed by 73 CE and the so-called Jewish War came to an end.

Masada has taken on the meaning: 'Israel will never fall again.'

A Roman coin commemorating the end of the Jewish War showed a proud Roman soldier beside a weeping widow. On it were the words *Judea Capta* (Judea captured). To celebrate its tenth anniversary in 1958, the State of Israel minted a coin with the words *Israel Liberata* (Israel Freed). Notice the illustration of freedom.

Even so, there remained fierce Jewish resistance and, in 132 CE, Simon bar Kosiba freed Jerusalem from Roman rule for three years, before his revolt was crushed and he was killed. The revolt is known as the Bar Kochba Revolt. Simon had been given the name 'Bar Kochba' meaning 'son of a star'. After 135 CE, many Jews were forced to join the dispersed communities (the Diaspora) living in other countries, notably Babylon.

I) The Torah Remains

In the first century CE, there were different groups of Jews. By far the largest of these was the Pharisaic party. Their study of the written Torah and their detailed working out of its meaning, the oral Torah, became the essence of Judaism, enabling it to survive when the Temple perished. Most influential among the Pharisees were Hillel and Shammai, who both founded schools for the study of the Torah; Jochanan ben Zakkai, who set up a centre at Yavneh (Jamnia) where, about 100 CE, it was decided which books of the Hebrew Bible were regarded as sacred scripture (see Chapter 3); and Akiva who, besides suffering martyrdom in the Bar Kochba Revolt, was a man of great scholarship. The title that came to be given to these Jewish teachers was 'Rabbi'.

J) What's to Come?

On the basis of what we have seen so far, it should now be apparent that the three fundamental ideas of Judaism are God, the Torah, and Israel (both the people and the land). There must surely have been many times when the Jewish people longed for God to rule the world, to establish his kingdom. As time went on and the kings of Israel failed to live by God's laws, the hope grew for a descendant of David who would truly show the qualities of an anointed king and usher in God's reign of peace. The roots of this hope for a Messiah (Mashiach, 'anointed one') are in the Bible. Look especially at Isaiah 11:1–10.

It was not until the time of the rabbis, however, under the difficulties of Roman rule, that the Messianic hope became fully developed. From the thinking of the rabbis there emerged the idea of a human figure who would be sent by God to bring in an altogether new era. All the peoples of the world would

Extension Section

i)   Rabbi Akiva is the hero of *The Source*, an historical romance by James Michener (Secker and Warburg, 1965). See what you can find out about him from this or other books.

ii)   The following extract from *The Jewish War* by Josephus, a Jewish historian of the first century CE, gives a vivid picture of the Roman destruction of the Temple:

> *While the Sanctuary was burning, looting went on right and left, and all who were caught by the Romans were put to the sword. There was no pity for age, no regard for rank; little children and old men, laymen and priests alike were butchered; every class was held in the iron embrace of war . . . Through the roar of the flames as they swept relentlessly on could be heard the groans of the falling . . . Many who were wasted with hunger and beyond speech, when they saw the Sanctuary in flames, found strength to moan and wail . . .*

Turn to Chapter 16 and find out when and how Jews commemorate this event and to Chapter 6 to see when and how Jews celebrate regaining the whole city of Jerusalem. What do you think about such annual remembrances?

iii)   Another Jewish sect in Roman times was the Essenes. Find out about them. Many books will give you information, especially books on the Dead Sea Scrolls. The Essenes are generally believed to be the community who lived at Qumran, by the Dead Sea, where the scrolls were found.

be united and recognise God. The dead would be resurrected. So the Pharisees believed, though another first-century Jewish group, the Sadducees, rejected the idea of resurrection.

There have been people who have claimed to be the Messiah at various times in Jewish history, notably Bar Kochba and, in 1665, a

Turkish Jew called Shabbetai Zevi. Jews believe, however, that the Messianic Age has clearly not dawned. Many Jews pray daily for its coming and with it the rebuilding of the Temple and the restoration of the sacrificial system. Others emphasise not so much the traditional details and a particular figure as an age when people will live in a world filled with the peace and justice looked forward to by Isaiah.

Questions

A Matter of Fact

1 When did the term 'Judaism' become widely used? (A)

2 What name was originally given to the Jewish people? (B)

3 Give the two names of the third patriarch. (B)

4 What is the Exodus? (D)

5 State two of the Noahide laws. (D)

6 Which nation defeated the Babylonians in 538 BCE? (F)

7 When was the second Temple built? (F)

8 When did the Maccabean revolt begin? (G)

9 Which Jewish sect believed in armed resistance to the Romans? (H)

10 What happened in the following years CE:
a) 37; b) 70; c) 132? (H)

11 Where did Jochanan ben Zakkai set up a centre for learning? (I)

12 Which group developed the biblical idea of God's kingdom into the Messianic hope? (J)

Vocabulary

Give the Hebrew words for the following:

1 teaching or direction (D)

2 anointed (E)

A Question of Understanding

Try to give at least two religious explanations in answer to each of the following questions.

1 Why is it appropriate to describe the Bible as a book about God and his people? (B)

2 Why, according to the Bible, does God make a covenant with Israel? (C)

3 A Victorian nanny is reported to have said: 'Go and see what the children are doing and tell them not to.' Why would it be misleading to suggest that God, giving the Torah, resembles this nanny? (D)

4 Why were keeping the Sabbath and not

intermarrying important to Jews after the return from exile in Babylon? (F)

5 Why was Antiochus IV fiercely opposed by the Jews of his kingdom? (G)

6 Compare Isaiah 2:1–5 and 9:6–7 with Isaiah 11:1–9. How are these passages linked with belief in a Messianic Age?(J)

Over to You

Answer these questions fully, giving your reasons, and stating arguments both for and against where appropriate.

1 How important do you think it is for Jews to know their own ancient history?

2 'A Judaism without God is no Judaism. A Judaism without Torah is no Judaism. A Judaism without Jews is no Judaism.' Do you agree?

Assignment

Choose one person or group of people significant in ancient Jewish history. Then

Either:

a) Design and write a page of a newspaper, imagining you were there at the time of the events.

Or:

b) Prepare a presentation (with appropriate pictures and music) for your class.

In either case, bring out:

i) what the person(s) did;
ii) why it was important;
iii) your personal reaction to it.

Possible resources are Volume 1 of *Chronicles*, a set of imitation newspapers covering the period from Abraham to Ezra (from JEB); slides of Masada (from the Slide Centre); David Kossoff's novel *Masada* (Fount, 1975); *Living Judaism*, a tape–slide sequence (from the Council of Christians and Jews).

2

People of God: In Medieval and Modern Times

- In medieval and modern times, Jews were scattered across the world. Jews originating from eastern countries were called **Sefardim** and those from western countries **Ashkenazim**.
- Their treatment varied greatly from country to country and period to period. In medieval Spain, for example, Jews at first flourished under Muslim rule. Christian rule in the Middle Ages often meant religious persecution, though there were spells of tolerance and freedom.

- As the modern period began, with the French Revolution, persecution became racially rather than religiously based.
- Such anti-Semitism culminated in the Holocaust, the destruction of six million Jews in Germany and German-occupied countries.
- This changed the Jewish world dramatically, wiping out major centres, notably Poland, and challenging long-held beliefs about God's purposes for his people.

A)   Still God's People?

In ancient times the Jews lived in Palestine, Babylonia, and Egypt, the area which we now call the Middle East. In the Middle Ages, Jewish communities continued in these places and, as we shall see in Chapter 4, they exercised enormous influence on the development of Judaism. Nonetheless, our geographical horizons need to widen considerably if we are to understand Jewish life and thought in medieval and modern times. Jews are now scattered throughout the world. Each country has a different history and needs to be considered separately.

However, this is not a history book and our interest is not simply with historical facts, but with what these events meant for Jews and

their faith. In the twentieth century came the most shattering event in Jewish history, the Holocaust. The twentieth century also saw the historic founding of the State of Israel. We should remember that neither of these events came 'out of the blue' and we need to pick out from the long history of medieval and modern Jewry some of the most significant moments.

B)   Spain in the Early Middle Ages

In the first century CE a new religion emerged in Palestine. This was Christianity. In the seventh century came the beginning of another religion, Islam. Interaction between the adherents of these two religions, Christians and Muslims, became crucial in Jewish history. For a long time, Christianity was viewed by the Romans as a threat, but in 312 the Emperor Constantine converted to Christianity. He then made it increasingly difficult for Jews to practise their faith and to exercise their full rights as citizens. Such restrictions continued even after the collapse of the Roman Empire in 410.

Islamic rule, which by the eighth century extended from India to Spain, brought for some time much better conditions for Jews.

WORLD HISTORY		JEWISH HISTORY
Empire of Islam		*Golden Age*
Middle Ages and Renaissance		*Persecution and Expulsion*
Dark Ages begin	500	Age of Gaonim
Muhammad		
Muslim conquests		
	1000	
		Rashi
Crusades		Crusader massacres
		Maimonides
	1300	
		Expulsions from England and France
		Inquisition
		Marranos
Renaissance begins		
Columbus		Expulsions from Spain, Portugal
Michelangelo	1500	
Reformation and Enlightenment		*Age of the Ghetto*
Luther		Ghettos established
Rise of Protestantism		
Catholic Counter-Reformation		
		Shulchan Aruch
Galileo	1600	Settlement in Holland
Thirty Years' War		
		Shabbetai Zevi
Cromwell		Settlements in England, America
Enlightenment begins	1700	Chasidism
		Vilna Gaon
		Germany – Moses Mendelssohn
American Independence		
Modern Era		*Age of Uncertain Freedom*
French Revolution		Emancipation
Napoleon		
Industrial Revolution	1800	Non-Orthodox movements
Communism, Socialism		Russia: Haskalah – Repression – Migration to U.S.
		Dreyfus Case – Herzl – Zionism
World War I	1900	Balfour Declaration
Russian Revolution		
World War II – Nazism		Holocaust
United Nations		State of Israel established
"Third World"		Arab-Israeli wars

We are today so accustomed to the presentation of Jews and Arabs as mutual enemies that it may be hard to understand why the period of Islamic rule over the many Jews in Spain is referred to as the Golden Age. The reason is that Jews and Arabs both flourished, learning from and inspiring each other. The Arabs had a flair for mathematics and the sciences, and in the area of literature, too, Jews owed much to their Muslim rulers. There was a flowering of Jewish poetry and philosophy. One of the great poets of this period was Judah Halevi (1021–69) and the most famous philosopher was Rabbi Moses ben Maimon (1135–1205), called Maimonides. We shall see his impact on Jewish thought, as he tried to combine the idea of divine revelation with that of human reason, at many points in future chapters.

The life of Maimonides illustrates, however, how fragile were the good relations between Spanish Jews and Muslims. Fanatics insisted that Maimonides either convert to Islam or leave the country. He left and eventually settled in Egypt. Nor was Islam the only threatening religion. From the late eleventh century until the fourteenth century, Spain was in turmoil as Christianity and Islam struggled for supremacy.

C) Europe in the Middle Ages

Most of Europe was ruled by Christians, with power concentrated in the Church and the aristocracy. Under their head, the Pope, Christians began military campaigns against the Muslims in control of Jerusalem. These campaigns were known as the Crusades. Though directed at Muslims, the Crusades involved violent attacks on Jews encountered by Christians on their way to Palestine. Once they reached Jerusalem, the Crusaders not only killed their main target, the Muslims, but also burnt alive the Jews in their main synagogue.

Even the preparations for the Crusades whipped up hostility to Jews. A notorious instance of this was in England in 1190. As the armies of Richard I (the Lionheart), set out for Palestine on the Third Crusade, they stirred up grudges against Jews in towns along the east coast of England. Trapped in Clifford's Tower in York, many Jews took their own lives rather than surrender. Others were killed by the Christian mob.

Jews and Christians gather at Clifford's Tower in 1988 for an act of remembrance and reconciliation. Why was such an act necessary? What thoughts on this might have been in the minds of those pictured here?

The roots of such resentment against Jews in England and other European countries were both religious and economic. The Church at that time taught that the Jews had killed Christ and that their Passover ceremonies involved the blood of Christian children. The second accusation is called the 'blood libel'. Jews outside Muslim Spain were barred from many professions. There was one particular job, however, which they were encouraged to do, and that was money-lending. Nowadays, those requiring capital for some business venture turn to bankers, who lend them money and charge interest. In the Middle Ages, Christians were forbidden to lend at interest, and so non-Christians were very useful middlemen between the people needing to borrow and those with the money, namely Christian princes. The Jews became such middlemen and consequently were despised, as people resented being in debt and accused Jews of charging excessive interest rates.

Though some Christian leaders spoke up for Jews, the dominant attitude of the Church was hostile. Laws were passed by the medieval Church to keep Jews in a state of humiliation. Jews were compelled, for instance, to wear a special hat or yellow badge so that they could be clearly identified and kept separate from Christians. These decisions (many of them taken at a series of meetings known as the Lateran Councils) became canonical law, the law of the Church. Sadly, they later provided Nazi Germany with a model for its Nuremberg laws.

D) Expulsions

Not content with isolating and humiliating their Jewish populations, many rulers tried to enforce conversion. We have already seen the refusal of Maimonides to convert to Islam. There were also attempts to convert Jews to Christianity.

In Spain, 'disputations' were held. These were informal debates, conducted by a government official, between a representative of Judaism and a representative of Christianity, each trying to demonstrate the truth of his beliefs. The Jew was placed in an impossible position, as presenting a weak case left him open to scorn and presenting a strong case made him seem a threat to Christian power. Some Jews were consequently compelled to leave Spain. Others chose to be baptised into the Church rather than face persecution. Many of these 'new Christians', both in Spain and Portugal, remained secretly loyal to Judaism. The Catholics hated them because of both their attitude to Christianity and their professional success. They called such Jews *Marranos*, 'pigs', and tried to root them out in what is termed the Inquisition. Finally, in 1492, King Ferdinand and Queen Isabella of Spain signed a royal edict, expelling 150,000 Jews. This was not officially abolished until 1968.

For some years, France had been ejecting Jews and then taking them back for their skills. In 1496, however, it too expelled them. Only in the seventeenth century did Jews move back there. Jews had already been expelled from England in 1290. There were no new settlements there until Cromwell allowed Jews to return in the mid-1660s.

Italy did not actually expel Jews, but in 1516 a decree was passed in Venice limiting them to the northern sector of the city. This was the first official *ghetto* (the Italian word for the nearby cannon factory). This simply legalised what had been practised for centuries, namely compelling Jews to live in the less pleasant areas away from the Christian population.

E) The Ashkenazim

Many of the Jews expelled from Spain fled eventually to the Netherlands, where the Protestant Church at first offered greater tolerance than the Catholic Church and its Inquisition. These Jews of Spanish origin were called the **Sefardim**, from the ancient Hebrew name for Spain, **Sefarad**. Jews from other 'eastern' countries were also called Sefardim. To the Netherlands in the mid seventeenth century came also another stream of Jewish immigrants, this time from Eastern Europe. They were called the **Ashkenazim**, from **Ashkenaz**, the Hebrew name for Germany. The Ashkenazim now include French, English, East European, American, and other 'western' Jews. The Ashkenazim had a different experience of the Middle Ages from that of the Jews in Spain. Their two main centres were Germany and Poland.

The fortunes of Jews in medieval Germany varied considerably. Oppression in the thirteenth century led many of them to flee to Poland. There they developed the language known as Yiddish, a German dialect containing elements of Hebrew, Polish, and Russian. Though the language is not widely spoken by modern-day Jews, some Yiddish words are still in common use, such as, **shul**, meaning 'synagogue'. Growing Protestant oppression

A model of Zabludow Synagogue, Poland, 17th century, from the collection of Yeshiva University Museum. During the age of the ghetto, Poland was the main centre of European Jewry. The synagogue, the focus for Jewish community life, helped Jews retain their faith in the face of opposition and persecution.

Sefardim and Ashkenazim.

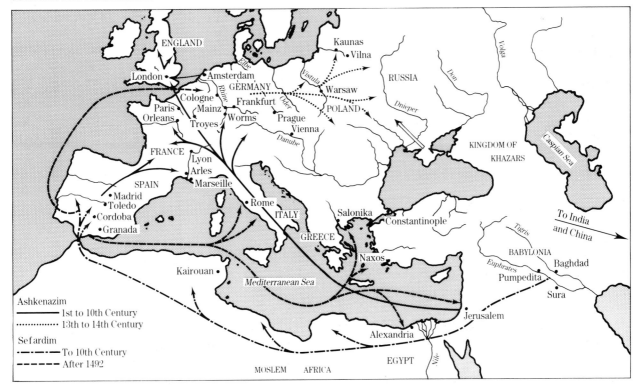

at the time of the Reformation of the Church led to further migration to Poland. Jews were now fleeing from both German Catholics and German Protestants. In the seventeenth century, however, there was a reverse migration westwards, bringing many Yiddish-speaking Ashkenazim back to Germany. There, in the period known as the Enlightenment, many Jews flourished. A notable example of this is Moses Mendelssohn (1729–86). The Enlightenment stressed Science and Reason, and Mendelssohn tried to combine this new secular (non-religious) learning with Jewish thought and belief. He translated the Hebrew Bible into German and became the leading figure in the Jewish Enlightenment Movement, **Haskalah** in Hebrew.

In Poland, too, Jewish fortunes swung. By the mid-sixteenth century, Poland had the biggest Jewish community in the world. There many Jews served as landlords. By the mid-seventeenth century, however, the Ukrainian Cossacks defeated the Polish army and tortured and massacred Jews. Many now fled to Germany. Out of this troubled period in Poland developed the Jewish movement known as Chasidism (see Chapter 5).

Extension Section

i)   Find out more about the Crusades. An encyclopaedia will give you information on routes taken, for example. A story by the Israeli writer, Amos Oz, offers a frightening picture of violence against Jews. Entitled 'Crusade' it is published, together with 'Late Love', a story about an Israeli professor's fears for the treatment of Russian Jews, under the title *Unto Death* (Flamingo, 1986).

ii)   One of the most famous of the disputations took place in Barcelona in 1263. It was between Pablo Christiani and Moses ben Nachman. **Ben** is the Hebrew word for 'son of' (the Aramaic **bar** has the same meaning). The Greek way of indicating 'son of' was to add 'ides' to the name. So Moses ben Nachman was called Nachmanides. Which other example of such a name have you come across in this chapter? There is a film (from CTVC Films/Video Library) about this particular disputation. It is entitled *The Disputation* and features Toyah Wilcox.

iii)   Though the basic practices of the Sefardim and Ashkenazim are the same, there are still differences, for example, of custom and in the pronunciation of the Hebrew language. Listen to illustrations of their different sorts of music on the JMD tape. The tape also includes music relating to particular periods in Jewish history.

iv)   For a portrayal of seventeenth-century Jewish life in Poland, see Isaac Bashevis Singer's *The Slave* (Penguin, 1962). Other books by this Nobel Prize-winning author include *The Manor* (Penguin, 1967), and *The Estate* (Penguin, 1969), illustrating life in nineteenth-century Poland.

F)   France in the Modern Period

The modern period is usually considered to begin with the French Revolution in 1789. This date may not sound very modern, but it marks the beginning of an era in Jewish and in world history. The 'liberty, equality, and fraternity' of the French Revolution came for the Jews of France in 1791 with a decree of equal rights for Jews from the National Assembly. An important figure in implementing such emancipation was Napoleon, who set up a supreme Jewish council. Jewish hopes soon faded, however, after Napoleon's defeat at Waterloo. Jews were again urged to convert to Christianity to escape discrimination.

More dangerous than the flaring up of old religious hatreds was the development of organised anti-Semitism. In the Middle Ages, anti-Jewish feeling was stirred up by pressure groups afraid of losing power and privilege. Often it was the Jew's religion that was opposed. This anti-Judaism was in the modern period turning into hostility towards Jews simply on the grounds of their race. Jews belonged to the Semitic race and the idea was growing that this somehow made them inferior. Worse still, some people concluded that supposedly superior races had the right to exterminate others. This philosophy is usually associated with Adolf Hitler in twentieth-century Germany, but it can be seen to have begun much earlier. Hatred of Jews, not for religious or economic reasons but because of their blood, found striking expression in France in 1894. A Jewish army captain, Alfred Dreyfus, was accused of treason and imprisoned for 12 years before being found innocent. His being Jewish provided sufficient reason for blaming him for France's problems.

G)   In Russia

Similar developments took place in Russia as the modern period began. Russian anti-Semitic activity was formalised by laws in 1795 and 1835. These limited Jews to living in a certain area near the western border. By 1897, five million Jews lived within this 'Pale of Settlement', as it was known. Between 1871 and 1907, there were seven *pogroms* (the Russian word for 'mass violent attacks') on Jews. These received added impetus when, in 1881, the Tsar was assassinated and Jews were blamed. Many fled the Pale to settle in America or Palestine. Some came to Britain, settling in London, Hull, Bradford, Tyneside, Merseyside and Manchester.

The Russian Revolution of 1917 lifted the restrictive laws on Jews remaining in Russia, but the new regime soon launched an onslaught against religion. The resulting persecutions of Jews were for years hidden from the world, with thousands being refused

permission to emigrate. In the 1950s and 1960s, however, more Jews became free to leave the USSR, most of them going to America or to the newly created State of Israel, formerly Palestine. Ironically, the greater freedom granted to Jews, as to other religious groups, in the 1980s and 1990s, has resulted in America restricting the number of Jewish immigrants from the USSR. Visas are no longer automatically granted because, it is argued, Jews no longer need to leave the USSR to escape oppression.

North America, nonetheless, has the largest Jewish community in the world. It began in the sixteenth century, when the Dutch helped Jews to settle in New Amsterdam, later to be called New York. Then there were mass movements of Jews from Russia and Europe between 1881 (the time of the pogroms) and 1914 (the beginning of the First World War). America granted freedom of religion from 1791 and, as we shall see (Chapter 5), was a vitally important country for developments in Judaism.

H)   The Holocaust

The First World War cost Germany dear in men, territory, and money. The inflation and unemployment which followed left Germans desperate for a solution. The party which was eventually elected was the National Socialist (Nazi) Party. In 1933, Hitler became Chancellor of Germany. The solution offered by the Nazis was to remove groups of people who could be seen as a barrier to the restored greatness of Germany. Gypsies and the mentally handicapped were among these groups, but the chief threat to the racial purity of the 'master-race', the Aryans, was considered to be the Jews. Hitler stripped them of their rights by the Nuremberg laws of 1935. A Jew could not, for instance, be a German citizen, exercising a political vote or holding public office. As we have seen, Hitler did not invent anti-Semitism. Racist theories, combined with

A Czech girl about to be deported.

the need for someone to blame, had shown themselves earlier in a number of countries. They now culminated in the so-called Final Solution, the attempted total extermination of the Jewish people.

By 1942, Hitler was at the height of his power, his armies having taken over most of the European mainland and North Africa, and being within miles of major Russian cities including Moscow. Wherever they went, German troops killed the Jews. Those who resisted, such as in the Warsaw ghetto in 1943, were slaughtered on the spot. Others were taken to concentration camps, where most of them were gassed. Altogether six million Jews were murdered. Former Foreign Minister of Israel, Abba Eban, has suggested that, in order to grasp the enormity of this, we think of the Second World War as having three million minutes. This means that for the six years that the German war-machine operated, Jews were killed at an average of one every 30 seconds. This has become known as the Holo-

caust, which means 'widespread destruction, especially by fire'. Jews often call it the **Shoah**, the 'whirlwind'.

I) Responses to the Holocaust

At the time of the Holocaust, most of the world did little to help Jews. Many nations closed their doors to those Jews trying to escape Nazi rule. However, Denmark and Holland defended their Jewish citizens, and individuals rescued and hid them. These individuals are remembered, alongside the six million Jews, at the Holocaust memorial in Jerusalem.

The memorial is called **Yad Vashem** which is the Hebrew for a 'monument'. Yad Vashem is a whole complex, housing, among other things, photographs and belongings of Holocaust victims. An avenue of trees has been formed, called the Avenue of the Righteous, by planting a tree in the name of each 'righteous Gentile' (a Gentile is a non-Jewish person) who helped a Jew. Many people visit Yad Vashem, especially on the day which many Jews set aside as Holocaust Remembrance Day, **Yom Hashoah**. (Its date in the Jewish calendar is shown on p. 127). In some countries, including Britain, there is a charitable trust called Yad Vashem. Like the memorial, it is dedicated to keeping alive the memory of the six million.

Remembering the victims of the Holocaust is thought by Jews of many different experiences and outlooks to be vitally important. Those who surrender their lives rather than betray their Judaism are called 'holy ones', **kedoshim**. Their martyrdom is regarded as 'sanctifying the Name of God'. The Hebrew for this is **Kiddush Hashem**. Those killed in the Holocaust had no choice in the matter. They died simply because they were Jews. Many now try to make sense of this by regarding the whole slaughter as Kiddush Hashem.

The Wall of Remembrance, Yad Vashem. The right-hand sculpture is *The Last March* – the final deportation of Jews to the death-camps – and the left-hand sculpture is *The Ghetto Uprising* – Warsaw, 1943.

Country	Jewish Population September, 1939	Jews Killed	Percentage of Jewish Deaths
Poland	3,300,000	2,800,000	85%
USSR (occupied territory)	2,100,000	1,500,000	71.4%
Rumania	850,000	425,000	50%
Hungary	404,000	200,000	49.5%
Czechoslovakia	315,000	260,000	82.5%
France	300,000	90,000	30%
Germany	210,000	170,000	81%
Lithuania	150,000	135,000	90%
Holland	150,000	90,000	60%
Latvia	95,000	85,000	89.5%
Belgium	90,000	40,000	44.4%
Greece	75,000	60,000	80%
Yugoslavia	75,000	55,000	73.3%
Austria	60,000	40,000	66.6%
Italy	57,000	15,000	26.3%
Bulgaria	50,000	7,000	14%
Others	20,000	6,000	30%
	8,301,000	5,978,000	72%

The Holocaust – the destruction of European Jewry.

There have, in the years since, however, been other responses.

In its magnitude and inhumanity the Shoah is unique. Though others have been slaughtered before, during, and after the Holocaust, the Jews are the only group to have been marked out for total annihilation. Their suffering has seared into the outlook not only of those who survived the death-camps and of those whose relatives were killed but of all who are Jewish.

For those who hold the traditional belief in a good and powerful God, the Holocaust raises acutely the problem of innocent suffering. The question of why good people suffer is a very ancient one, raised in the biblical Book of Job and the Psalms. The Holocaust, however, may be said to challenge the whole scheme of things. For Jews believe that God is not only all-good but also active in human history. They believe that he is at work particularly in the Jewish people, to whom he has given a special role (see Chapter 3). How can all this possibly be reconciled with what happened to the six million?

Some Jewish writers have said that it cannot and that they are compelled to give up belief in God. What the Holocaust shows, they say, is the moral bankruptcy of human beings. We must now concentrate on human responsibility. Others feel that human responsibility is the very key to understanding how a loving God could allow the Holocaust. Having granted humankind the freedom to choose, God cannot intervene and take that freedom away, even when it is so appallingly misused. Some say that we must deny Hitler any posthumous victory by making sure that the Jewish people survive. Others are wary that this might suggest mere survival without considering its purpose. If Jews are the people of God, how should they be living and what should they be aiming at after the Holocaust? Responses to this question will be of the utmost importance when we come to consider what followed the end of the Second World War, the founding of the State of Israel (Chapter 6).

Extension Section

i)   Elie Wiesel, who survived the death-camps of Auschwitz and Buchenwald, writes: 'Jews can be for God or against God but never without God.' What do you think he means? He tells the powerful story of his childhood in *Night* (Penguin, 1987).

ii)   See what you can find out about the art and music that came out of the Holocaust, in particular from Theresienstadt (Terezin), the transit camp for Auschwitz. Listen also to the JMD tape.

iii)   Do some further research on the Holocaust. Useful resources include a pack, *Auschwitz*, and a video of pupils talking to survivors of the Holocaust (both from Holocaust Educational Trust). The film *Genocide* is available from Thames Television. There is also a GCSE topic book by Carrie Supple, entitled *From Prejudice to Genocide: Learning about the Holocaust* (Trentham Books, 1993).

Questions

A Matter of Fact

1   In which century did the Golden Age of Spanish Jewry begin? (B)

2   Name a medieval Jewish philosopher. (B)

3   When did the Third Crusade begin? (C)

4   Who expelled the Jews from Spain in 1492? (D)

5   In which city was the first official ghetto? (D)

6   What is Yiddish? (E)

7   Where were the two main centres of the Ashkenazim? (E)

8   Name a notable figure of the Jewish Enlightenment. (E)

9   What event marks the beginning of the modern period? (F)

10   What term means 'hatred of Jews because of their race'? (F)

11   Name the French army captain wrongly imprisoned in 1894. (F)

12   What is a pogrom? (G)

13   Which party did Adolf Hitler lead? (H)

14   What is meant by the Final Solution? (H)

15   Where is Yad Vashem? (I)

Vocabulary

Give the Hebrew word for the following:

1 Spain (E)

2 Germany (E)

3 Enlightenment (E)

4 whirlwind (H)

5 Holocaust Remembrance Day (I)

6 holy ones (I)

7 sanctifying the Name of God (I)

Over to You

Answer these questions fully, giving your reasons, and stating arguments both for and against where appropriate.

1 From your study of Jewish history, do you think that it is possible for people of different religions to live together peacefully?

2 Some people consider the Holocaust to be a manifestation of racism carried to its logical conclusions. Is that what it was?

A Question of Understanding

Try to give at least two religious explanations in answer to each of the following questions.

1 Why is the twentieth century specially significant in Jewish history? (A)

2 Why were Jews often resented in medieval Europe? (C)

3 Why were some Jews called Marranos? (D)

4 Why are there both Ashkenazi and Sefardi Jews in the Netherlands? (E)

5 Why has Russia been such a difficult place for Jews to live? (G)

6 How might a Jew reconcile what happened in the Holocaust with faith in God? (I)

Assignment

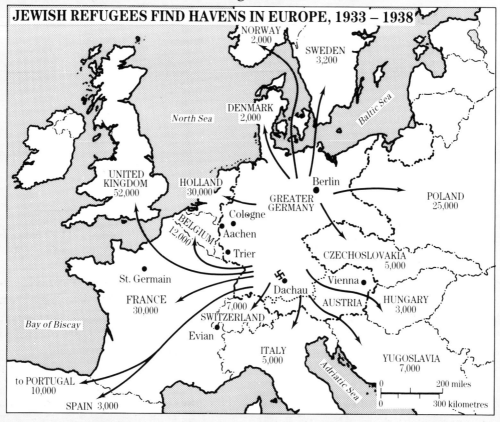

JEWISH REFUGEES FIND HAVENS IN EUROPE, 1933 – 1938

NORWAY 2,000
SWEDEN 3,200
DENMARK 2,000
North Sea
Baltic Sea
UNITED KINGDOM 52,000
HOLLAND 30,000
Berlin
GREATER GERMANY
POLAND 25,000
Cologne
BELGIUM 12,000
Aachen
Trier
CZECHOSLOVAKIA 5,000
St. Germain
Vienna
FRANCE 30,000
Dachau
AUSTRIA
HUNGARY 3,000
7,000
SWITZERLAND
Bay of Biscay
Evian
ITALY 5,000
YUGOSLAVIA 7,000
Adriatic Sea
to PORTUGAL 10,000
SPAIN 3,000
0   200 miles
0   300 kilometres

a) England was one country receiving Jewish immigrants shortly before the Second World War started. With the aid of a map or chart, indicate the other main movements of Jews to and from England in medieval and modern times.

Useful resources for studying Jewish life in England include the Heritage Trail (notes available) organised by Manchester Jewish Museum (which has many tape-recorded interviews with Jews who settled in Manchester, largely fleeing oppressive laws in Russia in the late nineteenth century); the London Museum of Jewish Life at the Sternberg Centre; the Jewish London Tour organised by the Board of Deputies; Maisie Mosco's novels, e.g. *Almonds and Raisins* (New English Library, 1979); and Jonathan Romain's *The Jews of England* (Jewish Chronicle Publication, 1985).

b) Explain why:

i) Jews were leaving Germany during the period shown in the map above;

ii) large numbers of Jews remained in Germany in 1938;

iii) Poland turned out to be anything but a safe haven;

iv) the following six years (1939–45) were so significant in terms of Jewish population.

c) Discuss whether the events of this period should be studied by non-Jewish pupils. If so, should this be in History, Religious Studies, both, or another subject altogether?

3

The Tenakh (Bible)

- The Hebrew Bible has three parts: **Torah** (Teaching), **Neviim** (Prophets), and **Ketuvim** (Writings).
- The first letter of each of these words, TNK, makes up the Jewish word for the Bible, pronounced **Tenakh**.
- The five books of the Torah are the most important. They give Jews the **mitzvot** (commandments) by which they are to live as people chosen by God for a special task.
- The Neviim describe God's activity in history. Individual prophets speak God's word to the people, sometimes offering hope, but more often denouncing their people's disloyalty to God. They appeal for just and truthful behaviour.
- The Ketuvim are very varied in content, style, and length. The best known are the Psalms, which are prayers or songs to God. They still feature prominently in Jewish worship.
- The Torah is read in the synagogue, followed by a reading from the Neviim. Some of the Ketuvim are read on special days in the Jewish Calendar.
- The text of the Bible is carefully handed on by scribes, and the ancient process of interpreting the text continues.

A)   The Hebrew Bible

The word 'Bible' comes from a Greek word, *biblia*, meaning 'books'. The Bible is a collection of books. To make clear just which these books are, we must remember that the Jewish Bible does not include the 27 books which Christians call the New Testament and include in their Bible. The New Testament presents a new faith, Christianity, which rests on a new covenant (or 'testament', which means the same as 'covenant'). Though Jews may study the New Testament to learn about Christianity, they do not regard it as sacred scripture and so it has no place in Jewish belief and observance. The Jewish faith rests on the original covenant, which Jews have no reason to call 'old' since they do not accept the new.

The first five letters of the Hebrew alphabet. All 22 letters are consonants. A system of dots and dashes below (and sometimes above) the letters shows people what vowel sounds to make in order to pronounce the words.

The Jewish Bible is the Hebrew Bible. All its books are written in Hebrew apart from part of Daniel, which is written in Aramaic, a very similar language. All the books of the New Testament, on the other hand are written in Greek. The Bible for a Christian is made up of both the Hebrew and the Greek books. The Bible for a Jew is made up of the Hebrew books, of which there are 24. Below is a list of them.

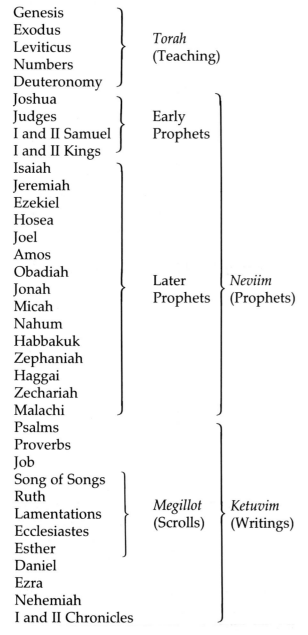

Genesis
Exodus
Leviticus   *Torah*
Numbers   (Teaching)
Deuteronomy

Joshua
Judges   Early
I and II Samuel Prophets
I and II Kings

Isaiah
Jeremiah
Ezekiel
Hosea
Joel
Amos
Obadiah
Jonah   Later   *Neviim*
Micah   Prophets   (Prophets)
Nahum
Habbakuk
Zephaniah
Haggai
Zechariah
Malachi

Psalms
Proverbs
Job
Song of Songs
Ruth
Lamentations   *Megillot*   *Ketuvim*
Ecclesiastes   (Scrolls)   (Writings)
Esther
Daniel
Ezra
Nehemiah
I and II Chronicles

You will notice that the books of the Hebrew Bible fall into three main sections: Torah,

Neviim, and Ketuvim. The first letter of each of these Hebrew words (TNK) gives us the Jewish name for the Bible, **Tenakh**. The word is more usually spelt **Tanach**. The Tanach is then the Torah, the Neviim, and Ketuvim. We now need to look at these three sections and at some of their most important contents.

B) Torah

The word Torah, as we saw in Chapter 1, means 'direction' or 'teaching'. It can be used to mean the whole of Jewish teaching based on the Bible, but the word is sometimes used specifically to mean the Bible. The Torah is then the same as the Tanach. In yet a third use, the word Torah is applied solely to the first five books of the Bible, sometimes called the Pentateuch (from the Greek word for 'five'). The Torah, in this its most specific and usual sense, is also called the 'five books of Moses', because of the belief that it was given directly to Moses on Mount Sinai.

The five books include accounts of the creation of the world and the life stories of the patriarchs (Genesis); the early history of the people in Egypt, their release from slavery, their presence at Sinai, and their wanderings in the wilderness (Exodus); the leadership of Moses, and the origin of the priesthood (Numbers); legislation ranging from the minute details about sacrifices to universal ethical precepts (Leviticus); and most important of all, the covenant made at Sinai and the obligations on which this covenant depends (Exodus and Deuteronomy).

C) Mitzvot (Commandments)

The obligations laid upon the Jewish people at Sinai are known as the **mitzvot**, which is the Hebrew for 'commandments' or 'obligations' (singular **mitzvah**). Of the total 613 mitzvot,

248 are positive and 365 are negative. Positive commandments (e.g. 'Honour your father and your mother.') and negative commandments (e.g. 'You shall not kill.') are seen together in ten of the best known of the 613. These ten come in a unit in both Exodus 20:1–17 and Deuteronomy 5:6–21. They are often referred to as the Ten Commandments or the Decalogue (Ten Words). The first of these commandments: 'I am the Lord your God, who brought you out of the land of Egypt, out of the house of bondage.' is actually a statement, which sets all the other commandments in context. From the relationship with God, established at the Exodus, all else follows.

According to one tradition, there are exactly as many seeds in the pomegranate as there are mitzvot in the Torah. Some say the positive mitzvot correspond to the bones in the body (248) and the negative mitzvot to the days of the solar year (365).

The second of the Ten Commandments (Exodus 20:3–6; Deuteronomy 5:7–10) puts starkly the main consequence, namely, that the Israelites must have no other god or try to make any physical representation of God. Imagine you are asked to define the term 'God'. This is no easy task. Whether or not you believe in him, you may well include in your definition something about God being different from everything else, God starting everything off and keeping it going. If God is understood as the sole creator and sustainer of everything that exists, it must follow that there cannot be any other gods. God, being God, can only be one. This is proclaimed with crystal clarity in 'Hear, O Israel: the Lord is our God, the Lord is One.' (Deuteronomy 6:4), the heart of Jewish belief.

The mitzvot can be divided not only into positive and negative, but also into ritual (to do with worship) and ethical (to do with morality). 'Remember the Sabbath day to keep it holy' is a ritual mitzvah and 'You shall not steal' a moral mitzvah. Look up the full Ten Commandments and divide them into ritual and moral.

A further distinction between mitzvot can be made. This is between those for which the reason is obvious (e.g. 'You shall not kill.') and those for which the reason is far from obvious (e.g. 'In the seventh month, on the first day of the month, you shall observe a day of solemn rest, a memorial proclaimed with blast of trumpets . . .'). The first sort are called **mishpatim** (judgements) and the second **chukim** (statues). Jews differ over whether it is right to try to work out reasons for the chukim and even over whether it is essential to keep them. The Bible, however, does not raise either question. All the mitzvot are to be kept.

D) The Chosen People

Jews who today follow the traditional teaching to keep all the mitzvot base their conviction on an idea frequently expressed in the Torah and elsewhere in the Bible. This is that God has chosen them to be a special people. We saw in Chapter 1 that, according to Exodus 19:6, they are to be 'a kingdom of priests and a holy nation'. These words give us the clue to understanding the idea of a chosen people.

Some people find the very idea of God choosing people offensive. Nowadays this includes some Jews. They feel that any reference to their being chosen should be omitted from Jewish worship. This would mean a great many omissions from the Prayer Book, and most Jews prefer to explain the idea rather than reject it. The explanation is that God needs people who will play a special role in his plan for humanity, people prepared to obey his will. He chooses the Jews. It is not that they are better than other people, any more than priests, who in ancient Israel represented the people before God and God before the people, were better than non-priests. They are simply called to a different kind of work. Their task is to keep God's Torah and thereby be a holy nation, a nation set apart. This finds clear expression in the following prayer spoken before the Torah reading in the synagogue:

> Blessed art thou, O Lord our God, King of the universe, who hast chosen us from all peoples, and hast given us thy Torah.

Objections to God choosing anyone usually rest on the idea that God is somehow limited, that he is not God of the world. On the contrary, a choosing God must in the nature of the case, be a universal God, a God of 'all the earth' (Exodus 19:5). A little girl once saw a film in which twins featured. Taken with the idea of being a twin, she pestered her mother for months, asking if she could have a twin. This was, she eventually realised, a ridiculous request. Her mother did not have the option of making her a twin. Choosing involves possible options. So God must be God of all in order to choose anyone.

You may still ask, however, why God chose the Jews. The ancient rabbis concluded that the Jews were the only ones who would take on the job. When you think how many mitzvot there are, you may see why. To be chosen to play or run for your school or county might, besides being a privilege, entail much hard work. To be chosen to obey the Torah, for life, is perhaps a privilege many people would rather do without.

Some people say that no human beings can possibly understand God's reasons and so

Being chosen is not always a pleasure. As a Jewish quip puts it: 'Thou hast chosen us from among the nations; isn't it time to choose someone else?'

should not try to. Others object that the oddness of the chosen people lies not in God choosing the Jews but in his having to choose at all. Why could he not make the whole human race the means of fulfilling his purpose for the world?

The famous twelfth-century philosopher, Rabbi Moses ben Maimon, says that we simply do not know, any more than we know why God created the world so that strawberries grow in some countries and not in others. A famous twentieth-century theologian, Rabbi Louis Jacobs, suggests that we remember that 'all the great achievements of humanity have been made by particular people living in a particular way.' Shakespeare's plays could have been produced only by an Englishman writing in English and in England, because no literature can be produced in the abstract. Yet millions of people who are not English gain greatly from the plays. So the Jews have a particular experience of God from which come particular demands. 'But', Jacobs writes, 'what came out of it all and, Judaism believes, what will come out of it, is for all humanity.' (*The Book of Jewish Belief*, Behrman House, 1984).

E) Neviim

If you look back at the list on p. 24, you will see that there are 19 names in this, the second section of the Tanach. In fact, the last 12 books are so short that they are counted as one book, the Book of the Twelve.

The English translation of the Hebrew word Neviim is 'Prophets'. I wonder what, if you were turning to these prophetic books for the first time, you would expect to find in them? Probably you would expect predictions about the future, since a prediction is generally what we mean nowadays by a 'prophecy'. When we turn to the Neviim, however, we find that the future is not their main concern.

The first four books, known as the Early Prophets, are predominantly concerned with the past. They tell the history of the people from their entry into Canaan until the destruction of Jerusalem more than 500 years later. As they tell the history, the writers of Joshua, Judges, 1 and 2 Samuel, and 1 and 2 Kings are not interested in the bare facts, but in what they believe to be the meaning of the facts. If you were asked about a friend, you would not simply say, for example, 'He is 180 centimetres tall with blue eyes and curly blond hair.' Anybody could find that out without really knowing the person. You are more likely to say something about his character and what he means to you. So the writers of these historical books are concerned to draw out the meaning of the facts for their readers, the people whose history it is.

As we saw in Chapter 1, the chief character in history as presented in the Bible is God. The Early Prophets try to make sense of history in terms of God's character and also to teach what God requires of people. In some of these books, prophetic figures appear, notably Elijah. Elijah recalled both people and king to the worship of one God and to traditional moral standards (see the story of the contest on Mount Carmel in 1 Kings 18 and of Naboth's vineyard in 1 Kings 21). In this way, the prophet functioned as a spokesman for God.

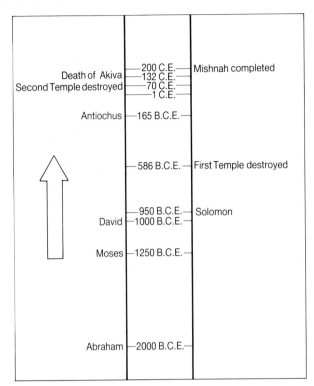

Time line.

The books of the Later Prophets all take their names from prophetic figures who spoke on God's behalf, presenting the past, the future, and most importantly the present from the perspective of faith. These books are again divided: 'Minor Prophets' (so-called not because their message is unimportant but because these twelve books are quite short) and 'Major Prophets', the long books of Isaiah, Jeremiah, and Ezekiel.

We have already seen some expressions of Isaiah's hope for the future (p. 8). Most of his prophecy, however, is concerned with speaking out against the immorality of his time. Look, for example, at Isaiah 1:21–3; 5:8–12 and note some specific criticisms. The prophet also appeals for change:

> . . . cease to do evil,
> learn to do good;
> seek justice,
> correct oppression;
> defend the fatherless,
> plead for the widow.

> *(Isaiah 1:16,17)*

Part of the complete scroll of Isaiah (the oldest biblical manuscript) found near the Dead Sea and now displayed in Jerusalem's Shrine of the Book.

They were probably grouped together because they were collected and accepted as scripture last of all. They include various types of literature. The Psalms are hymns which were sung in the Temple. They still play a prominent part in Jewish worship. Notice references to them when you study prayer, the synagogue, and the festivals. Proverbs is largely made up of wise sayings, and Job depicts the struggles of a good man suffering.

The next five books, or **Megillot** (scrolls) as they are known, are quite short. The first is a love poem; the second tells of a Moabite woman's devotion to her Israelite mother-in-law and her God; the third laments the destruction of Jerusalem; the fourth asks questions about the meaning of life and morality; and the fifth tells a story from the time of Persian rule. Each of the five Megillot is read at a special time in the Jewish year. Ecclesiastes, for example, is read at the Festival of Tabernacles. Note the other four names from the list on p. 24 so that you can recognise them later in this book.

Extension Section

i)   Imagine a friend is describing your character. She might say that you are kind, sympathetic, and a good listener (provided you are these things). Write a description of God's character from the picture you have gained from the Bible.

ii)   Look up Micah 6:8. How far do you think that this is a good summary of prophetic teaching?

The Tanach often inspires the windows in a synagogue. The Hebrew words on this one are from Psalm 100: 'Serve the Lord with gladness! Come into his presence with singing.'

F)   Ketuvim

Ketuvim means 'Writings'. All the remaining books of the Bible are included under this heading. The Ketuvim are essentially what is left when the Torah and Neviim are removed.

The Book of Daniel tells the story of faithfulness in time of persecution; Ezra and Nehemiah (counted as a single book) present life in Israel after the exile; and Chronicles reviews history from the beginning of the world to the end of the Babylonian exile.

G) The Bible in Jewish Life

From ancient times the Torah has been read publicly in the synagogue. It is the focus of Sabbath worship, and the Festival of the Rejoicing of the Law celebrates the completion of the cycle of readings from all five books. Another festival, Weeks, celebrates the reception of the Torah. A portion of the Neviim is also read each week. The Ketuvim feature less in public reading, but we have noted the importance of the Psalms in Jewish worship and the reading of the five Megillot on special days in the Jewish Calendar.

Though nowadays not all Jews take the same view about how God's word was received, all regard the Bible as inspired by God. Because of this, the Bible is the source of all Jewish teaching. The Jews have rightly been called 'the people of the book'. Though other books, especially the Talmud and the Prayer Book are vitally important, they and other Jewish writings stem from the Bible and from what it teaches about God and his will.

In order to pass on this teaching accurately, the greatest care has been taken throughout the centuries by those copying the Hebrew text. The present text of the Bible is known as the Masoretic text, from the Hebrew word **masorah** (tradition or 'what is passed on'). It dates back to the ninth century. The accuracy of the copying is demonstrated by the fact that the Dead Sea Scroll of Isaiah, written some eight centuries earlier, is exactly the same (apart from minor differences) as the Masoretic text of Isaiah. Many Jews believe that the Masoretic text goes right back to Moses.

The Hebrew Bible has been not only copied but also translated and commented upon. The earliest translations were into Greek (the *Septuagint*) and Aramaic (the **Targum**). The most famous commentary was made by Rashi (an abbreviated title for Rabbi Solomon ben Isaac), who lived in northern France, 1040–1105 CE. His comments are often printed alongside the biblical text.

Since the nineteenth century, some Jews have engaged in what is called biblical criticism. This suggests, for instance, that the Torah was written not by Moses at God's dictation (the view of Jews for over two millennia) but by a variety of human hands and over some centuries. Biblical criticism explains the different periods and literary styles reflected in the Book of Isaiah by suggesting that behind the book lie two or more prophets. There was Isaiah of Jerusalem, living before the Babylonian exile, then another prophet, living during the exile. Most Orthodox Jews reject all biblical criticism, especially of the Pentateuch, as incompatible with the Jewish faith.

The Torah scroll, **Sefer Torah**, is hand-written by a special scribe on special parchment and with special ink.

Questions

A Matter of Fact

1 What name do Jews give to their Bible? (A)

2 What is the Pentateuch? (B)

3 Name one book in the Bible where you would look for:

a) laws on sacrifice;

b) the stories of Abraham, Isaac, and Jacob;

c) an account of the wilderness wanderings;

d) creation stories;

e) the covenant laws;

f) details of the priesthood. (B)

4 How many positive mitzvot are there? (C)

5 Name one of the Early Prophets. (C)

6 How many Minor Prophets are there? (E)

7 Name one Major Prophet. (E)

8 Which book in the Bible contains hymns used in worship? (F)

9 Which eleventh century rabbi wrote a famous commentary on the Torah? (G)

Vocabulary

Give the Hebrew words for the following:

1 teaching (A)

2 obligations (C)

3 judgements C)

4 statutes (C)

5 prophets (E)

6 writings (F)

7 scrolls (F)

8 tradition (G)

A Question of Understanding

Try to give at least two religious explanations in answer to each of the following questions.

1 Why do Jews believe in one God rather than in many? (C)

2 Why are some Jews unhappy with the idea of their being the chosen people? (D)

3 Why is 'forthteller' a better definition of 'prophet' than 'foreteller'? (E)

4 Why is the third section of the Bible given the rather general heading of 'Writings'? (F)

Over to You

Answer these questions fully, giving your reasons, and stating arguments both for and against where appropriate.

1 Look back at the words of Isaiah on p. 27. Why do you think the prophets often spoke in short rhythmic phrases of poetry rather than in the language of prose?

2 Why do you think many Jews reject the ideas of biblical criticism? How far do you sympathise with their misgivings?

Assignment

Read Deuteronomy 7:6–11 and then answer the following questions:

a) i) What is the 'house of bondage' (v.8)?

ii) What is another word for 'covenant' (v.9)?

iii) How many mitzvot (v.9) are there?

iv) Deuteronomy is set out as a series of addresses by Moses to the people about to enter the promised land. Choose two other books of the Bible (one from the Neviim and one from the Ketuvim). Select one chapter from each book and give a brief description of its contents.

b) What do Jews think is the purpose of the mitzvot? Explain, with examples, the difference between 'statutes' and 'judgements' or 'ordinances' (v.9).

c) How odd
Of God
To choose
The Jews!
Write a reply which you think best defends God's position.

4

The Development of Jewish Law

- The Torah can be divided into the Written and the Oral Law. The Written Law is found in the Bible. The Oral Law gives the details of the Written Law. Originally passed on by word of mouth, it was eventually written down.
- The Oral Law is found in the Talmud, a combination of **Halachah** (Law) and **Aggadah** (story).
- The Talmud has two parts, **Mishnah** and **Gemara**. The Mishnah records the discussions of rabbis in the first two centuries of the Common Era. The Gemara contains explanations of the Mishnah by rabbis who lived some generations later.

- There are two Talmuds, the first from Palestine and the second from Babylonia.
- After the close of the Talmudic period, a question and answer system developed. Specific queries on specific occasions were sent to great rabbis. This system is called *responsa* (responses), and it continues today as new questions arise.
- Another way in which a decision could be found with speed and ease was by looking at a code, a summary of the Oral Law.
- Some questions are taken to the **Bet Din**, the rabbinical court.

A) The Point of It All

To most of us the idea of law governing every aspect of our lives is offputting. The very word 'law' has the ring of restriction and boredom about it. To observant Jews, however, the Torah is far from being a burden and dull. The Torah is God's gift. It is the communication of his will for his people and the study and practice of it is their privilege.

By the time of Ezra, the Torah was regarded as regulating every sort of activity. The Ten Commandments are a good example of the range of the Torah, making no division between sacred and secular. But the Ten Commandments and all the other laws in the Torah need interpreting. After all, what does it mean to 'honour your father and your mother' in concrete terms? Leviticus 19:18 says: 'You shall love your neighbour as yourself', but what does this amount to? Deuteronomy 24:1 says that a man wanting to divorce his wife must write her 'a bill of divorce', but how and in what circumstances is he allowed to do this?

Those who succeeded Ezra as experts in the Torah made it their business to discuss these practical questions. They believed that the answers lay in the principles of the Torah as given to Moses. These principles, however, needed interpreting. People needed to make

---

sense of them as new circumstances arose. Schools were, therefore, set up, where the teachers (rabbis) studied very carefully the text of the Torah. They also studied the discussions which had been handed on by word of mouth.

Two of the earliest and most famous of these rabbis were Hillel and Shammai. It is interesting to note that Hillel and Shammai, who taught in the first century CE, often disagreed. Indeed, different opinions on what to do and how to do it were what made this discussion, the Oral Torah, alive.

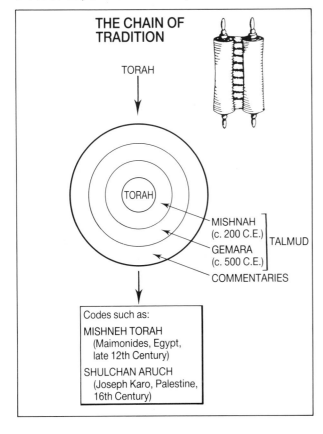

THE CHAIN OF TRADITION

TORAH

TORAH

MISHNAH (c. 200 C.E.)
GEMARA (c. 500 C.E.) } TALMUD

COMMENTARIES

Codes such as:

MISHNEH TORAH
(Maimonides, Egypt, late 12th Century)

SHULCHAN ARUCH
(Joseph Karo, Palestine, 16th Century)

B)   The Mishnah

As time went on, there was felt the need to start writing down these exchanges of opinion. Imagine if you were asked to remember all the different points of view expressed by a group of people, without making any notes and for a long time. It was important that

what the rabbis said was remembered, for it was not just interesting discussion. It was considered vital for helping people follow God's Law, to live life God's way.

The name given to this way, or Law, is **Halachah**, which comes from the Hebrew verb 'to go'. Halachah is the Jewish Law, showing the way to follow God, the route that God requires. Halachah, with its detailed rules, became, in the time of the rabbis the foundation of Jewish life. So collections of these rules began to be made. It is believed that a major collection was made by Rabbi Akiva and another by Rabbi Meir. All these collections were studied and discussed at length by the teachers who lived in the first two centuries of the Common Era. The teachers of this period were called **tannaim** (singular **tanna**). They would repeat this teaching material. Each collection, therefore, was called a **mishnah** (a repetition or learning). If you think about it, repeating something helps you learn it.

Most of these collections of rabbinic opinion were finally gathered together and edited by Rabbi Judah the Prince (Hanasi), who lived from 135 to 217 CE. This collection became what we call **the** Mishnah. Some other discussions of the Tannaim, which did not find their way into the Mishnah, are called **Tosefta** (addition).

The Mishnah contained so much material that it was divided into six sections, called orders. Each order deals with a particular area of Jewish life:

1   Seeds – agricultural laws, e.g. which crops to leave for the poor;
2   Appointed Times – Sabbath and the Festivals, e.g. how to celebrate the Passover;
3   Women – marriage laws, e.g. who can marry whom;
4   Damages – law proper, the law courts, and criminal law, e.g. how to examine witnesses;
5   Sacred Things – sacrifices, e.g. which sacrifices are acceptable;
6   Purities – ritual impurity, e.g. how people can become pure or impure.

Even then, each section is very long. It is, therefore, divided into shorter units, called tractates. There are 63 tractates.

A life-long study.

C) Completion

The Mishnah was edited about 200 CE, but, in the centuries following, people still needed clarification of God's Law for their specific circumstances. The tractates of the Mishnah were much discussed by the rabbis who lived after the Tannaim. Their discussions came, in turn, to be written down, not in a formal way, as though everything were cut and dried, but rather in the form of case studies. The talk of these wise men would be lively, as they worked out what the Torah meant in real-life situations. The written result is, therefore, rather like the transcript of a tape-recording. It is about thirty times the length of the Mishnah and it is called the **Gemara** (completion). The Gemara completed the discussions of the Mishnah and so marked a major stage in the development of Jewish Law.

These written discussions, the Gemara, were not written out on their own, but always alongside the part of the Mishnah on which they were based. The Mishnah and Gemara combined were called the **Talmud**, from the Hebrew for 'to learn'. There were two Talmuds, one compiled in Palestine about 400 CE and the other in Babylonia about 500 CE. The Babylonian Talmud, edited by Rabbi Ashi and his disciple Rabbi Ina, was more extensive and became more authoritative than the Palestinian Talmud. It is still very important for Jewish life and study today.

A page from the Talmud. In the centre is the Mishnah passage and the Gemara text. On either side are commentaries on the Talmud (mainly from the Middle Ages).

D) Different Sorts of Writing

The line of development runs from the Torah, through the Mishnah to the Talmud. Within the written stages of development we find two sorts of material. You will have realised from Chapter 3 that most of the Torah is in the form of Law, but there are some parts that are in the form of narrative or story. Just as traditions developed about the legal parts of the Torah, so traditions developed about the narrative parts.

As legal traditions came to be written down (Halachah), so narrative traditions were also recorded. The name given to this narrative material is Aggadah (story or telling).

There are, therefore, two sorts of writing: Halachah, which gives the 'way' people should live, and Aggadah, which gives the 'story' of such living. Halachah gives, for instance, the detailed treatment of the laws regarding work on the Sabbath. Aggadah gives encouragement to keep the Sabbath, with stories about people who have kept it.

It is not always easy to separate these two types of writing. In the Talmud, most of the material is Halachah, but some is Aggadah. There are other books which are mainly Aggadah. These books are called **Midrashim**, and they exist independently from the Talmud. The best known is a collection on the five books of the Torah and the five Megillot, called **Midrash Rabbah** (the Great Midrash). Midrash means 'searching' or 'rooting out'. It is a technical term for interpretation, exploring the meaning of the text.

Extension Section

Aggadah tells the story that on Sabbath eve two angels, one good and one bad, accompany a man home from synagogue. If he finds everything ready for the Sabbath and the right atmosphere, the good angel says: 'May the same happen next week', and the bad angel has to respond: 'Amen' ('so be it'). But if the household is not ready for the Sabbath, the bad angel has his say: 'May the same happen next week', and the good angel, against his will, has to respond: 'Amen'. What does this story teach?

E)   Responsa

The Talmud was vast and hard to find your way around. People, therefore, turned to their rabbi to find out what they should do. Between 650 and 1050 CE, there were some very learned men heading the rabbinic academies

in Babylonia. Each of these held the title **Gaon** (Excellency). Rabbis from many countries sent the **Gaonim** (plural) questions. In reply, they gave answers (*responsa*). These questions were often about situations which would not have arisen in the days of the Talmud. Such questions still arise, and so responsa are still needed. For example, the Talmud says that you cannot kindle a fire on the Sabbath. A Jew in Britain nowadays is hardly likely to want to rub together two sticks of wood to light a fire, but he may want to put on his electric fire on the Sabbath. Can he do so?

F)   Codes

If you have been present at a discussion between people with different points of view, you will know how confusing it can be. What, you may ask, was finally decided? People looking up the Talmud to find out how they should live could easily get lost in the discussion. People needing the 'bottom line' of the decision needed a guidebook or summary. To meet this need, codes have been written, in which the major decisions are summarised, without going into all the discussion.

One such code, which has been very influential, was written by Maimonides. It was a difficult period for Spanish Jews (see Chapter 2), and Maimonides was anxious that they kept their Law. In the introduction to his code, he writes:

> *At this time, the tribulations have become heavy ... and the wisdom of our wise has vanished, ... hence all the commentaries ... of the Gaonim ... have become difficult to understand, ... not to speak of the Talmud proper ... calling for wide knowledge, wisdom, and much time for research ... Hence I Moses ben Maimon, ... have studied all these books and determined to ... prepare a clear digest of all the works ... so that the entire Oral Torah shall be arranged clearly for everyone ... I have called this work 'Mishneh Torah' (Repetition of Torah), since henceforth anyone who first reads the Written Torah and then this book will know the entire Oral Torah ...*

Codes are a sort of filing system.

The most important of these Jewish law codes is called the **Shulchan Aruch** (the Prepared Table). This sixteenth-century code was written by Rabbi Joseph Caro. Caro was Spanish, but after the expulsion of the Jews from Spain he settled in Palestine, at Safed, a major centre of Jewish learning. There he compiled his code. Most Sefardi Jews accepted the Shulchan Aruch. A few years later, it was also accepted by Ashkenazi Jews, once notes had been added to it by an Ashkenazi rabbi, Moses Isserles. The notes were referred to as the **Mappah** (the Tablecloth), for the Prepared Table.

G) Bet Din

There still arise situations where experts in Halachah are needed to judge what is right. There is, therefore, in many towns with a sizeable Jewish population, a **Bet Din** (a rabbinic court). Making up the Bet Din are three highly qualified and experienced rabbis. They judge civil disputes according to Jewish Law when both parties agree to attend in preference to a secular court. Their main work, however, is to make decisions on religious matters, notably dietary laws, divorces, and conversions. High standards of fairness are required of these rabbinical courts, in accordance with their origin in the Law of ancient Israel:

You shall appoint judges and officers in all your towns which the Lord your God gives you, according to your tribes; and they shall judge the people with righteous judgement. You shall not pervert justice; you shall not show partiality; and you shall not take a bribe, for a bribe blinds the eyes of the wise and subverts the cause of the righteous. Justice, and only justice, you shall follow, that you may live and inherit the land which the Lord your God gives you.

(Deuteronomy 16:18–19)

Questions

A Matter of Fact

1 Who were Hillel and Shammai? (A)

2 Who edited the Mishnah? (B)

3 Which tractate deals with the Sabbath and Festivals? (B)

4 What was combined with the Mishnah to form the Talmud? (C)

5 Which Talmud was edited by Rabbi Ashi and Rabbi Ina? (C)

6 What is Midrash Rabbah?

7 In which country did the Gaonim teach? (E)

8 Who wrote the Mishneh Torah? (F)

9 Name another Jewish law code. (F)

10 Who wrote Ashkenazi comments on this code? (F)

Vocabulary

Give the Hebrew words for the following:

1 way or going (B)

2 repetition (B)

3 a teacher (in the first two centuries CE) (B)

4 story or telling (D)

5 searching or rooting out (D)

6 rabbinic court (G)

A Question of Understanding

Pair up the illustrations in this chapter with one of the following captions:

1 Will we ever get to the bottom of this?

2 What's the bottom line? I need to know.

3 The links in the chain.

Over to You

Answer these questions fully, giving your reasons, and stating arguments both for and against where appropriate.

1 How might stories, such as those of Jewish Aggadah, inspire people to live better? (Give an example if possible.)

2 Suggest a question with which someone might approach the Bet Din. Do you think the matter could be just as easily settled in a secular court?

Assignment

A man may not dig a cistern, nor may he dig a trench, vault, water channel, or washerman's pool, unless it is three hand's-breadths away from his neighbour's wall; and he must plaster it with lime ... A man may not open a baker's shop or a dyer's shop under his neighbour's storehouse, nor may he keep a cattle stall near by ... His wall may not be built within four cubits of his neighbour's roof gutter, so that the other can set up his ladder to clean it out.

This is part of a Mishnah tractate from the order, 'Damages'. For many quotations from another tractate, see my worksheets, *Understanding Judaism* (Hodder and Stoughton, 1989).

a) Write out and learn the law in Leviticus 19:18 which the above Mishnah could be said to clarify.

b) Why was the written law so much discussed? Why was this discussion eventually written down?

c) Write a modern version of the above Mishnah and then explain to someone what you think are the advantages and disadvantages of having detailed laws on such matters of behaviour.

5

Orthodox, Reform, and Liberal Movements

- There are two main types of Judaism: Orthodox and Progressive. They hold different views about the authority of the Torah.

- Orthodox Jews believe that the Torah is totally God's word as revealed to Moses and is binding on Jews for all times. The interpretations found in the Talmud and Law Codes are also binding as they are part of the Torah.

- Orthodox Jews believe that Judaism means observing as many of the commandments as possible without questioning God's will.

- In Britain, there are two Progressive Movements: the Reform and the Liberal. They believe that only the moral commandments are forever binding. Ritual laws may need to be adapted or sometimes abandoned in modern circumstances.

- Reform and Liberal Jews believe that theirs are equally valid forms of Judaism, and they stress the values and practices which they hold in common with Orthodox Jews.

A) Who Is a Good Jew?

Before the State of Israel was established in 1948, the question: 'Who is a Jew?' was seldom asked. The question which was debated was: 'Who is a good Jew?' We have already seen (in Chapters 1 and 2) that being Jewish means belonging to a people with a certain history and heritage. But if someone born Jewish grows up uninterested in this history and not valuing this heritage, is he or she a good Jew? To be a good Jew must surely be something more than being just a good person.

We are studying Judaism as a religion and religion involves particular beliefs and prac-

tices. So what are the beliefs and practices of a good Jew? The Jewish people have a long history, involving many different settings and neighbours. As they have tried to work out the answer to this question, especially in the last two centuries, different groups of Jews have come to different conclusions.

We noted in Chapter 2 that many changes of thought were brought about in the Enlightenment. How did Jews react to these changes? Traditionally, Jews saw the origins of their beliefs and practices in the revelation at Sinai. The Torah was the foundation of doctrine, observances, and customs. There was believed to be an unbroken chain of tradition between the Written Torah found in the Hebrew Bible and the Oral Torah eventually laid

In which country is Mount Sinai situated?

down in the Talmud. With so much change going on around them, could Jews still believe this?

B) Orthodox

People who practise traditional Judaism are called Orthodox. The word 'orthodox' means 'right belief'. It is in some ways a misleading term, for Judaism is concerned as much, if not more, with right practice as it is with right belief. The better term would then be 'orthoprax', 'right practice', indicating those Jews who keep the commandments. Those Jews whom others refer to as Orthodox prefer to call themselves 'observant', as they observe the mitzvot. They feel that they represent the only true Judaism and that others have changed their practices, and the beliefs on which they rest, in a way that betrays Judaism.

There are varieties of Orthodoxy, even within one country such as Britain, but they are all agreed in their stress on the Torah (written and oral) as coming from God and therefore binding. Many of the 613 mitzvot cannot be kept nowadays, because they relate to worship in the ancient Temple in Jeru-

salem, but those that can, ritual and ethical, are regarded as all of equal importance. Orthodox Jews do not cut themselves off from Western culture and modern insights. Rather they think that these can be combined with Jewish tradition. They think that it is not for them to decide which aspects of God's Law still hold. The Torah, they say, needs, and has always needed, interpretation, but if it is abandoned, Judaism disappears.

They believe that Judaism requires people thoughtfully to work out their faithfulness to God, slowly evolving the tradition. Jews must find ways of fulfilling the Torah in modern circumstances, rather than letting the circumstances dictate which parts of the Torah are acceptable. If there are difficulties or apparent contradictions in parts of the Torah, Jews must go back to first principles to see what it is God really demands. For example, the Torah forbids the use of fire on **Shabbat** (the Sabbath). When electricity first came into practical use, the rabbis had to explain how it could be used in accordance with the original ruling.

The Orthodoxy described here is known as Modern Orthodoxy, because it takes account of the changes that have taken place in the last two centuries and tries to make traditional Judaism clear and attractive to modern Jews. In Germany, a model was provided by Samson Raphael Hirsch (1808–88). He taught that the Torah could be combined with the new,

Study at Jews' College, established in 1885 to provide rabbis, cantors, and teachers for the Anglo–Jewish community.

secular learning. His approach is, therefore, sometimes called Neo (New) Orthodoxy.

The Modern Orthodox community in Britain is mainly represented by the United Synagogue, an organisation formed by the joining of five synagogues in the late nineteenth century and now comprising some 70 synagogues. Orthodox Jews have established their own schools and colleges. The best known Higher Education institutions are Yeshivah University in New York and Jews' College in London.

C) Ultra-Orthodox

There is a different sort of Orthodoxy from the one just described. It is sometimes known as Ultra-Orthodoxy. Ultra-Orthodox Jews stress not only the demands of the oral and written Torah but also the values and practices of Jews in the late Middle Ages. They think that in this period Jews were 'Torah-true' (wearing earlocks, for example, in accordance with Leviticus 19:27, 'You shall not round off the hair on your temples.') and that present-day Jews should be very suspicious of beliefs and practices which have been influenced by modern conditions and ideas.

Not all Ultra-Orthodox Jews think in exactly the same way, so there are different Ultra-Orthodox groups. One of the most important of these groups or movements is the Chasidic movement. Its main influence today is in Israel and America, but there are Chasidic communities also in Britain, notably in Manchester and Newcastle-upon-Tyne.

Chasidism began in Eastern Europe in the eighteenth century. The word **chasid** means 'pious' and had been used of devout Jews, resisting opposition to their faith, in the second century BCE. The Chasidim of the eighteenth century were not only a resistance movement but also a revivalist movement. They wanted to revive the hope and faith of Jews who felt disappointed and oppressed in Poland and surrounding countries (see

Chapter 2). They were enthusiastic and joyous in their worship, which was highly charged emotionally. They stressed selfless devotion and personal union with God. The effort to rise above ordinary experience to a feeling of oneness with God is called mysticism. Such mystical yearning is expressed in this Chasidic song:

> *Wherever I go – You!*
> *Whatever I think – You!*
> *Only You, You again, always You!*
> *You! You! You!*

If this were set to modern music, it would sound like a love song and in a way that is what it is; but what it expresses is love not for another person but for God.

What impression does this picture give of Chasidism?

The mystical tradition, known in Judaism as **Kabbalah**, is not strong amongst twentieth-century Chasidic Jews. It has, however, greatly influenced two recent Jewish theologians, Martin Buber and Abraham Heschel. Some Chasidic movements today stress reason and meditation rather than emotion. This is true of Chabad Chasidism, also called Lubavitcher Chasidism, having originated in the Russian town of Lubavitch. Today the Lubavitcher run an active educational programme with centres around the world (e.g. Stamford Hill, London).

Chasidism was founded by Israel ben Eliezer, who lived from about 1700 to 1760. He became known as the Besht, which is an abbreviation of Baal Shem Tov, 'Master of the Good Name', the 'Good Name' being the Name of God. He was given the title Baal Shem Tov because of his healing and other wonder-working. He was a charismatic figure and so were the Chasidic leaders who succeeded him. They were known as **zaddikim** (Righteous Ones). Each zaddik (singular) was thought to be specially close to God by virtue of his personal qualities and training. By mediating between God and other people, he could inspire followers and bring them closer to God too.

Not all the zaddikim who lived after the Besht were as genuine as he was. Many rabbis became increasingly dismayed at the amount of trust people had in these zaddikim, and in the 1770s a counter-movement began. Its members were called the **Mitnagdim** (opponents). They were led by a scholar from the Lithuanian capital, Vilna. He became known as the Vilna Gaon.

Eventually a compromise was reached, and the Mitnagdim recognised the inspiration of the zaddikim, whilst the Chasidim acknowledged the learning and piety of the rabbis. At its best, eighteenth-century Chasidism was characterised by a glowing faith, and the same is true of modern-day Chasidism.

Extension Section

i)   Many Chasidic songs, particularly from Poland, express the mystical element. Listen to some (e.g. tape of *Hasidic Greatest Hits* from JMD) and describe their mood.

ii)   Below is the opening of Chaim Potok's novel, *The Chosen* (Penguin, 1970). Read the extract and then describe or illustrate the appearance of Chasidic (here spelt 'Hasidic') Jews. The rest of the novel gives an illuminating picture of the tension between Chasidism and a more modern outlook. There is also a film of this story. See also the sequel, *The Promise* (1971) and *My Name is Asher Lev* (1973), which illustrates the authority of the **rebbe**, the Chasidic term for rabbi.

For the first fifteen years of our lives, Danny and I lived within five blocks of each other and neither of us knew of the other's existence.

Danny's block was heavily populated by the followers of his father, Russian Hasidic Jews in somber garb, whose habits and frames of reference were born on the soil of the land they had abandoned. They drank tea from samovars, sipping it slowly through cubes of sugar held between their teeth; they ate the foods of their homeland, talked loudly, occasionally in Russian, most often in a Russian Yiddish, and were fierce in their loyalty to Danny's father.

A block away lived another Hasidic sect, Jews from southern Poland, who walked the Brooklyn streets like specters, with their black hats, long black coats, black beards, and earlocks. These Jews had their own rabbi, their own dynastic ruler, who could trace his family's position of rabbinic leadership back to the time of the Ba'al Shem Tov, the eighteenth-century founder of Hasidism, whom they all regarded as a God-invested personality.

About three or four such Hasidic sects populated the area in which Danny and I grew up, each with its own rabbi, its own little synagogue, its own customs, its own fierce loyalties. On a Shabbat or festival morning, the members of each sect could be seen walking to their respective synagogues, dressed in their particular garb, eager to pray with their particular rabbi and forget the tumult of the week and the hungry grabbing for money which they needed to feed their large families during the seemingly endless Depression.

The sidewalks of Williamsburg were cracked squares of cement, the streets paved with asphalt that softened in the stifling summers and broke apart into potholes in the bitter winters. Many of the houses were brownstones, set tightly together, none taller than three or four storeys. In these houses lived Jews, Irish, Germans, and some Spanish Civil War refugee families that had fled the new Franco regime before the onset of the Second World War. Most of the stores were run by gentiles, but some were owned by Orthodox Jews, members of the Hasidic sects in the area. They could be seen behind their counters, wearing black skullcaps, full beards, and long earlocks, eking out their meager livelihoods and dreaming of Shabbat and festivals when they could close their stores and turn their attention to their prayers, their rabbi, their God.

D) Reform

The Bevis Marks synagogue is the oldest Sefardi synagogue in Britain. It was from this community that some Jews broke away to found the first British Reform synagogue.

In Britain today, as in many other parts of the world, there are Jews who are not Orthodox but Progressive. They have a different view of what makes a good Jew from the Orthodox, basing their thinking on a different view of the way God speaks to human beings and what

he requires of them. Progressive Jews number about 20 per cent of British Jewry and they fall into two main groups: Reform and Liberal. Reform Jews make up two-thirds of the non-Orthodox Jews in Britain. The first British Reform congregation was founded in 1840, when some London merchants broke away from the established Orthodox synagogues to form the West London Synagogue. In 1941, this, and the other Reform communities which had grown up, formed the association which is now called the Reform Synagogues of Great Britain (RSGB).

The *Jewish Year Book* states the purpose of the Reform movement as:

> *to promote a living Judaism, to interpret the Torah in accordance with the spirit and needs of the present generation, and through its positive, constructive, and progressive view of Jewish traditions raise and maintain a high standard of Jewish religious life throughout the country.*

The aim of Reform Judaism is then to renew and strengthen Judaism. To understand how it tries to do this, it is necessary to go back to the beginnings of the Reform Movement, which were not in Britain but in Germany.

E) The Origins of the Reform Movement

After the French Revolution and the Napoleonic Wars, Jews in Western Europe were given the right to vote and other freedoms that had been denied to them. As they became more involved in Gentile society, some Jews converted to Christianity. Others, however, tried to change Judaism to meet their new needs. Their aim was to stay Jewish, and to this end they *re*-formed Judaism. The first of these reformers, a German called Israel Jacobson, did not set out to create a new religious movement. Rather, he tried to update Jewish services by introducing prayers in German, rather than in Hebrew, and by having the musical accompaniment of an organ, making Jewish worship more like that of the Christians. Jacobson also reassessed and reformed some important Jewish beliefs.

As we have seen in Chapter 3, Jews believe that God speaks, communicating his will to people. The question which Jacobson and other eighteenth-century thinkers, Jewish and Christian, raised was: how does God speak to people? You might ask the same question nowadays of someone who claimed that God had spoken to him. God is not a physical being with vocal chords, so how does God speak to people? How does someone know that God is speaking to him and telling him what is right and true? Is it possible that someone might not really be hearing God, or at least be misunderstanding God, and therefore pass on to other people his own ideas, which may be mistaken?

Orthodox Jews before, during, and after the time of Jacobson give a clear answer to these questions. They say that God spoke to Moses on Mount Sinai and gave him the whole Torah. He spoke in a non-physical way and dictated the written Torah and the oral Torah, which was passed on by Moses and eventually written down (see Chapter 4). All these words of God are as delivered to Moses and must not be changed.

The Jews who began the Reform Movement in Germany felt unable to believe that God spoke in this way and that Moses and the rabbis passed on without error God's word. They believed that the Torah was as much the product of human beings as of God. The Bible, they said, was a human book, in that it was people's expression of what God was like and what it meant to serve him. This would explain apparently contradictory statements in the Bible. It would also mean that laws which seemed in more modern times to be unhelpful could be disregarded. For example, according to Jewish Law, a **Cohen**, that is, a man descended from the old priestly families, cannot marry a woman who has been divorced, though other Jews can. Reform Jews argued, and still maintain, that this Law does not fit modern life when Jewish priests no longer exist. According to Reform Jews, Jewish Law can and should be changed when Jews begin to live in a different situation from that in which the Law was originally given.

The Torah is only the word of God as interpreted by human beings, who can make mistakes. So each generation of Jews should be selective, fulfilling only those laws which seem right in the light of new knowledge and understanding. This, Reform Jews believe, is in line with the views of the early rabbis, who themselves recognised development and change and sought to interpret for people what Judaism meant in each situation.

F) Reform in America

Though the Reform Movement began in Germany, its centre soon became North America. Many Jews had emigrated to this New World and Reform Judaism seemed particularly well-suited to their way of life and attitudes. Reform rabbis were imported from Western Europe to lead the new congregations in America. The most important of these was Isaac Mayer Wise. Wise was responsible for

YOU SHALL NOT BOIL A KID IN ITS MOTHER'S MILK (Exodus 23:19)

the two main institutions of the Reform Movement: the Union of American Hebrew Congregations, established in 1873 (today nearly 800 synagogues belong to this union), and the Hebrew Union College, founded in 1875.

In the early days of American Reform Judaism, there was a division between those such as Wise, who made what they considered to be moderate changes to Orthodox Judaism, and others, notably Kaufmann Kohler, who had more radical views. Kohler's views prevailed at an important meeting in Pittsburgh in 1885. These involved radical changes in synagogue, home, and personal life. For instance, men and women sat together in synagogues, most food laws were dropped, and confirmation replaced Bar Mitzvah, the Jewish coming of age ceremony at 13. In Germany too there was disagreement between reformers such as Abraham Geiger, with moderate views, and the radical Samuel Holdheim, who wanted to abandon all mitzvot.

Many American Jews, especially after the arrival of some strongly traditional Jews from Eastern Europe in the 1890s, thought that the Pittsburgh Platform (as the decisions of the 1885 meeting were known) had gone too far. Traditional symbols, mitzvot, and ceremonies were, they felt, important in giving Judaism

The Columbus Platform called for 'distinctive forms of religious art and music'. This is a modern Kiddush cup.

meaning and keeping it alive. At another conference of Reform rabbis, in 1937, a new statement was accepted of the 'Guiding Principles of Reform Judaism'. This statement was known as the Columbus Platform, since the meeting took place in Columbus. The Columbus Platform took a more positive view than the Pittsburgh Platform not only of Halachah (the complex of laws regulating Jewish life) but also of the importance of Palestine as a Jewish homeland (see Chapter 6).

Extension Section

i)   Listen to examples of Reform and Liberal synagogue music on the JMD tape and suggest how they differ from Orthodox music.

ii)   For recent statements of British Reform, for example, on women, intermarriage, the Prayer Book, write to Reform Synagogues of Great Britain, The Manor House, 80 East End Road, Finchley, London N3 2SY.

G)   Reform Today

Though the more radical wing dominated American Reform Judaism in the second half of the nineteenth century, there has this century been a general movement back to tradition, especially on the role of Israel in teaching justice, freedom, spirituality, and morality to the non-Jewish world. Reform Judaism in Britain has continued to be moderate and it too shows an increasing appreciation of ritual rules such as food and Sabbath restrictions. There remains at this point, however, a vital distinction between Reform and Orthodox Judaism. According to Orthodox Judaism, all the mitzvot are binding. According to Reform, only moral laws are binding. Ceremonial laws have to be assessed to see how valuable they are in preserving Judaism in each age. Reform

Judaism does not spell out exactly what you should do to be a 'good Jew'. Those who are Reform, however, believe that it is not an easy option compared to being Orthodox. This is made plain in the 1976 Centenary statement of American Reform Rabbis, which summarises the duties of a Reform Jew as:

creating a Jewish home centred on family devotion; lifelong study; private prayer and public worship; daily religious observance; keeping the Sabbath and the holy days; celebrating the major events of life; involvement with the synagogue and community; other activities which promote the survival of the Jewish people and enhance its existence.

Extension Section

i) Study the figures on male synagogue membership (from *British Jewry in the 80s*) printed below and then answer the following questions:

a) Which is the larger of the two Progressive groups?
b) What is another term for Ultra-Orthodox?
c) What, if anything, surprises you about the figures given?

ii) For recent Liberal statements on matters such as Zionism, Jewish Status, Death and Mourning, write to the Union of Liberal and Progressive Synagogues, The Montagu Centre, 109 Whitfield Street, London W1P 5RP.

MALE SYNAGOGUE MEMBERSHIP IN THE UNITED KINGDOM, 1983

	Congregations	Membership	Percentage
Right-Wing Orthodox	35	3,482	4.4
Central Orthodox	221	55,606	70.5
Sephardi	13	2,120	2.7
Reform	36	12,030	15.3
Liberal	23	5,661	7.2
Total	**328**	**78,899**	**100.0**

H) Liberal

One third of British Progressive Jews belong to the Liberal Movement. Like Reform, Liberal Judaism's purpose is to promote, purify, strengthen, and preserve Judaism. Liberal Jews believe that their practice of Judaism has the best chance of commending itself to modern Jews. A prominent Liberal, Rabbi John Rayner, writes:

The Jewish Religious Union was founded in order to win back for Judaism those who were drifting away from it, to awaken in them a new understanding of their heritage, a new respect for it, a new commitment to it.

The Jewish Religious Union was a body founded in 1902 by a community leader and

Leo Baeck (1873–1956) was an important spokesman for Jews during the Nazi regime. Settling in England after the war, he stressed the need for both a consciousness of God and moral values.

This London college was founded in 1956 by the RSGB to train rabbis and teachers. Since 1964 it has been sponsored jointly by RSGB and ULPS. It is named after the leader of German Jewry here pictured.

social worker, the Honourable Lily Montague, together with two other distinguished scholars of the early Liberal movement, Claude Montefiore and Israel Abrahams. This body, now known as the Union of Liberal and Progressive Synagogues (ULPS), has over 25 congregations. Each is self-governing, but together they reflect a certain outlook which distinguishes them from Orthodox and, to a lesser degree, from Reform Jews.

Liberal Judaism started as a break-away group from Reform and generally represents a more radical position, being further away from Orthodox Judaism on questions such as Jewish status and the State of Israel (see Chapter 6).

Like Reform, Liberal Judaism stresses progressive revelation, the idea that people progress as God reveals his nature and purpose to them over time. Liberal Jews think that some truths are unalterable, but others can be discarded as people learn more. Liberal Judaism offers individuals general principles and a practical programme which they are free to accept, modify, or reject. This stress on the individual's choice, especially on matters of ceremonial, is seen by Liberal Jews as more, rather than less, demanding. It means that every Jew has to think for himself or herself what best serves the purpose of Judaism. This purpose is to lead humankind to the Messianic Age of brotherhood and peace.

Liberal Jews do not think that they can make Judaism anything they like. Rather they think that each individual has the big responsibility of working out what he or she ought to do. The crucial question is still: 'What does the Lord your God require of you?' (Deuteronomy 10:12). This may include ceremonies which are seen as valuable, such as Sabbath worship in the synagogue and observance of the festivals. Yet, argue Liberal Jews, Judaism must be dynamic, and if ceremonies appear meaningless in new circumstances they should be rejected.

Questions

A Matter of Fact

1 Who, according to Orthodox Judaism, received the oral law? (B)

2 What is the United Synagogue of Great Britain? (B)

3 At which British college are Orthodox rabbis trained? (B)

4 Where did Chasidism begin? (C)

5 When was the first Reform synagogue founded in Britain? (D)

6 Who began Reform Judaism in Germany? (E)

7 To which country did it soon spread? (F)

8 What Liberal organisation was founded by Lily Montague? (H)

9 What does ULPS stand for? (H)

10 Progressive revelation, abandoning Jewish moral law, tolerance of other religious positions, merging completely with non-Jewish society. Which of these would be unacceptable to Liberal Jews? (H)

Vocabulary

Give the Hebrew words for the following:

1 Sabbath (B)

2 pious (C)

3 righteous ones (C)

4 opponents (C)

A Question of Understanding

Try to give at least two religious explanations in answer to each of the following questions.

1 Why is 'Orthodoxy' not an entirely appropriate term? (B)

2 Why are some Jews Ultra-Orthodox? (C)

3 Why do Liberal Jews keep some ritual laws but reject others? (H)

Over to You

Answer these questions fully, giving your reasons, and stating arguments both for and against where appropriate.

1 What do you think about the view that Judaism is not so much a religion as a way of life?

2 State a Jewish belief with which you either strongly agree or strongly disagree. What difficulties do you think a Jew might have in living by this belief?

3 Self-discipline, firm belief, intolerance, fanaticism, sincerity. Which of these do

you judge likely to result from Orthodox Judaism?

4 Some would say that Reform Judaism has reformed itself. How would you explain the growing attention to ceremonial law amongst Reform Jews in recent years?

5 Liberal Jews say that having responsibility for your own beliefs and decisions can be harder than having it all laid down for you. Is this true?

Assignment

You are preparing to debate the motion: 'Reform Judaism is an easy option.' Divide into two groups, one for and one against the motion.

a) List the chief differences between Orthodoxy and Reform.

b) Write the main speech for your side, making clear your arguments.

c) Who do you think would win this debate if it were held in your class? Give your reasons. (You may like to hold the debate to see the outcome.)

6

Zionism and the State of Israel

- For more than 3000 years, Jews have lived in the land of Israel. Jews living elsewhere have always thought of it as the Holy Land.
- After centuries of foreign rule, many Jews dreamt of having Israel as their homeland. The belief in such a homeland is called Zionism.
- Zionism's most vigorous advocate was Theodor Herzl, who believed that a Jewish state was essential in the face of anti-Semitism.
- Over the past century, Jewish attitudes to Zionism have changed, generally becoming more positive.

- The State of Israel was established in 1948. Some Jews celebrate every year the date when Independence was declared and the date when, in 1967, the partitioned Jerusalem was reunified, giving Jews access to the Western Wall.
- Though a secular democracy, Israel has certain areas of legislation that are based on biblical law. Israel's existence as a state requires Jews, inside and outside the country, to work out what it means to be Jewish.

A) The Dream

As soon as we began our study, we saw that Judaism centred not only on a people but on a land. From the time of Joshua onwards, through centuries of foreign rule, there have been Jews living in the land of Israel, **Eretz Yisrael**. They have clung to it as their religious inheritance, promised and given to them by God. They have regarded it as the Holy Land.

It is not that they thought that God was limited to one particular part of the world. Rather, in this land, people felt they might be particularly aware of him. Some people have holy buildings where they may be more aware of God (in Judaism, first the Temple and then the synagogue). In this way, the land of Israel is spiritually higher than anywhere else, and so the Bible speaks of 'going up' to it. The word **aliyah**, now used of immigration to Israel, literally means 'going up'.

When the Holy Land was conquered, the hope was always of restoration. So the prophet speaks God's word to his people:

> I will restore the fortunes of my people Israel, and they shall rebuild the ruined cities and inhabit them; . . . I will plant them upon their land, and they shall never again be plucked up out of the land which I have given them.
>
> (Amos 9:14–15)

Those in exile longed for their homeland:

> *By the waters of Babylon, there we sat down and wept, when we remembered Zion.*
>
> (Psalm 137:1)

'Zion' was the name of one of the hills in Jerusalem. It has come to stand for the whole city and even for the whole of Eretz Yisrael. It is from this that we get the term 'Zionism', the belief that Jews should have a homeland in Israel.

Solitude, by the Jewish artist, Marc Chagall. Like many Jewish poets, the painter expresses the longing for faraway Zion. Notice the Torah scroll held by the exile.

The Zionist dream became particularly strong in Russia when, in May 1882, laws were passed limiting Jews not only to the Pale (see Chapter 2) but to certain rural areas within it. These small towns, or **shtetls**, became seriously overcrowded, and the laws seem to have been intended to rid Russia of Jews by starving them, converting them to Christianity, or encouraging them to emigrate. Many Jews remained in Russia, some of them forming what was called the Socialist Bund, a radical political movement seeking to bring greater freedom and fairness by means of revolution. Others, however, did emigrate to Britain, America, and Palestine. Those who went to Palestine were known as 'Lovers of Zion'. The communities which they set up were the forerunners of the **kibbutzim**, Jewish communities based on equality, collective ownership, and communal living. The word **kibbutz** (singular) means 'a gathering together'. Though there are now over 200 kibbutzim in Israel, the early settlement by Russian Jews was small and slow. Zionism was still largely a dream.

B) Dreams Can Come True

The man who did more than anyone to make the dream a reality was Theodor Herzl (1850–1904). This Viennese journalist was in France covering the Dreyfus case (see p. 17). Shocked by the hostility to Jews which he witnessed in supposedly modern, Republican France, Herzl came to the conclusion that anti-Semitism was incurable, and that only in a country of their own could Jews be safe. For the remaining few years of his life, Herzl put all his passion and energy into making the dream come true. He published his ideas in an influential document called *The Jewish State*.

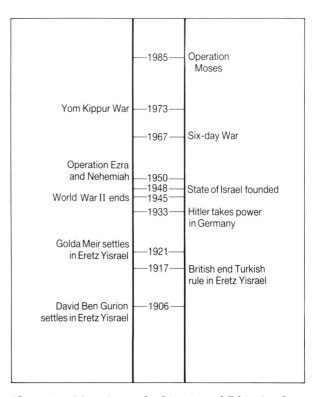

	—1985—	Operation Moses
Yom Kippur War	—1973—	
	—1967—	Six-day War
Operation Ezra and Nehemiah	—1950—	
	—1948—	State of Israel founded
World War II ends	—1945—	
	—1933—	Hitler takes power in Germany
Golda Meir settles in Eretz Yisrael	—1921—	
	—1917—	British end Turkish rule in Eretz Yisrael
David Ben Gurion settles in Eretz Yisrael	—1906—	

'Operation Moses' was the bringing of Ethiopian Jews (Falashas) to Israel.

There he stated:

The aim of Zionism is to create for the Jewish people a home in Palestine, secured by public law.

By becoming a citizen in his or her own country, the Jew would, Herzl believed, no longer be dependent on the fluctuating goodwill of others. In his campaign to persuade people of the need and practicality of this political Zionism, Herzl pursued all with influence, including the German Kaiser, the Turkish Sultan, the Pope, and the British Foreign Minister. He also called together for a conference like-minded Jews from all over the world. This was the first Zionist Congress and it assembled in Basel, Switzerland in 1897. There Herzl confidently announced that everyone would see the creation of a Jewish state in Palestine within 50 years. He was not far wrong, for the State of Israel was created in 1948.

C)   Changing Attitudes to Zionism

In the meantime, there was much opposition to Herzl's form of Zionism, not least from Jews. Though the Bible spoke of Jerusalem becoming the spiritual capital of the world (e.g. Isaiah 2:2–4), not everyone believed that it was for politicians to establish this. Divine intervention was what, according to Orthodox Jews, was required. All human beings could do was to live in obedience to the Torah until the Messiah should come. This is still the view held by Ultra-Orthodox Jews, who refuse to see in the present State of Israel any signs of the Messianic Age.

Jewish opposition to Herzl's proposals came from a number of other quarters. Those committed to Socialist revolution, such as the Bund in Russia, thought Jews should work for change in the countries where they were.

Nineteenth-century Reform Jews stressed the improvements which had come with the Haskalah. Emancipation meant that they were not longing to live in Eretz Yisrael. Liberal Jewish opposition was expressed by Claude Montefiore in a letter to *The Times* newspaper. There was the fear in many that the progress that had been made in the acceptance of Jews as loyal citizens of their respective countries would be reversed. Non-Jews might begin to think that Jews were interested only in a political homeland.

Israel's parliament, the Knesset. Notice the Israeli flag. It takes its blue and white colours from the tallit (prayer shawl). At its centre it has what has become a symbol for the Jewish people – the six-pointed star, known as the **Magen David**, the 'Shield of David'.

By the early 1900s, some of these attitudes were changing. The first Chief Rabbi of Palestine, Abraham Isaac Kook (1868–1935), tried to persuade his fellow Orthodox Jews that even a Jewish state in which many were unobservant was, in the final analysis, religious and to be supported. An Orthodox Zionist movement was formed in 1902. Its present members aim to make Israel a state faithful to the principles of Orthodox Judaism. To the extent that it is, they believe, it is the means of God's fulfilling his ancient promises.

Reform Judaism has also modified its position on Zionism. The Pittsburgh Platform of 1885 had stated:

We expect neither a return to Palestine, nor a sacrificial worship under the administration of the sons of Aaron, nor the restoration of any of the laws concerning the Jewish State.

Now that the State of Israel exists, however, most Reform Jews support it as a major means of preserving Judaism.

The Liberal Community in Britain recently declared:

our love for the Land of Israel, our solidarity with our brothers and sisters who dwell within its borders, and our commitment to the State of Israel. We rejoice in its existence, delight in its achievements, care about its security, seek its welfare, believe in its future.

The statement goes on to make plain, however, that the Liberal hope is for Israel to be a force for good for all the people of the Middle East and indeed for all humanity. Israel must strive to be 'a light to the nations' and try to reconcile its need for security with justice for all.

Extension Section

Read the following extract from the Centenary statement of American Reform Judaism and then put into your own words what Reform Jews feel about the State of Israel.

We are privileged to live in an extraordinary time, one in which a third Jewish commonwealth has been established in our people's ancient homeland. We are bound to that land and to the newly reborn State of Israel by innumerable religious and ethnic ties. We have been enriched by its culture and ennobled by its indomitable spirit. We see it providing unique opportunities for Jewish self-expression. We have both a stake and a responsibility in building the State of Israel, assuring its security and defining its Jewish character. We encourage aliyah for those who wish to find maximum personal fulfilment in the cause of Zion.

E) Establishing the State of Israel

The first major step towards realising the Zionist dream was taken in 1917. In this year, the British Foreign Secretary, Lord Balfour, wrote to the president of the English Zionist Federation, Lord Rothschild:

His Majesty's Government view with favour the establishment in Palestine of a national home for the Jewish people.

This letter is known as the Balfour Declaration.

In the First World War, British troops captured first Jerusalem and then all of Palestine from the Turks. After the war, the League of Nations gave the British a formal mandate to administer the area until it might be ready for self-government. Many people believe that, following the granting of this mandate in 1920, there was a chance for real peace in the Middle East. However, in 1939, the British government decided to go back on its 1917 commitment and establish an Arab-dominated state. In this, Jewish land-ownership and immigration were to be limited. Even the desperate need to settle displaced persons after the Holocaust did not alter the decision on limiting immigration. Arabs, feeling threatened by the number of Jewish immigrants already in the land, and Jews, angry and demoralised at the British verdict, became violent. Unable to deal with the situation, the British handed the problem over to the United Nations, which voted to partition the area into an Arab state and a Jewish state. As the British withdrew in 1948, the provisional Jewish government, under David Ben Gurion, declared the creation of a Jewish state to be named 'Israel'. He began:

In the Land of Israel, the Jewish people came into being. In this land was shaped their spiritual, religious and national character.

The date was 14 May and its equivalent in the Jewish Calendar (see p. 127) is now celebrated annually as Israel's Independence Day,

Yom Haatzmaut. Not all Jews feel it right to celebrate this day, but in some synagogues there are special services. In Israel, Yom Haatzmaut is a national holiday. Sirens herald a two-minute silence in which those who died in the conflict surrounding the Declaration of Independence are remembered. The conflict between Jews and Arabs had flared in 1947. Then, in 1948, the day after it was created, the State of Israel was invaded by all the surrounding Arab states: Egypt, Syria, Lebanon, Jordan, and Iraq. This war ended, after eight months, in an Israeli victory and extension of territory. Some Arabs stayed and became citizens of the new state. Others fled across the frontiers. These are the Palestinian refugees. The 1947–8 war is known as the War of Independence.

Jerusalem – city of peace? When he captured it from the Jebusites, King David saw that Jerusalem, on hills, would make a good capital. In the foreground, you can see the Western Wall of the Temple.

Extension Section

i) *Exodus*, by Leon Uris (Corgi, 1970), illustrates the connection between the experience of the Holocaust and the founding of the State of Israel. Arab–Israeli relations are explored in novels by Amos Oz, notably *My Michael* (Flamingo, 1984) and *In the Land of Israel* (1983). Oz is a member in Israel of 'Peace Now'. See what you can find out about this movement.

ii)   Find out what you can about the movements or organisations in this country which promote the Zionist cause.

F)   Further Conflict

Since the War of Independence, Israel has been involved in five major conflicts: the Sinai Campaign (1956); the Six Day War (1967); the Suez Canal (1969–70); the Yom Kippur War (1973); and the Lebanese War (1982). In the second of these, Egypt expelled the United Nations' peace-keeping force from Sinai and Gaza. Israel defeated Egypt, reconquering Sinai, and defeating Syria and Jordan. Israeli troops took the strategically important Golan Heights and the West Bank of the Jordan River. Their greatest jubilation came, however, when they captured the portion of Jerusalem that had been in the Arab sector since partition. In this section of the city was the Western Wall. As the only part of the Temple left after 70 CE, this is the Jews' holiest place.

Israel's Prime Minister, Golda Meir, meets the press on the Yom Kippur crisis.

They were now free to pray there and, within minutes of its liberation, the chief chaplain to the Israeli defence forces arrived and blew the **shofar** (ram's horn), while the Defence Minister placed between the wall's crevices a slip of paper on which he had written the prayer: 'Peace be upon Israel'. This event has given rise to another annual day of celebration, Jerusalem Day, **Yom Yerushalayim**. Huge crowds gather at the Western Wall on this day. In many countries, including Britain, some Jews celebrate the reunification of Jerusalem by services in the synagogue.

The Yom Kippur War takes its name from the fact that it began with a surprise attack by the Egyptians on **Yom Kippur**, the Day of Atonement, the holiest day in the Jewish year. The Arabs regained some territory but, after a month, were defeated.

So the conflicts continued. A ray of hope came in 1979, when a peace treaty was signed between Israel and Egypt. Egypt, however, stood alone among the Arab states in its implicit recognition of Israel's right to exist.

Egyptian President Anwar Sadat, American President Jimmy Carter, and Israeli Prime Minister Menachem Begin make an attempt at peace.

The Israeli invasion of the Lebanon in 1982, attempting to eliminate the Palestine Liberation Organisation, demonstrates some of the complexity of the whole area. This is further illustrated by the Palestinian uprising, the *Intifada*, begun in the late 1980s. Jews themselves, both in Israel and out, have conflicting views on what policies and strategies should be adopted. Israel's right to secure borders, when surrounded by Arab states, has somehow to be reconciled with a lasting peace, the **shalom** (peace) of the Hebrew (and the *salam* of the Arab) greeting, and the last request of important Jewish prayers. Only the ignorant or insensitive make snap judgements about how this can be done.

G) A Jewish State

The 'exiles' who have been gathered into Israel are from very many and very different countries. Attempts to recognise this diversity include having not one but two Chief Rabbis, one Sefardi and the other Ashkenazi. The diversity of the Jewish population, however, is wider than that, for by no means all Israelis are Orthodox Jews. Some belong to Progressive Judaism. Many others say their Judaism is not religious at all, but cultural. This raises sharply the question of how Israel's Jewishness should be expressed.

That Israel is a Jewish state can be seen at many points. Hebrew, the 'holy tongue', is its language, synagogues abound, Jewish festivals are officially recognised, and religious parties have considerable influence in the Knesset. All laws of status (marriage, divorce, and conversion) are in the hands of the rabbinic authorities (except, of course, for the non-Jewish population, who have their own religious laws). This means, for example, that there is no civil marriage, a Cohen cannot marry a divorcée (see p. 43), and non-Orthodox conversions are not recognised. The Law of Return (1950, 1954, 1970) guarantees any Jew who so desires immediate claim to Israeli citizenship. According to Halachah, a Jew is someone born of a Jewish mother. The main controversies arising from these laws are that Liberal Jews maintain that one Jewish parent should be sufficient to make someone a Jew and give him or her automatic right of return. Reform Jews argue that conversion to

Judaism under their regulations should also grant such a right of return.

Israel has no state religion, and the religious freedom of all citizens of whatever creed is safeguarded. How to work this out is a matter of debate, particularly for non-Orthodox Jews. Israel is, in reality, a modern state in an imperfect world. Its achievements are certainly remarkable in, for example, land reclamation, medical science, and Hebrew language and literature. Yet its contribution to the 'advancement of the entire Middle East' of which David Ben Gurion spoke in the Declaration of Independence has, in the opinion of many, yet to emerge. That it does emerge is vitally important for Jews who look to Israel for the expression of Jewish values. What happens in Israel matters to Jews everywhere.

Questions

A Matter of Fact

1 Which country passed the May Laws of 1882? (A)

2 What is a shtetl? (A)

3 Who were the 'Lovers of Zion'? (A)

4 Who wrote *The Jewish State*? (B)

5 What meeting took place in Basel in 1897? (B)

6 Which document of 1917 declared British support for a Jewish homeland in Palestine? (E)

7 Which Jewish leader declared Independence? (E)

8 When did Israel and Egypt sign a peace treaty? (F)

9 Which laws in Israel are under rabbinical jurisdiction? (G)

Vocabulary

Give the Hebrew words for the following:

1 The Land of Israel (A)

2 immigration to Israel (literally 'going up') (A)

3 a gathering together (A)

4 Israel's Independence Day (E)

5 Jerusalem Day (F)

A Question of Understanding

Try to give at least two religious explanations in answer to each of the following questions.

1 Why is the Land of Israel special to Jews? (A)

2 Why is Zionism so-called? (A)

3 How did the Dreyfus case influence Zionist thinking? (B)

4 Why is there Ultra-Orthodox opposition to Zionism? (C)

5 Why is Abraham Isaac Kook important in Zionist History? (C)

6 Why was the Six Day War so significant to Israel? (F)

Over to You

Answer these questions fully, giving your reasons, and stating arguments both for and against where appropriate.

1 How far do you think 'Seek peace and pursue it' (Psalm 34:14) sums up the Liberal Jewish attitude to the State of Israel?

2 Do you think it right that only the mother can give Jewish status?

3 David Ben Gurion said:

The State of Israel will prove itself not by material wealth, not by military might or technical achievement, but by its moral character and human values.

How far do you think this is true?

4 Do you think it possible for people of other religions to understand the importance to Jews of a Jewish state?

Assignment

You are preparing for a visit to Israel.

a) Over some weeks, collect information from the media about Israel, noting particular places and events.

b) Write a letter to a friend or relative about your forthcoming visit, explaining why you want to go.

c) In what ways do you think expectations of the visit for a Jew and for a non-Jew would be different?

Preparations for this assignment could include *Jewish Jerusalem* (from the Slide Centre) or *Jerusalem Within These Walls* (a video from Stylus). There are also songs of Israel on the JMD tape and on other tapes available from JMD, e.g. *My Israel Celebrates*, *Halleluyah* (Chasidic songs), and *Jerusalem: The Eternal City*.

7

Birth and Brit Milah (Circumcision)

- Vital moments in the life of a Jew are marked by customs going back to biblical times which have developed according to Halachah and local custom.
- **Brit Milah** (circumcision) is the oldest Jewish ritual to remain unchanged to the present day.
- Brit Milah does not make someone a Jew but symbolises his membership of the covenant people.

- A special ceremony, **Pidyon Haben** (redemption of the son), is sometimes performed when a woman's first child is a boy.
- A Jewish boy is given his Hebrew name at the Brit and a girl is named in the synagogue, usually on the first Sabbath after her birth.

A) A New Life

If someone asks you to tell your life story, you are likely to start with the moment of your birth. When and where you were born will form the beginning of your story. You may well go on to single out particular milestones in your life, such as starting school. When you are old, you will probably recall many of these as you look back on your life. Such milestones are sometimes marked by rituals or 'rites of passage'. A rite of passage is a ceremony in which people think about someone's passage from one stage to another.

Since the very first stage is birth itself, when a baby has independent existence, it is not surprising that the first such celebration occurs in the baby's earliest days. This is particularly true of Judaism, where the creation of a new life is a matter for great rejoicing.

You may have been asked how many children you would like to have. The question seems to assume that you *will* have children, even that everyone is under an obligation to have children. According to Judaism, everyone is. Genesis 1:28 and 9:1 say that it is a mitzvah to have children. Children are regarded as a great blessing, and we see in the Bible and Talmudic writings that the desire for children is strong. The desire for sons is especially strong, for they are the ones who play the social, economic, and religious roles ensuring the physical and spiritual survival of the Jewish community.

'Be fruitful and multiply' is the very first commandment in the Torah (Genesis 1:28).

B)   A Sign in the Flesh

It has been estimated that circumcision is practised by a seventh of the world's population, including people of Asia, Africa, Australia, the Pacific Islands, and North, Central, and South America. In ancient times, many peoples, including Egyptians and Moabites, practised circumcision, but for one people only circumcision was, and is, a wholly religious rite. For Jews, circumcision is a sign in the flesh of the relationship they hold with God. It is an external symbol of the covenant, begun with Abraham (Genesis 17:9–14). As such, the command for members of the community of Abraham to be circumcised has been kept with unbounded devotion. Martyrs died for it in the time of the Maccabees (1 Maccabees 1:61) and in the second century CE, the Emperor Hadrian hoped that by forbidding it he might destroy Judaism. Circumcision is fundamental to Judaism. Any male not born Jewish and wanting to convert to Judaism must be circumcised.

We know then what circumcision signifies. It is not something that turns a baby into a Jew, for, except in the case of a convert, being Jewish is a matter of birth and an uncircumcised Jew is, according to Halachah, still a Jew. It is an external symbol that this child will be brought up as a faithful Jew, a sharer in the covenant (Brit) of Abraham. But, we may ask, why this particular symbol? Why the covenant of circumcision, Brit Milah, the removal of the foreskin?

The Bible does not tell us why, but Jewish literature offers many suggestions. One is that it is appropriate for the sign of Israel's loyalty throughout the generations to be on that part of the body by which future generations are created. A second is that God creates an imperfect world, needing men's co-operation to perfect it. So circumcision makes a perfect male, without the useless foreskin. Man must not be satisfied with his natural condition but must perfect himself and serve God with every organ of his body.

George Eliot said that God cannot make a Stradivarius violin without Stradivarius. What do you think this writer meant?

Questions more easily answered are: where and when is the ceremony performed and by whom? Circumcision is a celebration not just for the family but also for the community. Between the ninth and nineteenth centuries CE, it was often held in the synagogue. Today the preferred place is the home, where a full service is held with a **minyan** (ten adult men required for public prayer) present if possible.

Some circumcisions occur in hospital, performed by a surgeon and with no prayers or other ceremony, but Orthodox, and many non-Orthodox, Jews think that this entails a sad loss of religious significance.

It should take place, in accordance with Leviticus 12:3, on the eighth day after birth, even if this is the Sabbath or the Day of Atonement. The only reason for postponing circumcision is if the baby is not strong enough. The baby's health is established by the doctor and the **mohel** (circumciser), a pious man specially trained in the techniques of the operation. It is a swift operation in which the foreskin of the penis is snipped, its inner lining removed, and a dressing put on to stop the bleeding.

The mother carries the baby in and hands him to a female godparent, who then hands him to the male godparent. These godparents are usually husband and wife, or brother and sister. The baby is then passed to the father. Important in the ceremony is the **sandek** (representative), the man on whose lap the baby is placed for the operation. Prayers follow. The father, who is charged with the responsibility of guiding the child in Jewish living, blesses God for circumcision, by which sons 'enter into the covenant of Abraham our father'. After the baby is named and a drop of wine held to his lips, he is returned to his mother.

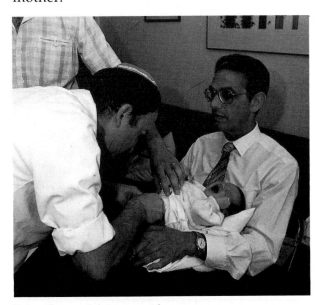

Being the sandek is a great honour.

Another important feature of the ceremony is the throne of Elijah, a special chair on which the father briefly places the baby before handing him to the sandek. This is an ancient custom, expressing the importance of Elijah's presence on this occasion. We see in 1 Kings 18 and 19; and Malachi 3:1; 4:5–6 the vital role of Elijah in defending and judging the Jewish people's loyalty to their covenant with God.

Reform Jews have developed for baby girls a ceremony called the 'Covenant of Life'. It is

an adaptation of the Brit, with God blessed for commanding 'us to sanctify life' rather than for circumcision.

Extension Section

i) Among observant Jews, a popular celebration is the 'Welcome to the Male Child'. This is held in the home, by Ashkenazim on the night following the child's birth, and by Sefardim on the night before circumcision. Suggest why Orthodox Jews would not hold a similar celebration for a baby girl.

ii)   *I am not yet born; provide me*
       With water to dandle me, grass to grow for me,
       trees to talk
              to me, sky to sing to me, birds and a white
       light
              in the back of my mind to guide me.

These words are from a poem by Louis MacNeice entitled '*Prayer before Birth*'. Compose, in poetry or in prose, a prayer before birth for a Jewish girl or boy.

iii)   Why do most Jews think it necessary to mark their covenant-status by a sign in the flesh? What do you think about a view held by the radical wing of Reform Judaism that the covenant of Abraham is purely spiritual, and circumcision, therefore, unnecessary?

C) Pidyon Haben (Redemption of the Son)

The Torah says that because God slew the Egyptian first-born and spared the Israelite first-born, the first-born belong to God. Moreover, the first-born son of the family had the privilege of being a priest, *Cohen*. In the time of Moses, the first-born sons forfeited this privilege by worshipping the golden calf (see Exodus 32). The tribe of Levi did not participate in this unfaithfulness, and so male members of one family from that tribe (Aaron's family) were given the great honour to be priests of God. It was originally God's intention, however, that all first-born sons should be priests. To be set free from this service, other first-born sons had to be 're-deemed', that is, 'brought back'. Redemption money had to be paid to a Cohen, a descendant of Moses' brother Aaron. The ceremony was called **Pidyon Haben** (redemption of the son).

The ceremony is still practised. If a woman's first child is a boy, he is regarded as belonging to God until he is redeemed. This is done by giving silver coins (or an article of value) to God, whose representative is a Cohen. So in this ceremony a Cohen is paid the modern equivalent of five shekels, in accordance with Numbers 18:16.

There is no Pidyon Haben if the father is a Cohen or a Levite, or if the mother is the daughter of a Cohen or Levite. Nor is the first-born son redeemed if the woman's first child was a girl. For the crucial verse, Exodus 13:2, says that it is what 'openeth the womb' that belongs to God.

The rabbis formulated Jewish Law by looking at every word of the biblical law and taking it literally. Therefore, a first-born son delivered by Caesarian section would not require Pidyon Haben, since he had not opened the womb in the natural way. Similarly, a mother whose womb had already been opened by a miscarriage or still-birth would not have Pidyon Haben for her first-born son.

Some non-Orthodox Jews think that girls should also be redeemed, as the idea of a priestly caste is out-of-date and there should, therefore, be no distinction between a boy and a girl. The ceremony, they say, is simply thanking God that the child has survived the first critical month of life. Certainly the element stressed in Pidyon Haben is dedication to God's service by the whole family. It takes place on the thirty-first day after the baby's birth, or on the following day if the thirty-first is a Sabbath or holy day. A baby who has lived thirty-one days is considered likely to thrive.

The Prayer Book gives the procedures. These include the Cohen asking the father which he would rather have, his first-born son or five shekels. After this token sum has been paid over, the Cohen returns the child to the father. The Cohen then pronounces the Aaronic or priestly blessing over the child:

The Lord bless thee and keep thee: the Lord make his face to shine upon thee, and be gracious unto thee: the Lord turn his face unto thee, and give thee peace.

D) What's in a Name?

Does it matter to you if someone gets your surname wrong? Do you know where your surname comes from? Unless you especially like it or are proud of some family connection, you may well not bother much about your surname.

Jews did not have family names at all until late in their history. In the eighteenth and nineteenth centuries, the governments of Austria, France, Prussia, Poland, and Russia required family names. Sometimes the government even assigned a family its name, and there are examples of officials being bribed to give a name with a pleasant meaning, for example, Rosenthal, valley of roses.

Many Jews simply adopted their fathers' first names as their surnames, for instance, Abrams, Jacobs, or Samuelson. A Jewish family might also take its name from its place of origin, for example, Warshawsky from Warsaw. Sometimes the name came from the occupation of the family, for example Schechter (a ritual slaughterer of cattle), or from the medieval custom of emblems, for example, Rothschild (red shield). As you could guess, Cohen and similar sounding names indicate priestly descent. People descended from the tribe of Levi might be called Levi, Levy, Levitt, or Leven.

Do you know why you were given your first name? Was it after a relative or someone famous? How do you feel if someone calls you

BIRTHS

Freedman To Nathan and Anne, a son, Joshua (on April 4th)
Goldstone To David and Susan, a son, Stephen...
Stein To Geoffrey and Ruth, a daughter, Deborah...

Jewish Birth Announcements.
There have been times when Jews have been denied a choice of names. In Nazi Germany, a medieval restriction was revived by which Jews were not to have non-Jewish names. Can you suggest why?

the wrong name? Even if you do not always know what your first name means, or even if it does not suit your character or appearance very well (for instance, you may be big for your age and still be called Paul, which means 'small'), you probably do not like being called the wrong name. For it is your first name which is personal and gives a sense of identity. In the Bible, the name says something about the person named. We see this idea in Exodus 2:10, where Moses receives his particular name because he is drawn out of the water. 'Moses' comes from the Hebrew word for 'to draw out'.

Before family names came into use, a Jew would have just his or her first or given name, together with that of his or her father. This would be in Hebrew, for instance, Yitshak ben Abraham (Isaac son of Abraham), or Miriam

Extension Section

i) In the Bible, personal names are significant. Look up the following passages and say whose name is changed and why:
  a) Genesis 17:3–5;
  b) Genesis 32:22–8 and 35:9–10.

ii) Lionel Blue, a Reform Rabbi, often to be heard on Radio 4's *Thought for the Day*, tells the following humorous story:

There was a Jewish guy who saw a Far-Eastern gentleman in a city restaurant. He was out of sorts, so he picked up a plate of noodles (as one does when one feels like that) and he poured it over the Chinese gentleman. 'That's for Pearl Harbour', he said.
'But I'm Chinese, not Japanese', said the oriental.
'Chinese, Siamese, Japanese, what's in a name?' said the Jew.
As he went to pay his bill, the Chinese gentleman suddenly hit the Jewish guy over the head with a salami. 'That', he said courteously, 'is for the sinking of the Titanic.'
'But', shouted the Jew, 'the Titanic was sunk by an iceberg!'
'Greenberg, Goldberg, iceberg, what's in a name?'

What other Jewish names can you find ending in 'berg'? See if you can discover what the names come from.

iii) At the Brit, the mohel says:

Our God and God of our fathers, preserve this child to his father and to his mother, and let his name be called in Israel _____ the son of _____.

Suggest some appropriate names, choosing them from the Bible or selecting other names that you know are Hebrew.

bat Amram (Miriam daughter of Amram). Every Jew still has such a given name. It is carefully chosen. Among Sefardi Jews, it is the name of a living relative who might be a guiding influence on the child. Ashkenazi Jews give the name of a deceased relative, or a biblical hero or heroine, especially if the name occurred in the week's synagogue reading from the Torah or Prophets. There has been a great increase in the usage of biblical names amongst Jews in Israel. The practice of using only a person's Hebrew name (first name) continues for important Jewish occasions, such as weddings.

Questions

A Matter of Fact

1 Genesis 17:12 gives eight days as the age for circumcision. Which other biblical passage gives this age? (B)

2 Where do we read of Jews being killed rather than break the command to be circumcised? (B)

3 Where are most Orthodox circumcisions performed nowadays? (B)

4 What is the throne of Elijah? (B)

5 What is 'the covenant of life'? (B)

6 What is the literal meaning of the word 'redemption'? (C)

7 Where in the Bible does it say that it is what 'openeth the womb' that belongs to God? (C)

8 Noting the law of Pidyon Haben relates to the woman and not to the man, which of the following require Pidyon Haben:

   a) the second baby boy of a woman whose first baby boy was delivered by Caesarian section;

   b) the first baby boy of a woman whose husband had had male children by a previous wife;

   c) the first baby boy of a woman who has previously miscarried;

   d) a baby boy who has an older sister? (C)

9 On what sort of occasion would someone's Hebrew name be used? (D)

Vocabulary

Give the Hebrew words for the following:

1 circumcision (B)

2 circumciser (B)

3 priest (C)

A Question of Understanding

Try to give at least two religious explanations in answer to each of the following questions.

1 Why is it regarded as a mitzvah to have children? (A)

2 Why is circumcision regarded as fundamental to Judaism? (B)

3 Why is there no Pidyon Haben if the father is a Cohen? (C)

Over to You

Answer these questions fully, giving your reasons, and stating arguments both for and against where appropriate.

1 After the blessing by the baby's father, all present respond:

> Even as this child has entered in the covenant, so may he enter into the Torah, the nuptial canopy [marriage], and into good deeds.

Put into your own words what is being wished for the child. Then say how important you consider each of these wishes, imagining you are the parent of the child.

2 What do you think about the idea that a girl should have Pidyon? (You may find it helpful to refer to Chapter 9.)

Assignment

a) Look at pictures of a Brit Milah (e.g. a filmstrip from the Board of Deputies, *Jewish Family Events – Brit Milah*). List all the main people involved, together with their part in the ceremony.

b) Explain how the various features of the ceremony create the mood of the occasion.

c) To what extent do you think it possible to enter into this mood if you are not yourself Jewish?

8

Bar and Bat Mitzvah

- After circumcision, the next major stage in a Jewish boy's life is when he becomes **Bar Mitzvah** (son of the commandment).
- From his 13th Hebrew birthday onwards, he has the obligations and privileges of an adult male Jew.
- The event is usually celebrated the following Sabbath in the synagogue.
- A girl becomes **Bat Mitzvah** (daughter of the commandment) at 12 years. Celebrations of this vary from community to community.

- Reform and Liberal Jews hold a confirmation ceremony for both boys and girls of about 16.
- Education is highly valued in Judaism, and there is a strong parental obligation to teach a child the faith from an early age.
- A Jewish child may go to classes at the synagogue. He or she may also attend a Jewish school and college.

A) Who's Responsible?

According to Jewish Law, parents are held to be responsible for their son's actions until he is 13 years old. Though boys mature at different rates, the Talmud lays down important landmarks in the life of a male Jew. Among them it sets down 13 as the age 'for the fulfilment of the commandments'.

Automatically, therefore, on his 13th birthday (that is, when he is 13 according to the Jewish Calendar. See Chapter 16) a Jewish boy becomes **Bar Mitzvah** (son of the commandment). This is not one commandment (mitzvah), but all the commandments (mitzvot) that go with being a member of the covenant people (see Chapter 3).

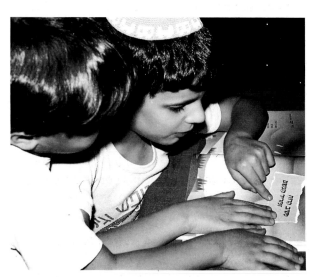

Learning Hebrew. As his Bar Mitzvah gets nearer, the boy will attend Hebrew classes at the synagogue, so that he can read at the Sabbath morning service.

Bar Mitzvah is then the term used for a boy who has become responsible for his own actions, who has gained his religious majority, who is subject to the same obligations and privileges as an adult regarding Jewish observance. Notably, he:

a) must put on tephilin (see Chapter 13) for his morning prayers;
b) can make up a minyan (required number for prayer);
c) is obliged to observe the fast days in full;
d) may be called up to the reading of the Torah.

Watch out for these activities when you read about prayer, the synagogue, and the festivals.

It would seem that Jewish families have from ancient times held a celebratory meal on a boy's 13th birthday. Since the late Middle Ages, however, there has been a ceremony to mark a boy's Bar Mitzvah. The term Bar Mitzvah can, therefore, refer to the boy or to the ceremony. The ceremony does not make a boy Bar Mitzvah. It merely marks the time when he becomes a 'son of the commandment'. If no ceremony were held, the Jewish boy would still be Bar Mitzvah once he was 13.

The ceremony is held in the synagogue on the first Sabbath after the boy's 13th birthday. The Bar Mitzvah himself will take part in the service. He may recite the blessing before the reading from the Torah. He may read the appointed passage from the Prophets, preceded by part of the Torah passage for that Sabbath. If he is thoroughly prepared, he may read the whole of the Torah passage. In this way, he demonstrates his competence to fulfil the demands of an adult male Jew. The boy's father acknowledges that his son is now ready to be responsible for his own actions by reciting the words:

Blessed be he who hath freed me from the responsibility for this child.

The service will often include words from the rabbi, encouraging serious commitment to the obligations of Judaism. These are directed

Bar Mitzvah reading the Torah. Boys sometimes travel all the way to the Western Wall in Jerusalem to celebrate the occasion.

specifically at the Bar Mitzvah but they offer his family and the whole community the opportunity to reaffirm their Jewish faith. After the service, the community often joins in a small celebration in the hall of the synagogue. There may be a further celebratory dinner with family and friends. The Bar Mitzvah is, however, the person and not the celebration, and the significance of this may get lost if, as sometimes happens, a huge banquet is held.

B) What About the Girls?

Judaism accepts that girls mature earlier than boys and sets their age of majority at 12. At 12, therefore, a Jewish girl becomes **Bat Mitzvah** (daughter of the commandment). Orthodox Judaism judges that, on reaching maturity, a girl does not assume the religious obligations of a boy: wearing tephilin, attending synagogue, making up a minyan, being called up to the reading of the Torah (see Chapters 5 and 9). However, from the age of 12, she begins to take on the many obligations which she does have as a Jew. She too is now responsible for her own actions.

Only in recent times has there developed a celebration of the girl becoming Bat Mitzvah. Practices vary from community to community. Synagogues may hold a ceremony of **Bat Chayil** (daughter of worth). This is usually on a Sunday and family and friends gather to hear the Bat Chayil read in Hebrew a passage of her choice. Often a number of girls, who have become 12 during the previous year, are jointly addressed by the rabbi, after each girl has read her passage. There might also be celebrations in the home.

Girls are often given Jewish books at their Bat Chayil.

Gaining in popularity are Bat Mitzvah ceremonies in the synagogue, modelled on the boy's Bar Mitzvah. This is especially so among Reform and Liberal Jews, who believe that there is no difference between men and women in terms of Jewish obligations and privileges. In the early days of Reform Judaism, the Bar Mitzvah ceremony was dropped altogether in favour of a ceremony of confirmation. This was a sort of group graduation ceremony, in which boys and girls aged 15 or 16 were considered old enough to 'confirm' or pledge their loyalty to the covenant at Sinai. Such confirmations still take place in Progressive Judaism, often at the Festival of Shavuot, since this festival celebrates the revelation of God at Sinai (see Chapter 18).

Confirmation was first introduced by Jews in nineteenth century Germany who were unhappy with the Orthodox distinction between male and female responsibilities. They were also worried by the way in which many boys fell away from their Hebrew studies once the Bar Mitzvah ceremony was over. Though these concerns remain, many Progressive congregations nowadays give the option of a Bar or Bat Mitzvah ceremony, provided the boy or girl gives a written pledge to continue his or her religious education until confirmation, to be held two or three years later. In Progressive Judaism, 13 rather than 12 is the age of a girl's Bat Mitzvah, suggesting equality with a boy.

Extension Section

i)   What have been the biggest milestones in your life? What do you remember about your hopes and fears at the time? Was there any particular 'rite of passage' marking this stage?

ii)   If possible, attend a Bar or Bat Mitzvah ceremony. Alternatively, see the filmstrip, *Jewish Family Events – Bar Mitzvah* (from the Board of Deputies).

iii)   What do you think might be the reactions of a Jewish boy whose parents want him to have a Bar Mitzvah ceremony but who themselves observe very few mitzvot?

iv)   Below is an extract from *Marjorie Morningstar* by Herman Wouk (Pocket Books, 1983). It describes a Bar Mitzvah in Manhattan. (Chapter 9 of *Almonds and Raisins* by Maisie Mosco (New English

Library, 1979), gives another interesting picture of Bar Mitzvah, this time in Manchester.) It is held in a Conservative synagogue (or 'temple' as some non-Orthodox Jews call it). Conservative Judaism began in the USA in the early twentieth century and now accounts for some 40 per cent of American Jews. In belief and practice, it lies somewhere between Orthodoxy and Reform (see Chapter 5). In the 1980s, a British version of Conservative Judaism began to grow. It is called the Masorti Movement. Read the passage and then answer the questions which follow.

It was strangely impressive, after all, when Seth stood before the Holy Ark draped in his new purple and white silk prayer shawl on Saturday morning, chanting his reading from the Book of Malachi . . . Seth's voice rang clear and manly over the massed rows of black skull-caps and white prayer shawls, sprinkled here and there with the frilly hats and rich furs of the women. It was a Conservative temple, so the men and women sat together. For years in the Bronx Marjorie had railed at the orthodox practice of separating the sexes; in the twentieth century women weren't second-class citizens, she said . . . Marjorie had little use for any version of the faith. She regarded it as a body of superstitious foolishness perpetuated, and to some degree invented, by her mother for her harassment. The parents managed to drag her to the temple once in a while on Friday evenings when she had no date, but it was always under protest . . .

But today, despite herself, the girl found awe creeping over her as her brother's voice filled the vault of the temple, chanting words thousands of years old, in an eerie melody from a dim lost time. A cloud passed away overhead and morning sunlight came slanting through the dome windows, brilliantly lighting the huge mahogany Ark behind Seth with its arch of

Hebrew words in gold over the tablets of the Law; Know before Whom you stand. Majorie had thrilled the first time her father translated the motto for her; and that thrill came back now as the letters blazed up in the sunlight. Seth sang on, husky and calm, and it occurred to Marjorie that after all there might be a powerful propriety in the old way of separating the men and women. This religion was a masculine thing, whatever it was, and Seth was coming into his own. The very Hebrew had a rugged male sound to it, all different from the bland English comments of the rabbi: it sounded like some of the rough crashing passages in Macbeth *which she so loved. She caught her breath as Seth stumbled over a word and stopped. The silence in the pause was heavy. He squinted at the book, and a murmur began to run through the temple. Seth glanced up, smiled at the bench where his parents sat, and placidly resumed his chanting. Marjorie unclenched her fists; the people around her chuckled and nodded at each other. She heard a woman say, 'He's a good boy.' She could have kissed him. Her little jealous pique was lost in a rush of love for her baby brother, the prattler with blond curls and huge eyes, fading in the tones of the chant as though he were being borne away by a ship. Time had taken him away long ago, of course, but only in this moment did she quite realise that it was so, and that it was for ever.*

i)   From which Book of the Prophets is Seth reading?

ii)   What objection has his sister, Marjorie, to the Orthodox practice of separating men and women in the synagogue?

iii)   What is her general attitude towards the Jewish faith?

iv)   Describe and explain the different feelings that come over Marjorie as she hears Seth chant the reading.

C)   Learning to be Jewish

In order to become Bar or Bat Mitzvah, obligated to carry out the mitzvot, a person has to know what the mitzvot are and how he or she should perform them. Imagine you are a young Jewish child. How are you most likely to learn your faith? You will probably learn it from those who bring you up, usually your parents. This will be not only from direct teaching but by example, as parents try to create an environment for Jewish living, teaching the prayers and symbols of the faith. The obligation of parents to transmit their Jewish faith is taken very seriously. It is laid down in Deuteronomy 6:6–7:

And these words which I command you this day shall be upon your heart; and you shall teach them diligently to your children, and shall talk of them when you sit in your house, and when you walk by the way, and when you lie down, and when you rise.

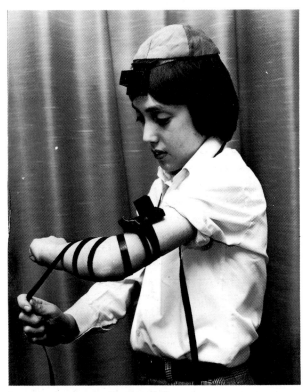

Learning to put on (lay) tephilin.

If the first impressions of Jewish life come from the home, the next come from the synagogue. In addition to the services, children will often attend Hebrew classes. While most learn their Jewish studies at these classes, some 15 per cent of Jewish children of school-age also attend a Jewish school. The Jewish school has a long history. The importance of educating people in the Torah goes back to the last few centuries BCE, after the rebuilding of the Temple. To meet the needs of the time, popular instruction developed.

During the first century CE, the High Priest, Joshua ben Gamla, set up elementary schools in the Holy Land. In this period and right into the Middle Ages, Jewish schooling was for boys only. By 1900, however, the education of girls had become an established feature of Jewish life.

In Britain, there have been Jewish schools since the nineteenth century, but the numbers greatly increased during the 1950s and 1960s. In addition to the normal curriculum, Jewish schools provide instruction in Hebrew, the Bible and, in secondary schools, the Talmud.

Talmudic studies are the main component of Jewish Higher Education, particularly for boys. The institutions are known as **yeshivot** (singular **yeshivah**). There, studies also include the Bible and Law Codes, together with Midrash (see Chapter 4) and Jewish philosophy. Girls too will study these subjects if they go on to Higher Education at seminaries. They usually have a structured three-year course, while boys spend varying numbers of years in yeshivot. (Some British Jews feel they want to study at one of the many yeshivot in Israel, and spend time there, often at considerable cost to themselves.) Many study for several years and some then go on to further training to become rabbis. In Reform and Liberal Judaism, women also may train as rabbis.

The deep respect given to Jewish learning can be seen in the treatment afforded to religious books. Worn-out scrolls, Bibles, and Prayer Books are not thrown away, but buried with dignity and care. In ancient times, disused religious items were put in a storage place called a **genizah**.

Two sayings, the first Talmudic and the second Midrashic, clearly sum up the Jewish attitude to education:

Children who attend school are not to be removed from the study of the Torah even for the building of the sanctuary.

Whoever has a son occupying himself in the study of the Torah is as though he never dies.

Extension Section

i)　Below are some of the courses offered to Jewish adults by the Spiro Institute for the Study of Jewish History and Culture. (Many synagogues also provide courses.) Imagine you are:

    a)　a woman of 23, unable to get a job;
    b)　a housewife whose children have grown up;
    c)　a retired businessman.

State in each case which course you would choose to follow and why:

Drama of the Synagogue
Jewish Humour
Russian Jewish History
Arab–Israeli Conflict
Beginners' Hebrew
Bible as Archaeology
Human Rights
Jews in the Modern World

(ii)　See what you can discover about Jewish education in Eastern Europe. The film *Yentl*, in which Barbra Streisand plays a woman determined to have a full education, is a possible source of information.

iii)　Below are part of the prospectus of a Jewish primary school and a recollection by the headmaster of a Jewish secondary school of his childhood in a non-Jewish school. Read them and then say what you think are the advantages for a Jewish child in Britain of attending a Jewish school. Do you think there may be any disadvantages?

Jewish Studies
Limmudei Kodesh

The School is a Jewish School and therefore Hebrew and Jewish Studies play an integral part both in the School Curriculum and the School Day. A fully qualified and experienced staff is employed by the Board of Religious Education of the United Synagogue to foster and develop this part of the curriculum.

Positive links with Israel are an essential part of the Jewish Studies curriculum. To this end the School has established a twinning programme with the Maimon Primary School in Jerusalem. Each year a group of 4th Year children take part in a two-week Study Tour of Israel and stay with families from the Maimon School.

The Hebrew language is used intensively as a means of tuition and communication in all Limmudei Kodesh lessons throughout the year groups in the School. The aim of the programme is for the children to achieve a competency in the use of Modern Hebrew by the time they leave School.

There is a Jewish Studies Committee comprising Governors, Headteacher, Head of Limmudei Kodesh Department and local Rabbis, which is specifically concerned with the programme of Hebrew and Jewish Studies.

In primary school I was one of three who stood outside the hall listening to the beautiful hymns and carols and it is not surprising that this little seven year old once crept in. To my amazement, when the headmistress said 'Let us pray' everybody started to look at the floor. I could only assume that someone had lost something so I also began to scan the floor to see if I could find it. Suddenly the headmistress said 'Thank you' and everyone looked up. It took me a year to discover how she knew without anyone saying that the item had been found!

Questions

A Matter of Fact

1 Which Jewish book gives 13 as the age for becoming Bar Mitzvah? (A)

2 When is the event celebrated in the synagogue? (A)

3 What part may the boy play in the service? (A)

4 With what words does the father acknowledge that his son is now responsible for his own actions? (A)

5 At what age does a girl become Bat Mitzvah? (B)

6 State one obligation which Orthodox Jewish girls do not have. (B)

7 Where is the Bat Chayil ceremony held? (B)

8 During which festival do Progressive Jews often hold a confirmation ceremony? (B)

9 Where in the Bible are Jewish parents commanded to instruct their children? (C)

10 What is a yeshivah? (C)

Vocabulary

Give the Hebrew words for the following:

1 son of the commandment (A)

2 daughter of the commandment (B)

3 daughter of worth (B)

A Question of Understanding

Try to give at least two religious explanations in answer to each of the following questions.

1 Why should you speak of a boy's 'becoming Bar Mitzvah' rather than 'having a Bar Mitzvah'? (A)

2 Why do some Jews discourage lavish celebrations of a boy's Bar Mitzvah? (A)

3 Why do some Progressive Jews have reservations about having a Bar Mitzvah ceremony at all? (B)

4 Why do some Progressive congregations prolong Jewish education beyond the age of 13? (B)

5 'Train up a child in the way he should go and when he is old he will not depart from it.' (Proverbs 22:6). How might Jewish parents put this into practice? (C)

Over to You

Answer these questions fully, giving your reasons, and stating arguments both for and against where appropriate.

1 What do you think are the marks of an emotionally and spiritually mature person? How far do you think a Jewish girl of 12 and a Jewish boy of 13 can be mature?

2 'The pupil who gives up the piano or guitar or flute at 12 or 13 has wasted his or her time. The Bar or Bat Mitzvah who stops learning has wasted his or her time.' How far do you agree with these statements?

3 'Religion is caught not taught.' How far do you think this is true of Judaism?

Assignment

a) Imagine you are going to interview someone in the week he becomes Bar Mitzvah. What questions would you ask him about his preparations for the following Saturday?

b) Explain why the Bar Mitzvah ceremony is important to
   i) the boy's family and
   ii) the wider Jewish community.

c) If you were a Jewish girl belonging to a Reform community, which ceremony do you think would mean more to you: the Bat Mitzvah or the confirmation? Give your reasons.

Women in Judaism

- In the times of the Bible and the Talmud, women depended on and were obedient to men.
- Changes in society have led Jews to reassess the position of women.
- Orthodox Jews follow the traditional ruling that women do not have to perform mitzvot (obligations) belonging to a particular time of day. As a result, women do not lead public worship.
- Progressive Jews express the equality of the sexes by allowing women to perform the same roles as men.
- The home is vitally important in Judaism. It is women who often bear great responsibility for Jewish homelife.
- Laws of family purity are practised by Orthodox Jews as an expression of the value of sex within marriage.

A) The Way It Was

We have seen that Judaism traditionally makes a clear distinction between a boy and a girl. There are different rites of passage. Some people may find this odd, even unfair. They believe that equality between the sexes is what should be aimed at. Jews who belong to the Progressive Movement feel that this is so. The role of women in Judaism is then an area which different groups of Jews see differently. What to one group is a positive attitude is seen by others as negative. To try to understand the traditional position of Orthodox Judaism, we need to remember the society in which Jewish Law originated.

Biblical society was patriarchal. The man was clearly the head of the family and the woman depended on him and obeyed him

(see Genesis 3:16). It is not that the women mentioned in the Bible were weak. This is far from true when we consider such women as Miriam, Deborah, and Esther. Generally, however, their role was not a public one. It lay in supporting their husbands and in raising a family. They were not expected to do anything which might interfere with this role. Because of this, women were exempt from or excused positive mitzvot (obligations) which had to be carried out at a specific time of day. The woman, therefore, was freed from the obligation of praying, say, in the morning, when she was preoccupied with her home and children. This and other exemptions were intended to free the woman for what she had to do.

The Jewish man had a mitzvah to pray in the morning, afternoon, and evening. Though he could pray at home, his prayer was improved by praying with a minyan, the smallest communal unit. The rabbis took the words in Proverbs 14:28: 'In a multitude of people is the glory of a king' to mean that the more people there are gathered for prayer, the greater the honour paid to God, the King of Kings. If you imagine that the Queen was coming to your area, you would expect people to turn out in force so, the thought is, a 'crowd' gives God his royal welcome. The man also had an obligation to wear certain symbols connected with prayer at specific times (see Chapter 13). The woman, however, could pray when she found it convenient and at home.

B)   The Way It Is

These rules still govern Orthodox practice. A woman may pray in a synagogue at specific times, but she is not obliged to. Because she is not obliged to, she may not count in a minyan of those who are obliged. Nor may she lead others who are fulfilling their obligation. The Talmudic principle is that only a person who is himself obligated to perform a mitzvah may perform that mitzvah on behalf of someone else. Orthodox Judaism, therefore, does not allow women to read the Torah, to lead the prayers, or to preach in the synagogue. There is also the thought in the Talmud that a woman's voice and appearance might prove to be a distraction to the man's prayers.

The Reform position on all these matters is that times have changed. Women are no longer dependent on men and subordinate to them. Not all women will find their fulfilment in being married and in having children. What about women who are single, divorced, or widowed? Therefore, women should share with men the privileges and obligations of Jewish living. How this is to be worked out in practice is being grappled with in the different branches of Judaism. Reform Judaism thinks that the fact that women have not participated as equals with men in the past does not mean

A rabbi.

that they should not participate now. Reform, therefore, counts women as part of the minyan, allows women to read in the synagogue, and to become cantors and rabbis. The Liberal position is much the same as the Reform.

We saw in Chapter 5 that Progressive Judaism feels that it is sometimes necessary to break out of Halachic norms in order to express Jewish values in new circumstances. There is certainly much heart-searching discussion going on about all sorts of questions that relate to women's relationships with men. Orthodox Judaism, however, insists that Jewish Law is followed. It recognises that new situations and perspectives arise, but says that these must not lead to any abandonment of Halachah. Modern society must not, according to Orthodox Jews, dictate the terms for Jewish living. Rather, modern trends should be examined carefully in the light of Halachic principles. This, they say, is very much the case with the growth in women's freedom and responsibility. Halachah should develop, as it has always done from Torah, through the Talmud, codes, and responsa, to find ways of expressing sexual equality. This is a demanding task, nowhere more so than in the home.

C)   Home: a Woman's Place

Traditionally, Jewish women have to keep the negative mitzvot, those that begin, 'Thou shalt not . . .' They have also to keep the positive mitzvot that are not bound to particular times. There are, however, certain things that women are obliged to do at particular times – for instance, fast on the Day of Atonement and eat unleavened bread at Passover. Such things are of major importance for all Jews, men and women. All the specific obligations of a woman can be carried out at home, and this is the important point.

In ancient times, the rabbis did not allow women to be witnesses or to become learned in the Torah. This would have required women to enter the public area. The rabbis did, however, acknowledge the influence of women and encourage great respect for them. To our modern minds, the confining of women's activity to the home may seem very limiting. 'She's just a housewife' is clearly meant to be insulting. To understand the traditional position, we have to realise how important the home was and, many would say, is.

Freeing their husbands to study the Torah, the women bore the responsibility for the home. They had the mitzvah to have children and in the home they brought up and taught the children. There, the women set the tone for Jewish family life. From the Orthodox point of view then, to say that a woman's place is in the home is to value women and their role very highly.

All that goes on in the home should, it is believed, be expressive of Judaism. This is symbolised by the mark of the Jewish home, the **mezuzah** (plural **mezuzot**). The mezuzah is a parchment scroll on which are written two passages: Deuteronomy 6:4–9 and 11:13–21. These two passages command the Jew to write God's words on the doorposts of his house. In this way, the occupants of the house have a constant reminder of God and his Torah. The two passages are hand-written on a strip of parchment, rolled up and, usually nowadays, placed in a mezuzah case. It is the parchment, however, and not the case, which is vital. The parchment takes its name from the Hebrew word for doorpost.

The mezuzah is fixed to the front doorpost. Many Jews have a mezuzah on the doorpost of each room of the house used for living. They touch the mezuzah and then their lips when they enter or leave a room. The mezuzah is then a permanent visual aid, reminding the Jew of God's commands in his or her homelife.

Fixing the mezuzah is an important occasion. Authorities differ on whether it should be placed horizontally or vertically, so it is placed slanting (upwards towards the room as you enter).

D) Sex

Rabbinic tradition stresses that sex is to be enjoyed. It is a creative act, the most intimate expression of a relationship. Whilst retaining a modesty and reserve, the Torah is strikingly frank and explicit. A married couple are encouraged to have sexual relations on Shabbat, partly in imitation of God's creativity, but mainly because Shabbat is meant to be a happy time. The Talmud rates physical satisfaction highly. The husband should have thought for his wife's pleasure during intercourse. It even gives rules about what the woman can expect from her husband. A man who works away from home, for instance, must not let his absences deprive his wife of sex for too long.

The Mishnah sets a minimum for sexual intercourse: people who do not need to work for a living – every day; labourers – twice a week; ass-drivers – once a week; camel-drivers – once every thirty days; sailors – once every six months.

This consideration of a woman's right to sexual satisfaction sounds quite modern. Not so modern-sounding is the restraint attached to sex in Judaism. With the emphasis on the pleasure of sex goes an equally strong emphasis on the discipline of sex. Sex is to be part of a relationship, physical and emotional.

Early in their history, the Jews were commanded to avoid the sexual practices of their neighbours, notably adultery. Sex was to be confined to marriage, where it was designed to deepen the relationship. This remains the Jewish view. There is no suggestion that sex is bad, or that the celibate life is specially holy. On the contrary, it is the very goodness and holiness of sex which leads to this insistence that sex belongs within a permanent relationship.

E) Separateness

Traditional Judaism has the idea of family purity. It too is linked to the belief that sex, as a God-given capacity, is something to be enjoyed yet never taken for granted. The laws of family purity are seen as the key to marital happiness, consideration, and respect. The idea is that during her period, and for seven days afterwards, a woman does not have sexual intercourse. She is **niddah** (separated) from physical contact with her husband. Any longings he might have during that time will just have to wait.

The laws of niddah are given in Leviticus 15:19–24; 18:19; 20:18. These revolve round the idea of ritual purity. Anything and anyone coming into contact with the Temple must stay pure. This purity was thought to be lost by contact with defiling substances, such as a dead body. Most people did not have to worry about being impure in this way, as they were not dealing with holy things in the Temple. But people like priests had to purify themselves if they had been defiled. This they did by washing themselves. This was nothing to do with being sinful. It was more like a courtesy to God, in the same way that, nowadays, a mechanic or a painter would have a wash before going to a party. There is nothing wrong in coming into contact with oil or paint, but to take it with you into someone else's house would be disrespectful. The Jews thought that certain substances left a sort of invisible dirt which needed ritual cleansing.

We are not absolutely sure why menstrual blood came to be regarded as a defiling substance. Leviticus gave the rule about a menstruating woman, however, and the rabbis later extended the period of separation to a minimum of 12 days.

That the besieged Jews on Masada took trouble to construct **mikvaot** (plural of mikveh) shows how vital ritual purity was.

Extension Section

It has been suggested that the idea of menstrual blood being defiling has to do with the fear the ancients had of unknown forces. They feared the mixture of life and death forces in conception and childbirth. For such fears in medieval times, see the novels of Isaac Bashevis Singer, e.g. *The Slave* (Penguin, 1962).

F) Ritual Cleansing

The cleansing process for a married woman after her menstrual period or after childbirth is an interesting one. (A woman who is about to be married also goes through the process, as her previous periods are considered to have rendered her niddah.) It involves going to a **mikveh**. The word means 'a gathering'. The gathering is of water. For all ritual cleansing, of people and of objects, water which has gathered naturally, rain water, is needed. A stream, river, pond, lake, or ocean constitutes a mikveh. Needless to say, Jewish women do not go rushing naked into the nearest stream, river, pond, lake, or ocean. Rather, they go to a specially constructed pool (a mikveh). Tap water, heated and disinfected, can top up the pool, but the pool is made in such a way that rain water is gathered to form an essential part of it.

The point of the mikveh is not physical cleansing. The mikveh has a bathroom attached, in which the woman prepares herself for the mikveh, removing nail polish, for example, so that nothing comes between her and the pure water. It is a spiritual cleansing. Purity and impurity in Jewish thought are nothing to do with hygiene, but are to do with a spiritual state. We see this idea in the fact that men too have the custom of immersion. This is on the eve of Yom Kippur (the Day of Atonement) when they are getting rid of anything that comes between them and God. Some men immerse themselves in a mikveh on the eve of Shabbat and festivals. But regular immersion is a mitzvah only for women. They usually go as soon as possible after the twelfth day ends (in Jewish thinking, this is at sunset rather than at midnight) so that the 'separateness' from their husbands does not last any longer than is necessary.

It is obvious that these rules demand great restraint. Those who keep them argue that they help keep a marriage fresh, encouraging respect and appreciation. The Talmud suggests that after immersion in a mikveh, a wife is like a bride again. Most towns with a sizeable Orthodox population will have a mik-veh. In recent years, there has been an increase in the number of Jews using a mikveh. Reform Judaism rejects the whole concept of niddah, and so Reform communities do not have a mikveh.

When she is ready each woman enters the mikveh. A female attendant checks that the immersion is complete.

Questions

A Matter of Fact

1 What term is given to the sort of society indicated in Genesis 3:16? (A)

2 Name one woman in the Bible. (A)

3 Which branch of Judaism does not count women in the minyan? (B)

4 Which branches of Judaism have women rabbis? (B)

5 What is written on a mezuzah? (C)

6 Where exactly do Jews fix a mezuzah? (6)

7 Where in the Bible do we find the laws of niddah? (7)

8 What sort of water is needed for a mikveh? (F)

9 When does a woman go to the mikveh? (F)

Vocabulary

Give the Hebrew word for the following:

1 doorpost (C)

2 separated (E)

3 immersion pool (literally a 'gathering' of water) (F)

A Question of Understanding

For each of the following statements, say which explanations are correct.

1 Biblical society was different from our own because:

a) women were weaker than men;

b) women did not play a public role;

c) men outnumbered women. (A)

2 The Talmud exempts women from mitzvot linked to time because:

   a) women are such bad time-keepers;

   b) only Jewish men are allowed to pray;

   c) women cannot guarantee to be free from family responsibilities at particular times. (A)

3 Jews believe that intercourse should only be within marriage because:

   a) they do not acknowledge the power of the sex drive;

   b) they think the sex drive needs directing;

   c) they think sex is meant to deepen a marriage. (D)

Over to You

Answer these questions fully, giving your reasons, and stating arguments both for and against where appropriate.

1 An Orthodox male blesses God for not having created him a slave, a Gentile, or a woman. By this he means that he is grateful for the privilege of all the mitzvot. Why do non-Orthodox Jews not say this prayer? It you were a Jewish woman, do you think you would be happy about this prayer?

2 The apparently archaic idea of niddah is said by those who uphold it to have great value. It gives a woman independence at a time when she may not feel too comfortable, and the resumption of marital relations corresponds with the time of month when she is most ready to conceive. What do you think about these ideas?

Assignment

a) Ask members of your class to sum up the main points of ritual purity.

b) On the basis of their answers, list the advantages and disadvantages for a Jew of practising these laws nowadays.

c) Imagine you are taking part in a debate between an Orthodox Jew and a Reform Jew on the role of women in Judaism. Which side would you prefer to speak on and why?

10

Marriage and Divorce

- Judaism thinks that men and women are most fulfilled through the special relationship of marriage.
- This depends on the partners being loyal and faithful to each other.
- A Jewish marriage is called **kiddushin** (sanctification).
- It always takes place under **chupah** (a canopy), a symbol of the marital home.
- The most important moment is the giving of the ring.

- A marriage contract, a **ketubah**, states the man's responsibility to provide for his wife.
- A Jewish wedding can only take place when both partners are Jewish, either by birth or by conversion.
- Judaism allows divorce if a marriage fails.
- For all except Liberal Jews, this requires a **get** (a divorce contract).
- The divorce procedure is conducted at a Bet Din (rabbinic court).

A) Why Marry?

Consider the following quotations from the Talmud:

Your wife has been given to you in order that you may realize with her life's great plan; she is not yours to vex or grieve. Vex her not, for God notes her tears.

Be careful not to hurt your wife, because woman is prone to tears and sensitive to wrong. Be careful about the honour of your wife, for blessing enters the house only because of the wife.

A man who has no wife is doomed to an existence without joy, without blessing, without experiencing life's true goodness, without Torah, without protection and without peace.

It is clear that Judaism rates marriage very highly. It is seen as the way to physical and spiritual fulfilment. Sex is stressed not just in order to produce children, but also for the way in which it can express and deepen love. The above quotations speak of the wife being given to the man. This reflects the patriarchal society at the time of the Bible and the Talmud. The idea that it is man who begins the relationship and man who, at times, ends it comes through in the traditional Jewish marriage and divorce rites.

However, if you look again at these words from the Talmud, you may get the feeling that Judaism sees not the man but the woman as central. She is the one on whom man depends. He needs her for 'life's great plan'. She is nearer to God in her sensitivity. It has been suggested that this is why a woman does not have to perform so many mitzvot. Prayer comes more naturally to her. What do you think about the idea of woman's spiritual superiority?

From the beginning, it is seen to be God's design that there are male and female (Genesis 1:27) and that a man should cherish a woman in an intimate relationship (Genesis 2:24). Judaism presents the woman as the home-builder. The hallowing of the home is expressed in the woman's special mitzvah, the mikveh, and in all the food laws which the woman has to maintain. Even in times when girls were given little Jewish education, they were thoroughly trained in these laws. For both man and woman then, marriage is seen as desirable. It is in the ties and obligations of marriage that God is to be hallowed.

This idea is very clearly expressed in the Hebrew word for marriage, **kiddushin** (sanctification). Marriage is a sacred relationship, a setting apart. In marriage, one woman is set apart for one man. Faithfulness, loyalty, and mutual respect are expected in Jewish marriage. Polygamy was not actually forbidden until about 1000 CE. The evidence suggests, however, that for centuries earlier monogamy had been the norm in Jewish life.

B) The Marriage Ceremony

Jewish weddings can take place on any day of the week except Shabbat and festivals. These days are already joyful and legal transactions are not allowed then. A Jewish religious ceremony is a legal transaction, and in this country there is no need for a civil ceremony. There are also periods of mourning, personal and national (see Chapters 11 and 20), when such happy events as marriages cannot be held. Most Jewish weddings take place on a Sunday, usually in the afternoon. This is often a

Choose two pictures and say what thoughts they evoke about marriage.

Under the chupah.

convenient time for people travelling some distance.

It is always held under a **chupah** (a canopy). Often the chupah is elaborately decorated and supported by four poles covered with flowers. Sometimes it is simply a prayer shawl held over the heads of the couple. The chupah symbolises the marital home. As the ceremony begins, the bride joins the bridegroom, who is already under the chupah. Also under the chupah are relatives and those conducting the marriage ceremony. Usually the chupah is in a synagogue, but sometimes the ceremony takes place in the open air.

Though there are some variations, the Jewish marriage ceremony generally takes a set form:

- Initial blessings of wine and marriage;
- The ring;
- The marriage contract;
- The final (seven) blessings.

The marriage ceremony was originally in two parts, with about a year between them. The first part, the betrothal, took place in the bride's home. The couple became legally bound to each other but did not live together. This first part is now what is known as the initial blessings. A cup of wine is blessed as a symbol of joy. Both partners drink from it. They share their joy. The actual marriage used to be when the bride entered the chupah. There the ring would be given, the contract read, and further blessings said over wine. The betrothal and marriage ceremonies are now combined.

The crucial moment now, as then, is when the bridegroom places the ring on the bride's finger. In most congregations, this is the forefinger of the right hand where it can be displayed most clearly to the witnesses. (It is later transferred.) The bridegroom says the words:

Behold, thou art consecrated to me by this ring, according to the Law of Moses and of Israel.

These words are important legally and religiously. They constitute the vows of Jewish marriage, though in some Liberal ceremonies in this country, both the man and the woman recite the English words: 'With this ring, I thee wed . . .' Reform congregations mainly follow the traditional form, but it is usual for the bride at this point to give the groom a ring, while making the same declaration. The vows 'until death do us part' are not part of Jewish marriage. A life-long commitment is implied, but Judaism does not believe that people can promise this.

After the giving of the ring, the person conducting the wedding (usually a rabbi, though any observant Jew familiar with the Law can officiate) reads out the marriage contract, the **ketubah**. The ketubah is in Ara-maic, and often an English summary of it is read. The ketubah is the written marriage settlement. It states the practical commitment of the husband to provide for his wife. It protects her by guaranteeing her a share in the husband's estate in the event of divorce or his death. Sometimes the ketubah is drawn up and signed during the ceremony. In some communities the bridegroom reads and agrees to the ketubah before the ceremony begins. In Reform communities, there is often a simple marriage certificate, which both bride and groom sign.

The marriage closes as it began with blessings recited over a cup of wine. Both partners drink from this second cup, again symbolising their resolve to share everything during their life together. The seven blessings link the couple with the story of creation, the history of Israel, and all its future hopes. They are recited again at the end of the wedding reception. Traditionally, they are recited at the end of the celebratory meal, held in a different home for each of the seven nights following the wedding.

Other features that often accompany a Jewish wedding are:

- fasting before the ceremony, as the couple prepare themselves for a solemn as well as joyful occasion;
- music from the choir;
- a sermon from the rabbi;
- the breaking of a glass (the groom steps on it), symbolising the destruction of the Temple and the couple's awareness that, whilst they are happy, others may be sad;
- a brief period where the couple are left in a private room, signifying their new status as man and wife.

This is quite a plain ketubah. Especially among Sefardim, it is often colourfully decorated.

C) Choosing a Partner

Perhaps you have heard the song from *Fiddler on the Roof*, 'Matchmaker, matchmaker, make me a match'. There are still matchmakers today. (You may know some unofficial ones!)

They make it their business to introduce people they think are suited. The decision to marry is, of course, the couple's. However, it is more usual for Jews to meet their prospective partners informally like everyone else. If their work and leisure activities take them into predominantly Jewish circles, the likelihood is that one Jew will marry another Jew. However, most Jews do not live in isolation from non-Jews, and there is always the possibility that a Jew will fall in love with a non-Jew. What happens then?

Love is not easily legislated for, and the various branches of Judaism wrestle with their official reactions to intermarriage. Orthodox, Reform, and Liberal Jews all lay stress on Jewish culture, and this is more likely to be preserved if it is something which both partners share. Jews who keep the food laws (see Chapter 12) may have difficulty if they marry non-Jews, unless, of course, the non-Jew con-

verts. Conversion is a very big step, involving a long period of education in Jewish beliefs and practices. Judaism does not normally seek converts, so the question arises: is it better to encourage conversion when a prospective partner is not Jewish or to risk alienating the Jewish partner by making a mixed marriage difficult? How are those appointed to judge in such matters to decide how genuine are both the love and the desire to convert?

One thing is clear. Jewish marriage is about a Jewish home. Therefore, no one who is not Jewish, either by birth or conversion, can be married in a synagogue. In this country, acts of parliament stipulate that both partners must be 'persons professing the Jewish religion'. Nor are rabbis allowed to participate in non-Jewish marriage ceremonies. Honesty is the aim. People must be clear whether they want a Jewish marriage or not, and not try to have it both ways.

Extension Section

i) For a good description of a girl's conversion to Judaism because of its importance to her fiancé, see Rosemary Friedman's novel, *Rose of Jericho*, pp. 42, 43, 112, 113, 197, 201–4 (Futura, 1984). For other insights into the family friction often caused by intermarriage, see Maisie Mosco's trilogy, *Almonds and Raisins*, *Scattered Seed*, and *Children's Children* (see page 22 for details). From these or other sources, see what you can find out about attitudes to intermarriage.

ii) The graph below shows a sharp decline in synagogue marriages between 1972 and 1982. During this period, this decline was sharper than for other types of marriage. What explanations can you think of for this? What do you think a Jewish couple may miss by not having a synagogue marriage?

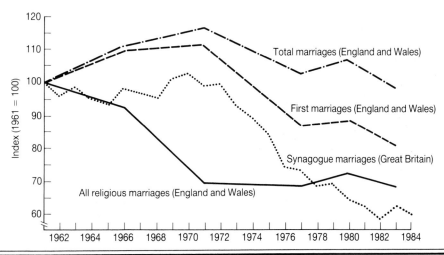

D) When It All Goes Wrong

You may well be aware of the rising divorce rate in Britain and in many Western countries. The rise amongst Jews has been slower than amongst non-Jews but, in recent years, it has come close to the national rate. Divorce is a very delicate area, and, for the people involved, usually extremely painful. It is unwise to generalise about its causes and its results. There are, however, a few important facts about divorce in Judaism.

From the very earliest times, Judaism has recognised that divorce may be necessary. We find in the Torah permission for divorce and the legal procedure for it. Deuteronomy 24:1 says that a man may divorce his wife if he has found 'some indecency in her'. You can imagine that the rabbis had difficulty over agreeing on what constituted 'some indecency'. Did it mean adultery, defined as the married woman having intercourse with someone other than her husband, or could a man divorce his wife for small things which did not please him?

In many people's thinking, who is to blame is an important question in a divorce. Until 1971, the British civil divorce law apportioned blame in that it set out the 'grounds for divorce'. Such grounds (e.g. cruelty) still exist in civil law, but there is now the fundamental 'ground' of the irretrievable breakdown of a marriage. Neither partner need have done anything that a court considers wrong. Yet the marriage may have failed and both partners want a divorce. Further complications arise, of course, if only one partner wants a divorce.

Jewish Law has always accepted the ground of marriage breakdown. It is not concerned with other people's judging and blaming. It simply recognises that marriages fail and grants a divorce, without establishing who has done what. If both partners have decided that they want their marriage ended, then the procedure is quite straightforward. Some may see this as devaluing marriage. Jews say, however, that marriage is an intimate relationship and that there is no point in staying in a marriage if the relationship has clearly broken down. If, however, a Jewish marriage is in serious difficulties, the couple is encouraged to make every effort to overcome them and to save their marriage. There is much sadness and regret in the Jewish community if divorce is the outcome. The belief is that God intended marriage to be for life. The Talmud says: 'If a man divorces his first wife, even the Altar sheds tears.'

E) The Divorce Process

A tractate of the Mishnah is devoted to the subject of divorce. It develops the basic procedure laid down in Deuteronomy 24. This rests on a man's handing his wife 'a bill of divorce', a get. It is at once striking that it is always the man who gives the get. The Torah makes this legal act necessary. No man is allowed simply to expel his wife nor, if a blameless woman refuses to accept a get, is there anything he can do about it. A woman, however, cannot give her husband a get. As with the ketubah, the certificate beginning a marriage, so with the get, the certificate ending it. The assumed legal superiority of the man goes back to biblical times.

There are many Jews who think that this inequality is unacceptable today. Liberal Jews do not have a get or any religious divorce procedure. A civil divorce dissolves the marriage. Reform Jews may follow the traditional procedure of a get. If, however, it is the woman who wants a divorce and the man will not grant her a get, the Reform Bet Din (rabbinic court) may issue a certificate of divorce. Reform feels that it is not fair that a husband can refuse a get, especially when his motives may not always be good. Orthodox Judaism does not accept such a certificate as a get and, without a get, a woman cannot remarry in an Orthodox synagogue. Indeed, it is considered that a woman without a get is still married, even after a civil divorce.

A woman whose husband is missing also remains married, unless there are very strong grounds to believe that he is dead. She is **agunah** (anchored). If she wants to remarry, she cannot according to Jewish Law. Reform Judaism rejects the idea of agunah. It regards a woman widowed if a civil court has declared her husband dead. She is then free to remarry in a Reform synagogue.

In most countries, there is a civil divorce before the religious divorce. In Israel, where laws of marriage and divorce are under rabbinical jurisdiction, a get is required for a woman to be divorced. Israel is the one country, however, where a man who refuses his wife a get can be compelled to grant her one by the religious court. This court has the power to imprison him if he refuses.

In all countries, it is the Bet Din, made up of at least three rabbis, which carries out the religious divorce. The rabbis preside over the actual handing over of the get, which is carefully prepared by a scribe and then signed by two witnesses. The get says: 'Behold you are permitted to every man.' (What words in the marriage ceremony do these words reverse?) The purpose of the get is to grant the wife freedom, and it is to her that the husband hands it. One or more of the partners can appoint a representative if they cannot appear in person. The formality and solemnity of the occasion correspond to those of the marriage ceremony. The couple are not appearing as adversaries in a civil court, but as people undoing before God the commitment they once made. The marriage was 'in conformity with the rabbis' rulings' and so, now, is the divorce.

The man hands his wife a bill of divorce. In what way do you think a divorcing couple might benefit from having this formal and final ceremony?

Questions

A Matter of Fact

1 What words legally bind the couple together? (B)

2 What comes before and what comes after the reading of the ketubah? (B)

3 Who signs the marriage certificate in a Reform synagogue? (B)

4 What symbolises the mixture of joy and sorrow in the ceremony? (B)

5 What does Deuteronomy 24:1 say a man must do before he can end his marriage? (D)

6 Where is a get handed over? (E)

Vocabulary

Give the Hebrew words for the following:

1 marriage or sanctification (A)

2 canopy (B)

3 marriage contract (B)

4 divorce contract (E)

5 anchored (E)

A Question of Understanding

Try to give at least two religious explanations in answer to each of the following questions.

1 Why is marriage given such a strong emphasis in Jewish life? (A)

2 Why are there two separate sets of blessings in the wedding ceremony? (B)

3 Why, if it discourages divorce, does Judaism permit it? (D)

4 Why is a woman whose husband is missing not allowed to remarry in an Orthodox synagogue? (E)

Over to You

Answer these questions fully, giving your reasons, and stating arguments both for and against where appropriate.

1 Do you think too much pressure is put on people to marry? Is this stronger among Jews than among non-Jews?

2 Do you think that it is important to marry someone who shares your religious beliefs? Is this particularly important for Jews?

3 What would you consider a good reason for someone to convert to Judaism?

4 Do you think that the Jewish divorce process is too easy?

Assignment

a) Describe or illustrate by a series of drawings the main features of a Jewish wedding ceremony. It may help to see the filmstrip, *A Seal upon thy Heart* (from the JEB) or the slide sequence, *A Jewish Wedding* (from the Slide Centre).

b) Explain the meaning of each part of the ceremony and of any symbols used.

c) Which of these ideas about marriage do you think is most important? Say why. Are there any ideas expressed in the ceremony with which you would disagree? Give your reasons.

Death

- Jews stress the sanctity of human life. Everything possible should be done to maintain health and sustain life.
- Judaism acknowledges the reality of death. It seeks to prepare people for death and to offer relatives ways of coming to terms with sadness and loss.
- Varied customs surrounding death come from different places and periods of Jewish history, but they are meant to express the equality of all human beings and the involvement of the community.
- Jews believe in an after-life, basing their ideas about this on their belief in a just and loving God.

A) Preparing for Death

It is sometimes said that death has replaced sex as the forbidden subject. People do not want to talk or even think about it. If a close relative or friend dies, we are likely to think and talk about death, but generally we keep off the subject. We fear death as something unknown, yet it is the one certainty of our life, though we may not know when and how we shall die.

In their funeral service, Jews affirm that one day God will conquer death itself, saying:

He maketh death to vanish in life eternal; and the Lord God wipeth away tears from off all faces . . .
(Isaiah 25:8)

Meanwhile, death is real and makes deep demands on people's faith and emotions. Many rituals have grown up, enabling Jews to express their feelings, values, and beliefs. As with marriage rituals, different, sometimes contradictory, explanations are offered for death rites. Perhaps we would be wrong in seeking a single and logical explanation for each ritual. Our task is to look at the main practices of Jews today and to see if we can establish the purposes and ideas behind them.

Though people can and do die young, we tend to link death with old age. Judaism regards old age as a distinction and demands respect for it. The Torah warns against disregarding old people, thinking that they have had their day. On the contrary, the old are to be respected for their experience and their wisdom.

Judaism does not gloss over death's approach but encourages people to be realistic about its inevitability and, sometimes, its unexpectedness. The Mishnah says: 'Repent one day before thy death'. Since nobody can know when this will be, the saying urges daily repentance. If it is clear that someone old or

Suggest two areas of conflict that might have arisen to prompt these comments.

sick is dying, the death-bed confession should be recited either by the dying person or, if he or she is unable, by those present, helping him or her to die as a Jew. This confession, largely from the Shulchan Aruch, is found in the Prayer Book. It begins:

I acknowledge unto thee, O Lord my God and God of my fathers, that both my cure and my death are in thy hands.

and ends:

Hear, O Israel: the Lord is our God, the Lord is one.

Ideally, every Jew dies with this proclamation of faith on his or her lips.

Extension Section

i)   What do you think it means to 'Honour your father and your mother' (Exodus 20:12)? Would a Jew think it right always:

a)   to obey parents;

b)   to give up work in order to care for an elderly parent?

Give reasons for your answers.

ii)   Do people get wiser as they get older? Explain why you are either grateful or resentful when older people give you advice. Is a Jew likely to feel differently about this?

B)   Coping with Death

Death is defined in Halachah as the end of respiration. In Orthodox thought, there must be no interference with the body. Unless the law requires it, Jews will always prefer there to be no *post mortem*. The Jew must be afforded respect and company. The family should not bear all the responsibility for this. Membership of a synagogue usually includes membership of a burial society, who make the necessary arrangements for the funeral. Many communities have such a society, made up of men and women considered worthy of attending to the dying and dead. It is called a **chevra kaddisha** (sacred society). Its members are not paid for their tasks of staying with someone as he or she dies, or for preparing the body for burial. This assistance, which can never be repaid, is regarded as a privilege.

Formal rules were established by the rabbis, responding to the emotions of the bereaved. Just before or soon after the funeral, Orthodox mourners keep the custom of formally tearing their clothes as a sign of deep grief. Though not required by Reform Judaism, this may offer an outlet for emotion.

To express spiritual cleanliness, the body is washed ritually in the home or the mortuary and then clothed in the plainest white garments, including a **kittel**, a smock-like garment, worn by Jewish men on the Day of Atonement (see p. 162). It is placed in a simple, unpolished coffin with a **tallit** (prayer shawl) around the shoulders if the deceased is a man. One of the shawl's fringes (see p. 106) is cut, to indicate that the dead are not subject to mitzvot. The coffin is covered with a plain black sheet.

The funeral should take place as soon after death as possible as a mark of honour, but not on Shabbat or the first and last days of festivals. The funeral ceremony is held in a hall in the cemetery grounds and stresses the merits of the person who has died and trust in God's justice. Then everyone fulfils the mitzvah of escorting the body to the grave.

Reform Judaism does not object to cremation, but Orthodox Jews believe that the Torah indicates that man must return to the dust (Genesis 3:19). The purpose of burial is that the body can decompose and return naturally to the earth, and be physically resurrected in

Those present at the burial help cover the coffin with earth. However painful, the finality and reality of death need to be recognised.

the Messianic Age. In biblical times, the body was buried, without a coffin, in direct contact with the soil. This is still the practice in Israel.

The end of the funeral marks the beginning of mourning. One expression of this is the parting greeting to the mourners gathered in the hall afterwards: 'May God comfort you among those who mourn for Zion and for Jerusalem.' This is also said by those who visit the mourners in the week after the funeral. A popular greeting at this time is: 'I wish you a long life.' You may think this an insensitive greeting to someone bereaved, but it expresses the important Jewish belief in the sanctity of life. Life is to be lived.

The other sign that mourning begins after the funeral is the reciting of the **Kaddish**. Kaddish is the Aramaic word for 'holy', 'set apart', 'sanctified', and the prayer takes its name from the opening line which affirms the holiness of God:

Magnified and sanctified be his great Name in the world which he hath created according to his will.

Children are obliged to recite the Kaddish at the funeral of a parent and daily for 11 months following the death. When there are no children, it is recited by other relatives or someone specially engaged for the purpose. In this way, children and parents are united in their loyalty to God. For this prayer focuses not on the dead but on God's name, praying that the world will acknowledge its holiness. It points forward to the establishment of God's kingdom with its promise of resurrection.

In this prayer, the mourners affirm that, although he has bereaved them, God is still their God. By reciting such a prayer when bereaved, they are saying that they continue to accept that God is the ruler of the universe even though they are at a low point of their lives. They acknowledge that life, in God's world, goes on. The Kaddish has been the affirmation of mourners since the Middle Ages in Germany, but the prayer itself goes back to Talmudic times. Spoken by a leader with a response by the congregation, some form of it is always offered in public prayer by Jews throughout the world.

C) After Death

How can you tell when someone is very sad? This is not always easy, as people do not all behave alike. Despite the variety of people, however, there are certain common reactions, particularly to deep loss. If you have not experienced this yourself, you might ask a relative or friend how he or she felt in the year following a close bereavement. If you do, you are likely to be told about different stages of grieving.

Whilst it would be wrong to expect everyone to recover at the same pace, Jews believe that there should be a gradual return to the rhythm of normal life. Once home from the funeral, close relatives of the deceased, be they father, mother, son, daughter, brother, sister, husband, or wife, spend the first seven days in deep mourning, surrounded by friends and relatives.

This seven-day period is known as **shiva**, the Hebrew for 'seven'. It involves various expressions of intense mourning. Men do not shave and hair is not cut, as a sign of withdrawing from society and its concern with physical appearance. The mourners need their strength, however, so the first meal is prepared by friends. Throughout shiva, members of the community support the mourners by gathering to hold services in the home. The first three days of grief are particularly intense and during them the mourners cannot count in the minyan. During shiva, they may leave their home only on Shabbat. They do not join the synagogue congregation until after Shabbat has been welcomed on the Friday evening, as the joy of this welcome would be inappropriate for them.

Following shiva there is a further period of restrictions. This is known as **sheloshim** (30). It lasts 30 days after the funeral (see Deuteronomy 34:8). The mourner returns to work, as undue mourning would be a rebuke to God, but festivities such as parties and dances are ruled out. All religious festivals, however, are

During shiva the mourners sit on low seats.

observed during shiva and sheloshim. (Can you suggest why?)

After 30 days, normal life is resumed, except for someone mourning a parent. In this case the restrictions of sheloshim continue for a full year after the funeral. At the end of the year, the children observe **Yahrzeit** (anniversary). This is a day of reflection and repentance, and so some Jews fast on it. On the eve of Yahrzeit they light a special Yahrzeit candle, which burns for 24 hours. They may attend synagogue and recite Kaddish. They may study the Torah, and give to charity.

On Yahrzeit, the children visit the grave, often leaving a small stone on the tombstone as a sort of visiting card. Tombstones are not erected at the time of burial, but within a period of several months to a year. A special ceremony is held at the unveiling of the tombstone. Relatives and friends are usually notified about this and attend. This and all the commemorations on Yahrzeit are intended to help in the bereavement process.

People recovering from bereavement often feel a sense of emptiness. They might wonder whether there is any future. Their wondering could well extend to the one who has died. What has happened to him or her? The Bible gives a predominantly gloomy picture. The dead, king or slave, good or bad, all go to a shady underworld where people are cut off even from God (see Job 7:9 and Psalm 88). The dead were believed to live on only in the form of their descendants. The idea of individual resurrection was a late arrival to Judaism. In the second Temple period, the Sadducees denied the idea, while the Pharisees emphasised it as an essential of faith, finding it inconceivable that God would be prepared to wipe people out at death.

Sometimes it is asked whether religion is this-worldly or other-worldly. Does it emphasise this world or the next? So far as Judaism is concerned, the answer is 'both'. We read in the Mishnah:

R. Jacob said, This world is like an ante-chamber to the world to come; prepare thyself in the ante-chamber, that thou mayest enter into the hall. He used to say, Better is one hour of repentance and good deeds in this world than the whole life of the world to come; yet better is one hour of blissfulness of spirit in the world to come than the whole life of this world.

Jews set aside special areas of land in which to bury the dead. Sefardi tombstones are placed horizontally and Ashkenazi tombstones vertically. These positions were probably influenced by Moslem and Christian customs respectively.

The purpose of human life is seen as communion with God and only in the world to come will this be fully enjoyed. In this world, there is a foretaste of it, as Jews exercise their freedom by choosing to obey God's mitzvot. The two worlds are quite different and yet there is a continuity between them. In his commentary on the Prayer Book, Rabbi Hertz says:

Resurrection of the Dead does not necessarily imply identity with the material composing the body when alive; rather that the sum-total of all our deeds and thoughts, habits and character, does not vanish into nought at the moment of death. There is for the soul in the World-to-come identity of personality with the soul in the earthly life.

Extension Section

i)   George Bernard Shaw defined hell as a 'perpetual holiday'. Louis Jacobs writes:

> *Descriptions of Heaven and Hell should be seen for what they really are, pure speculation about a state unlike anything we can experience in this life, but which people have tried to describe as best they can with the language they have.*

How would you describe Heaven and Hell? Do you think your views would be acceptable to Jews? Give your reasons.

ii)   A Jewish cemetery is called a 'house of eternity' or 'house of life'. What Jewish beliefs are expressed by these terms?

iii)   According to the Mishnah, Judah the son of Tema used to say:

> *At five years the age is reached for the study of the Scripture, at ten for the study of the Mishnah, at thirteen for the fulfilment of the commandments, at fifteen for the study of the Talmud, at eighteen for marriage, at twenty for seeking a livelihood, at thirty for entering into one's full strength, at forty for understanding, at fifty for counsel, at sixty a man attains old age, at seventy the hoary head, at eighty the gift of special strength, at ninety he bends beneath the weight of years, at a hundred he is as if he were already dead and had passed away from the world.*

What do you think about Judah's comments on each of the last six stages?

Questions

A Matter of Fact

1   What would a Jew hope would be his dying words? (A)

2   How does Halachah define death? (B)

3   What plain white garment is worn by a deceased Jew in his coffin? (B)

4   What two greetings may be offered to mourners in the week following the funeral? (B)

5   Apart from on Shabbat, where do mourners hold services during shiva? (C)

6   What does Yahrzeit mean? (C)

Vocabulary

Give the Hebrew words for the following:

1 sacred society (B)

2 seven (C)

3 thirty (C)

A Question of Understanding

Try to give at least two religious explanations in answer to each of the following questions.

1 Why should a Jew repent every day? (A)

2 Why are Orthodox Jews not cremated? (B)

3 How are

a) sheloshim

b) Yahrzeit

designed to help the bereaved? (C)

Over to You

Answer these questions fully, giving your reasons, and stating arguments both for and against where appropriate.

1 Can you suggest why Jews differ over whether it is permitted to switch off a life-support machine? Euthanasia is just one area of medical ethics where Jews have to try to work out what it means to follow their Law in modern times. What other areas can you think of?

2 Not all Jews sit shiva for a full week. What do you think might be gained and what lost by reducing this period of mourning?

3 What do you think Hertz means by the word 'soul'? Why is it so difficult to describe the after-life?

4 Which of the many customs associated with particular moments in Jewish life do you find the most interesting?

Assignment

a) Imagine you belong to a chevra kaddisha. What are your main tasks?

b) Explain why you carry out these tasks.

c) Like the biblical character, Job (see Job 1:21), Jews affirm the justice of God and the meaningfulness of life as they mourn. What point can you see to their doing this at a moment when they might feel that God is not just and life not meaningful?

12

Kashrut (Food Laws)

- The Torah gives Jews a system of laws dealing with food, which we might call dietary laws. They are known as **Kashrut**, from the word **kasher** or **kosher**, meaning 'fit', in the sense of what is permitted to be eaten.
- The laws are meant to set the Jewish people apart, obeying God even at the basic level of eating.
- Most of the food laws come in Leviticus 11 or Deuteronomy 14 or both. They mean that certain fish, poultry, and meat are forbidden, **trefah**.
- There are further restrictions on meat, notably that it must not contain blood. The meat is drained of blood by a particular method of slaughtering and a process of salting.
- There is a further law forbidding the mixing of meat and milk. This requires careful separation in both the preparation and the ingredients of a meal.
- Orthodox Jews believe that these laws come directly from God and must all be obeyed. Others adopt varying positions about their value.

A) You Are What You Eat

In the Bible and the Talmud, the Hebrew word **kasher** is used to mean 'right' or 'fit'. Kasher can be applied to a person who behaves properly, to a Sefer Torah or mezuzah properly prepared, or to food which is fit to be eaten. Food is judged fit not in terms of hygiene but in terms of what the Torah permits. This is the usual meaning of kasher today: food permitted to be eaten. The word has come into English via its Ashkenazi pronunciation, **kosher**. Kosher food is permitted food.

Its opposite, forbidden food, is said to be **trefah** (torn). Trefah was originally used of an animal attacked and killed by a predator, but the term came to be extended to animals with any defects and then to all forbidden food. Whatever is not kosher is trefah. Coming from the Bible, through the Talmud, and into the law codes, Judaism has a whole range of food laws. The name given to these laws is **Kashrut** (from kasher). The question arises: why do these laws exist? Why does it matter what food a Jew does or does not eat?

You may have come across people who feel that what they eat affects not only their physical health but their entire mental outlook. 'You are what you eat', they maintain. Whether or not we accept this, we cannot deny that eating is vital. It is a very common human activity. People may neglect all sorts of work and play, but they seldom forget to eat. Judaism teaches that in satisfying hunger, the most basic of all human appetites, people can demonstrate their belief in God and his demands. Obedience to the dietary laws is not required of all people, but it is, according to the Torah, required of the people of God, and this is because they are to be set apart, holy.

To express the holiness of the covenant people is the sole purpose of the dietary laws as stated in the Torah. Most of the laws come in one of two chapters: Leviticus 11 and Deuteronomy 14. Central to the first are the words:

For I am the Lord your God; consecrate yourselves therefore, and be holy, for I am holy.

and a rabbinic comment on the second says:

Sanctify yourself with the things that are permitted to you.

Whatever concerns of health and hygiene we may now detect in them, these laws have only one reason behind them: that they will discipline the Jewish people towards holiness. Maimonides wrote that they:

train us to master our appetites; to accustom us to restrain our desires; and to avoid considering the pleasure of eating and drinking as the goal of man's existence.

Kashrut is, therefore, about not always having what you like when you like. It starts with eating, elevating it into a means of distinctiveness. We see the consecrated nature of eating at many points in Jewish life. In the blessings both before and after a meal and in actions reminiscent of ancient priestly duties (for example, the washing of hands and dipping the special Sabbath bread in salt), the meal table becomes a sanctified place. The Talmud says: 'A man's table is like the altar.' But the purpose of Kashrut goes beyond eating. It is to encourage self-restraint generally. By exercising discipline in this area, people may culti-

vate a particular attitude to life. They remind themselves that they eat to live not live to eat.

B) Is It Kosher?

Everything that is not trefah is kosher. To know what can be eaten, a Jew must, therefore, find out what is declared trefah.

According to the list in Leviticus, this includes virtually every insect. Vegetables (all of which are permitted) must, therefore, be washed carefully to make sure there are no insects in them. Also included in the list (11:13–19) are many birds. It is not clear what characterises forbidden poultry. Some suggest that since they appear to be birds of prey it may be their association with cruelty. Not all the Hebrew names, however, can be translated with sufficient certainty for us to identify the birds, and in practice Jews tend to eat only those traditionally recognised as kosher: chicken, turkey, duck, and goose.

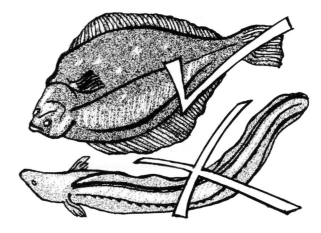

Kosher and trefah.

When it comes to fish, those which are forbidden are clearly identified. They lack fins and scales (Leviticus 11:10; Deuteronomy 14:10). To be kosher, fish must have both characteristics and, according to Halachah (the rabbinic elaboration of the biblical rules), the scales must be easily removable. A fish like sturgeon would thereby be ruled out.

Some have suggested that the prohibition is based on the revolting appearance of such fish as crabs and eels. They suggest the same explanation for snails, which are ruled out by Leviticus 11:9. However, those accustomed to eating crabs, eels and snails presumably do not find them revolting. Moreover, the Torah is not interested in giving a reason. These laws fall into the category of chukim, mitzvot whose reason cannot be known with any certainty.

Most of the remaining laws of Kashrut relate to animals. Those which are forbidden are identified by their not chewing the cud and not having cloven (completely parted) hoofs. To be kosher, animals must have both characteristics. If you think of the animals ruled out by this, pigs are the ones most likely to come to mind. There is the temptation to conclude that whether an animal is fit to eat has something to do with cleanliness, but this is not so. The Jewish writer Herman Wouk illustrates this by saying that a pig could be raised in an incubator, bathed daily, and slaughtered in an operating theatre, and the pork chops would not be kosher. Hygiene is not the point; ceremonial cleanliness is. As Leviticus 11:7 says:

> the swine, because it parts the hoof and is cloven-footed but does not chew the cud, is unclean to you.

The pig is unclean not in itself (a chicken is by nature hardly more clean) but to the people of Israel. The discipline is for them.

Jews may not eat even a permitted animal in its entirety. They are forbidden to eat animal fats, which used to be offered in sacrifice (Leviticus 7:1–4,22–5) and the part of the animal containing the sciatic nerve (in memory of a story in Genesis 32:25). Animals that have died of natural causes (Deuteronomy 14:21) or animals that have been killed by other animals (Exodus 22:31) – and by extension have any serious defect such as perforation of the lungs – may not be eaten either. Because 'the life of the flesh is in the blood' (Leviticus 17:11), the blood is sacred and may not be eaten. These points have important implications for the Jewish method of slaughtering animals. The crucial principle is the last one.

C) 'The Blood Is the Life'

Deuteronomy 12:23 sums up the point about blood: 'the blood is the life.' It is, therefore, too sacred to be eaten. Even a bloodspot in an egg renders the egg trefah. In the case of meat, as much blood as possible has to be removed. This involves two processes. Firstly, the animal must be killed by a single stroke across the neck with a finely sharpened knife. There must be no notch in the knife that might tear the animal's flesh while it is being killed and cause unnecessary pain. The animal's foodpipe and windpipe must be severed cleanly. There are many detailed rules, so only a skilled professional slaughterer, learned in the Torah, can kill the animal. He is called a **shochet** and the method is called **shechitah**, which means 'killing' (in the prescribed manner). Shechitah is designed to drain the meat of blood and to kill the animal with the minimum amount of pain. The bleeding is profuse, but the animal does not bleed to death, as is sometimes objected. The carotid arteries and jugular veins are instantly severed, cutting off the blood supply to the brain. The animal, therefore, loses consciousness before it can feel anything.

After shechitah comes salting.

Secondly, the remaining blood is removed by kashering (making fit). Nowadays this is usually the responsibility of the butcher or distributor. The specific process is known as 'salting', as the meat is covered with salt to extract the blood. The meat is first soaked in tepid water for half an hour to soften the texture and help the salt to extract the blood. It is then placed on a draining board, scattered with coarse salt, and left for an hour. It is then thoroughly rinsed.

Extension Section

i)   The Torah instructs Jews to care for their animals (see the fourth commandment). Inflicting unnecessary pain on animals is forbidden to both Jews and non-Jews (see Chapter 1). Jewish writings include the following:

> *A righteous man has regard for the life of his beast.*

> *Do not eat before you have fed your beast.*

> *No man may buy a beast, an animal or a bird until he has provided food for it.*

In the light of these sayings, what do you think will be the Jewish attitude to sports such as bullfighting? What bearing has all this on shechitah?

ii)   The Jewish method of slaughtering animals for food is sometimes attacked as cruel to animals. Find out about other methods and compare them with shechitah. (The Council of Christians and Jews provides a leaflet on the subject.)

D)   In the Kitchen

Even if the butcher does the kashering, observance of Kashrut makes heavy demands on the person in the kitchen. He, or more usually she, must follow another restriction. Three times in the Torah (e.g. Deuteronomy 14:21) we read: 'Thou shalt not boil a kid in its

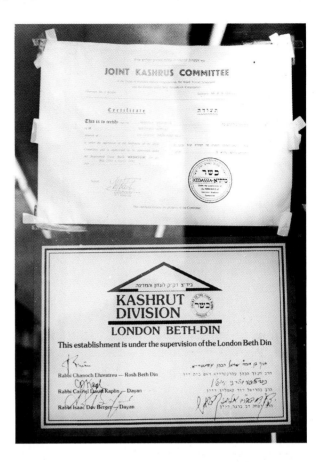

A kosher baker must display a licence from the rabbinic board recognising his food as kosher. Neither the ingredients nor the preparation of the food may involve anything trefah.

mother's milk.' 'Who would want to?' you might ask. Whatever practice this law originally referred to, rabbinic tradition has it that a kid in its mother's milk is given as an example of mixing meat and milk. Because of this law, meat and milk must not come into contact with each other. They must not be cooked or eaten together.

Think what this means in terms of kitchen utensils, crockery, cutlery, washing-up bowls, dishclothes, and teatowels! Such dual equipment, including separate sinks, would be taken for granted in an Orthodox household. Again we see the idea that the home is a sanctuary and all the demands take on a religious significance.

Think also what this particular law means in terms of menu! If you recall what you ate yesterday, you will soon see, unless you are a vegetarian, the way in which meat and milk items are mixed. Observant Jews cannot eat anything where these ingredients are mixed, nor can they eat meat or milk items straight after each other. Thirty minutes must be allowed between milk and meat and a much longer time, usually at least three hours, between meat and milk dishes, since meat takes longer than milk to digest.

Foods such as fish, that contain neither meat nor milk, are known as **parev** or **parve** (a Yiddish word for 'neutral'). They can be eaten with either milk or meat. You may think that this widens the choice considerably. It does when a Jew is choosing what he eats and how he prepares it. Meat is such a common ingredient, however, that this separation of milk and meat makes it extremely difficult for the observant Jew to eat in a non-Jewish home or in Jewish homes where Kashrut is not kept. This is, of course, part of the purpose of all these dietary laws. They are a reminder of distinctiveness. They require discrimination, recognising that the body and food are given by God.

Extension Section

i)   Increasingly, items bearing a label guaranteeing that they are kosher can be bought in British supermarkets. Kosher bakers and butchers, however, are harder to come by. Find out how far a Jew in your area would have to travel for such shops.

ii)   Devise a way of remembering the main dietary laws. The tape, *Baruch Learns his Brochos* (available from JMD) has a young boy using humorous, if rather corny, rhymes and catchy tunes.

E)   How Far Should You Go?

There are shades of observance of Kashrut. Many Jews observe everything with exact care, as a divinely-ordained means to self-discipline and purity. Some reject the idea of God's revealing these laws to Moses and stress that they are a means to an end, namely a holy life. People who hold this view may well keep some laws but not others. They may, for instance, never eat unkosher meat, but not bother having separate dishes for meat and milk. They may keep a kosher home, but be less particular in other people's homes or a restaurant. From the Orthodox point of view, such variations are unacceptable. The dietary laws are to be kept in their entirety. Liberal Jews, however, say that the individual must decide whether the laws are helpful to his or her spiritual development. Some Jews reject Kashrut altogether, saying that they are outdated or harmful to relations with non-Jews. Early Reform Judaism inclined to this position, but now accepts the possible value of observance. Most Jews would say that the dietary laws help to give a sense of personal identity and common bond.

Questions

A Matter of Fact

1 In which two chapters of the Bible would you find most of these food laws? (A)

2 Quote the words of the Torah which state the purpose of the dietary laws. (A)

3 What two characteristics must a fish have to be kosher? (B)

4 What makes pigs trefah? (B)

5 What does parev mean? (D)

Vocabulary

Give the Hebrew words for the following:

1 food laws (A)

2 permitted (literally 'fit') (A)

3 forbidden (literally 'torn') (A)

4 killing (C)

A Question of Understanding

Try to give at least two religious explanations in answer to each of the following questions.

1 Why does it matter to a Jew what he or she eats? (A)

2 Why does hygiene not determine which animals are kosher? (B)

3 Why is shechitah the method used by Jews to kill animals? (C)

4 Why is meat salted? (C)

5 Why would lamb chops not be followed by rice pudding in an observant household? (D)

Over to You

Answer these questions fully, giving your reasons, and stating arguments both for and against where appropriate.

1 What, apart from the taste of meat, do you think a Jew might lose by keeping Kashrut simply by becoming a vegetarian?

2 Discussion of 'Thou shalt not boil a kid in its mother's milk' fills as many as 28 pages in the Talmud and 11 sections and 62 sub-sections of the Shulchan Aruch. Why do you think this is?

3 What do you think about the opinion of some Jews that the laws of Kashrut make Judaism largely a gastronomic exercise?

Assignment

A useful preparation for this assignment might be the Jewish London Tour organised by the Board of Deputies, or Manchester Jewish Museum's occasional demonstration of Jewish cooking. Also of use is the video (from RMEP) *Judaism through the Eyes of Jewish Children*. In addition to the Jewish kitchen, the video introduces preparations for the Sabbath, Jewish symbolism in the home, and the synagogue service.

Below is a menu from a non-kosher restaurant. A Jew who keeps kosher strictly at home, yet is more flexible when eating out, has been invited for a meal at this restaurant.

a) Choose a four-course meal which she can eat, which is in keeping with the general laws of Kashrut.

b) Explain why a Jew keeping strictly to all the dietary laws would not be able to eat at all in this restaurant.

c) Which do you think makes more sense – to keep some of the laws of Kashrut or to keep all of them? Give your reasons.

Menu

— Starters —

Melon Cocktail
Egg Mayonnaise
Chicken Soup
Prawn Cocktail
Turkey Pate
Garlic Bread with Mushrooms

— Main Courses —

Lemon Sole
Chicken with Lemon and Almonds
Roast Beef and Yorkshire Pudding
Moussaka
Grilled Mackerel
Cheese and Asparagus Flan
Vegetarian Lasagne

— Desserts —

Sherry Trifle
Black Forest Gateau
Fresh fruit salad
Apple Strudel
Sorbet
Cheese and Biscuits

— Beverages —

Coffee
Tea with milk or lemon
Iced Tea
Perrier Water
Coca Cola

13

Prayer

- Prayer is communication between human beings and God.
- Jews have three daily prayer times.
- Prayer takes many forms. It may be spontaneous or set, individual or communal, said, sung, or silent. It reflects many different moods and emotions.
- Jews pray both at home and in the synagogue, usually in Hebrew. To help them they have a prayer book, the **siddur**.

- Siddur means 'order' and the Prayer Book contains set forms of prayer, many of them going a long way back in Jewish history.
- The whole person should be involved in prayer. How the Jew stands and moves and what he wears are designed to cultivate the right attitude and atmosphere.

A) Why Do Jews Pray?

Do you ever pray? If so, why do you pray and what do you pray for? Do you pray aloud? What do you expect to happen when you pray? The American psychologist, William James said: 'The reason why we pray is simply that we cannot help praying.' Prayer seems to stem from our human desire to communicate with a higher power. We do seem to need, for example, to tell someone when we feel particularly bad or particularly good about something. Sometimes, especially if we are distressed and asking for help, we may not express ourselves very clearly, but we are still somehow reaching out for something.

Jews believe that human beings should try to have a relationship with God and that when they reach out, God hears and answers.

'Prayer is asking for someone to get better.' Illustrate two other occasions on which it might be natural to pray and supply a caption for each, beginning 'Prayer is . . .'.

Jewish prayer assumes a relationship with God and this, like all relationships, makes demands on people. The idea is not to make

God fit in with how people are and what they want, but through prayer to become and to want what God intends. This notion of self-examination is expressed in the most common of the Hebrew words for prayer, **tephilah**. This probably comes from the Hebrew word for 'to judge'. So in prayer God is called on as judge of all our thoughts and desires.

B)   When Do Jews Pray?

Solomon's Temple was dedicated to prayer (see 1 Kings 8:27–30). It was also used for offering sacrifices in the morning and in the afternoon. So, in the Temple, sacrifice (or ritual) and prayer (or liturgy) were both offered. When people began to worship in synagogues (see Chapter 14), prayer replaced sacrifice. The times for prayer in the synagogue were taken from the times of the Temple sacrifices. The morning sacrifice was called the **shacharit** (from **shachar** meaning 'morning') and the afternoon sacrifice was called the **minchah** (offering). The parts of the sacrifices that were not eaten were burnt on the altar all night long and this gave a reason for another prayer time, the **maariv** (evening). These are still the three daily times of prayer for Jews.

In addition to the shacharit, the minchah, and the maariv, there is a further prayer time on Shabbat and the High Holy Days. This is called the **musaf** (additional), and it corresponds to the time of extra sacrifice offered in the Temple on the special days. The musaf often follows the Torah reading of shacharit, making a morning service of over two hours.

C)   What Do Jews Pray?

To most of us, three times a day would seem to be a lot of praying. Whatever do Jews find to say? Prayers, for the festivals come from a book called a **machsor** (cycle), as it covers the special occasions in the cycle of the year.

Other Jewish services, whether at home or synagogue, are taken from the main Prayer Book, the siddur (order). This 'order' refers to the order of worship, the set prayers offered at the various stages of the service. All Jews accept the siddur as the vital expression of their hopes and convictions. In this country, Orthodox Jews use *The Authorised Daily Prayer Book*; Reform Jews use *Forms of Prayer for Jewish Worship*; and Liberal Jews use *Service of the Heart*. ('Service of the heart' is a term the rabbis used for 'prayer'.)

Jews can pray anywhere. A synagogue is not strictly necessary.

The foundation prayers of all three main prayer books are the same and come from a variety of people and periods. Many of their phrases come from the Bible, especially the Psalms with their different sorts of prayer, including praise, complaint, and thanksgiving. It should be noted that nearly all the prayers are in the first person plural ('*Our* God' not '*My* God'), giving a sense of community.

The liturgy (words used in worship) evolved and was given shape by the rabbis of the Mishnah and Gemara. The first outlines of the siddur were prepared by the heads of the Babylonian academies in the ninth and tenth centuries. The Reform and Liberal Prayer Books also include some very recent prayers, and they leave out some parts of older prayers that Progressive Jews feel are no longer appropriate. They omit, for example, prayers for the restoration of the Temple. On page 103 is part of a prayer from the concluding service on the Day of Atonement. It comes from the special Prayer Book used by Liberal Jews on the High Holy Days. What features of the prayer and its language suggest that it was written in modern times?

Lord our God, we turn now to You once more to cry out our longing and the longing of all men and women for a beginning of the wholeness we call peace ... Ever and again, we now admit, we have turned our backs on You, and on our brothers and sisters, and murdered the dreams of our children: forsaking Your Law, denying Your truth, ignoring Your will, defacing Your beauty. The intelligence You have implanted within us we have applied to the arts of war; with the skill we have from You we make engines of terror and pain.

If set prayers are to have value, individuals will have to make them their own by praying with devotion or direction, **kavanah**. The Mishnah says that if a Jew prays without kavanah, then he will have to pray all over again, this time with kavanah. This is a point stressed by Maimonides, who himself added to the Prayer Book.

Extension Section

i) The famous Berditchever Rebbe once walked over to a group of his Chasidim after the Amidah prayer, shook hands with them and greeted them with 'Shalom Aleichem' (a Jewish greeting). The group looked surprised at this unexpected gesture. The Rebbe explained, 'I greeted you in this way because I could see from your expressions that you had no idea of the meaning of the words you were reciting. Rather were you thinking of the grain market in Odessa or the woollen market in Lodz. Now that you have returned from such a long journey, I extend to you a welcome back.'

Retell this story, setting it in present-day Britain.

ii) On the right is part of a leaflet illustrating the contents of the Reform Prayer Book. What point do you think the writer of this leaflet is trying to make by focusing attention jointly on synagogue and home?

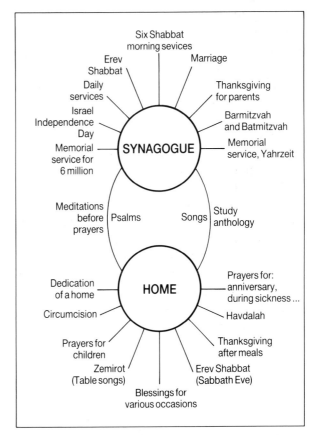

Extract from leaflet about *Forms of Prayer for Jewish Worship.*

There are, however, advantages to having a siddur. These may be listed. It:

- Gives a sense of being linked with great figures in Jewish history;
- Expresses experiences and emotions common to all Jews;
- Discourages selfish prayer;
- Gives Jews all over the world a unity;
- Provides a routine without which prayer might not happen at all;
- Helps those unable to pray spontaneously;
- Repeats familiar phrases, giving life a feeling of continuity and security.

D) The Main Prayers

The fundamental Jewish prayer is the **Shema**. Shema means 'hear' and is the first word of the Hebrew of Deuteronomy 6:4–9, which begins this prayer. The opening verse is:

Hear, O Israel: The Lord is our God, the Lord is one.

After Deuteronomy 6:4–9, the Shema continues with Deuteronomy 11:13–21 and Numbers 15:37–41. To recite these passages may sound more like study than prayer, but in Judaism, study is a prayerful activity. The Shema is a prayer in that it acknowledges God and affirms confidence and trust in him. Yet it is fundamentally a declaration of faith. It declares what is absolutely central to Judaism: that there is only one God and that he requires whole-hearted moral obedience. This belief is sometimes called ethical monotheism. The Shema has a central place in every Jew's morning and evening prayers. The opening sentence is recited as the Torah scroll is taken from the Ark on Sabbaths and festivals, and at other crucial moments.

Next to the Shema, the most important prayer is the **Amidah**. (It is often known as *the* prayer, Tephilah.) Amidah means 'standing'. The worshipper recites the prayer standing, facing Jerusalem. Originally the prayer had 18

blessings (so it is also known as the 18 Benedictions). They now number 19, all of which are said on weekdays; on Shabbat, the first and last three are said. The main feature of this prayer is that it makes requests. It asks God to satisfy spiritual needs, such as forgiveness, and physical needs, such as food.

Another Jewish prayer indicated by its name is the **berachah**. Berachah (plural **berachot**) means 'blessing'. A berachah is not one particular prayer. Rather it is a type of prayer. In it God is blessed, or praised. Each berachah begins with the words:

Blessed art Thou, O Lord our God, King of the Universe.

This acknowledges God as the source of all blessings. Then there is mention of a specific gift (e.g. over wine, the blessing is 'who createst the fruit of the vine'); or a mitzvah (e.g. at circumcision the blessing is 'who hast commanded us to make our sons enter into the covenant of Abraham our father'); or a wonder of nature (e.g. on seeing lightning the blessing is 'who performest the act of creation'). A fourth type of berachah is a longer prayer of general praise, but it either begins or ends, or both, with the words: 'Blessed art Thou, O Lord.'

A Jewish child learns to say berachot when very young. They become a part of his or her life, for instance, when getting dressed. (What do you think is the value of learning such prayers at an early age?)

The **Alenu** is a prayer which takes its name from the opening word in Hebrew. Alenu means 'It is upon us'. This prayer speaks of the obligation which is upon every Jew to respond to God's greatness and bring hope to the world. All nations will be united in abandoning idolatry and in recognising the one God. The Alenu was originally sung just at the New Year but now it concludes all services.

The Kaddish is another very important prayer. It appears in five different forms in the siddur, marking the end of sections of the service. (Make sure you remember from Chapter 11 what this prayer is about.)

E) Body Language

No movements or gestures are prescribed in the Bible, but a number have developed naturally to lend emphasis to prayer. Traditionally, bowing occurs at four important stages of the Amidah. Instructions on how to bow are in the Babylonian Talmud. They include bending the head and body forward when saying **Baruch Atah** (Blessed art Thou), and straightening first the head and then the body in order to be upright when saying **Adonai** (Lord).

What prayer might these people be saying?

Total prostration is allowed only at particularly sacred moments on the New Year Festival and the Day of Atonement. Many cover their eyes while reciting the first verse of the Shema to cut out any distractions. The practice of swaying in prayer is quite old. One of the many explanations offered is that it comes from Psalm 35:10 which begins:

All my bones shall say, 'O Lord, who is like thee . . . ?'

Opinion is divided, however, about its desirability. Some prefer being still when praying, whilst others think swaying gently can aid concentration. The Chasidim encouraged violent movement to bring about a sense of God's nearness. They stressed, however, spontaneity rather than fixed times for this.

Extension Section

i)   Besides structured prayer, there is in Judaism a tradition of spontaneous prayer. Jews can pray whenever they like and say whatever they like. If you were asked to pray in terms acceptable to a Jew, how might you begin?

ii)   Nearly all the prayers in an Orthodox service are in Hebrew. Suggest a reason for this.

iii)   Listen to the chanting of prayers (e.g. on the JMD tape). What do you find most striking?

iv)   Read the following passage and then put into your own words any one point the writer is making about prayer:

Daily prayer sometimes is uplifting, sometimes routine, but it always is reflective of a Jewish commitment. Formalised prayer is a way of bringing into one's own time and place the awareness of God's creation, the miracles of our having been saved, the blessings of life and love that we enjoy, the existential concerns that escape not a single one of us. Prayer also is a way of uniting oneself with the Jewish people. Less sublime, and perhaps more immediate, it is a way of marking one's time as a Jew and even in that there is great value. (Blu Greenberg)

F) Other Aids to Prayer

Can what you wear affect how you feel? Many people think that it can. There are three items worn by adult male Jews as reminders of God and their obligations to him.

The first is a prayer shawl, called a tallit. It is a white, square or rectangular garment, usually made of wool or silk. The most important feature of the tallit is the fringe, **tzizit**, in each of its four corners. You may sometimes tie a knot to remind you that you have to do something. The tzizit serve a similar purpose. They are a constant reminder of the mitzvot. They are worn in obedience to Numbers 15:37–41.

Orthodox Jews, and often Reform, wear the tallit during morning prayer in home or synagogue. Some, especially the leader of the service, wear it also during evening prayer. It is placed around the shoulders and sometimes over the head. (What effect do you think having it over the head might have on the person praying?)

There is also a garment called a **tallit katan** (a small tallit). This is worn by some Jews, under their usual clothes, throughout the day.

Tallit katan (tzizit).

It is often just called tzizit, as it is the fringes which form the important reminder of the mitzvot.

The second visual aid is **tephilin** (sometimes known as phylacteries). They are two

black boxes in which are placed four passages of the Torah which instruct the Jew to bind the Torah to his hand and between his eyes: Deuteronomy 6:4–9; 11:13–21 (the first two paragraphs of the Shema) and Exodus 13:1–10; 13:11–16. As with the mezuzah (see Chapter 9), the material for the tephilin comes from kosher animals, the words are written on the scrolls by a qualified scribe and checked about every three years to see that the writing has not faded, and they are treated with great respect.

'Get me to the shul on time.' This devout Jew was seen hurrying to morning prayer at his synagogue in Israel. To save time, he is already wearing what he needs for his prayers.

The tephilin are bound to the body: one to the arm opposite the heart and the other to the forehead. Thus they remind the Jew that he must worship God with his whole person, the heart and the head. (Which verse in Deuteronomy 6 says where God's words are to be placed?) Orthodox, and some Reform and Liberal males over 13 put on tephilin for morning prayer in the synagogue or at home. Because they stress obedience to the Torah, tephilin are symbols of the covenant (see

Chapter 1). They are not worn on Shabbat and festivals, as these themselves are signs of the special relationship of the Jews to God.

The third item is the **kippah**, sometimes called a **capel**, or a **yarmulkah**, a contraction of the Yiddish for 'fear of the King' (reverence for God). This is a skull-cap worn by most Jewish males when the Name of God is spoken, notably during prayer. Some wear a kippah, or other headcovering, all the time. Jewish men consider that keeping their heads covered expresses respect for God (just as some men think removing a headcovering expresses respect).

Music too can help people pray. Sometimes public prayer is spoken, as in Reform and Liberal synagogues, but often it is sung, or chanted, as in Orthodox synagogues. A probable reason for this chanting is that the sung voice carries further than the spoken one, and in early times some synagogues were very large indeed. The chant is led by someone professionally trained or a knowledgeable member of the congregation (see Chapter 14). It fits the mood of the prayers, buoyant and

exhilarating on the festivals, yet solemn and yearning on the Day of Atonement.

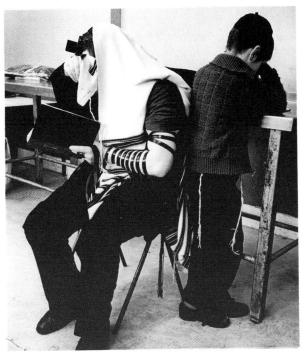

Make sure you can name all the special items worn by this father and son as they pray.

Questions

A Matter of Fact

1 What does siddur mean? (C)

2 What is ethical monotheism? (D)

3 Name two things asked for in the Amidah. (D)

4 At which prayer time are tephilin worn? (F)

5 Which of the following statements is true?

   a) Jews pray only in a synagogue.

   b) A mezuzah is a parchment scroll.

   c) There are three daily prayer times.

   d) Afternoon service is called maariv.

   e) The machsor contains the prayers for festivals.

   f) Orthodox Jews use *The Authorised Daily Prayer Book*.

   g) The Amidah is said standing.

   h) Kaddish is the same as Kiddush (a blessing recited over wine at the beginning of the Shabbat and festivals).

   i) A kippah is something Jews eat. (F)

Vocabulary

Give the Hebrew words for the following:

1 morning prayer (B)

2 devotion or direction (C)

3 hear (D)

4 blessing (D)

5 it is upon us (D)

6 fringes (F)

7 small tallit (F)

A Question of Understanding

Try to give at least two religious explanations in answer to each of the following questions.

1 Suggest three different endings to the blessing:

Blessed art Thou, O Lord our God, King of the Universe, who has hallowed us by thy commands and commanded us to . . . (D)

2 Why does a tallit have fringes? (F)

3 Why do adult males wear tephilin? (F)

Over to You

Answer these questions fully, giving your reasons, and stating arguments both for and against where appropriate.

1 What do you think is the difference between magical incantations and Jewish prayer?

2 Which of the three prayer times do you think would be the most difficult to fit into daily life?

3 'People have souls not clocks.' How might a Jew reply to this implied criticism of praying at set times?

4 Look back at the advantages of having a siddur. Do you think there are any disadvantages in having set forms of prayer?

Assignment

Either:

a) Learn the opening lines of one of the prayers mentioned in this chapter (e.g. the Shema). Try reciting them with bowing, then with eyes covered, and then swaying. Describe to someone in your class the various effects on your thoughts or emotions.

b) Using a Judaica kit (available from JEB), select an item a Jew might wear when praying and explain to someone why it is worn.

c) 'Better a little supplication with kavanah than a great deal without it.' Is this true? Try to find some people, of any religion, who pray regularly. Work out a few questions to ask them and record your questions and their answers.

Or:

d) Read the following extract. (In it, the words tallit, yarmulkah, and tephilin are spelt slightly differently from this chapter. Shuls are synagogues.)

Abraham was draping his prayer shawl around his shoulders. 'What're you looking at, David? You've never seen me put on my tallith before?' he snapped. He adjusted his yamulke which was inclined to slip off because his hair was so thick and took the phylacteries which must be worn to say the weekday morning prayer out of a little draw-string bag.

David watched him flex his left arm and lay one of the small leather boxes on the upper muscle, opposite his heart like the Law instructed, then wind the long black strap attached to the box round and round, the required seven times, all the way down to his wrist.

'You've never seen me laying my tephillin either?' his father said tetchily.

'I like watching you do it.'

'All right, so watch,' Abraham sighed. 'I'm not angry with you, David,' he added though he ought not to be talking whilst preparing for the prayer. 'It's just the way I feel, why should I take it out of you?' He laid the second little box on the centre of his forehead and tightened its straps at the back of his head, to hold it in place. Finally, he wound the dangling end of the first strap around his fingers.

'When I was very little, I used to think you looked funny like that, Father,' David confessed.

'But a big boy knows it's a serious matter, that inside the boxes are holy texts. "And thou shalt bind them for a sign upon thine hand and they shall be for frontlets between thine eyes, as a sign that we are the sons of our Father in Heaven and members of the community of our great and holy people".' Abraham quoted gravely. 'We lay them opposite our brain and our heart so that our thoughts and desires will be subservient to God, David. After you are Bar Mitzvah, we'll do this together in the mornings.'

'Can you get tephillin in England? I haven't got mine yet, have I?' David asked anxiously.

Abraham picked up his prayerbook and moved nearer the candle so he could read the print though he knew the words by heart. 'Don't worry, wherever Jews are tephillin are and everything else required for our devotions. In Russia they think if they burn down the shuls with the scrolls inside them, they'll be able to wipe out our religion, but for every one they burn another will rise in its place.' He stared at the candle flame pensively for a moment, then bent over his prayerbook.

Something in his father's expression made David want to get up and hug him, but he controlled the impulse. 'I hope you find a job soon, Father,' he said quietly instead.

(Maisie Mosco *Almonds and Raisins* New English Library, 1979)

Imagine you are David. Write a letter to a non-Jewish friend describing and explaining what you saw and how you felt during this morning prayer time.

14

The Synagogue

- 'Synagogue' comes from a Greek word meaning 'to gather together'. Originally it referred to the people assembling and then to the place where they gathered.
- Today a synagogue is a community centre with many functions.
- Its main function is worship, with the emphasis on prayer and reading.

- A cantor usually leads the congregation in worship.
- Synagogues are of many different types, depending on when and where they were built. There are also differences between Orthodox and non-Orthodox synagogues.
- The main features of all synagogues, especially the symbols, are designed to help people to worship God.

A)   The Start of the Synagogue

We cannot be absolutely certain about the beginnings of the synagogue. It is very likely, however, that there were such meeting places as long ago as the sixth century BCE. After the first Temple had been destroyed, and many Jews taken into exile in Babylon, there was probably a great need among the exiles to meet in an effort to keep their faith alive. It is also likely that, once the exile was over, synagogues existed side by side with the newly built Temple.

The Temple in Jerusalem was the only place where sacrifice could be offered. Places for study and prayer, on the other hand, could be built anywhere. From the Babylonian exile onwards, many Jews lived outside Israel. The command to visit the Temple three times a year became an impossibility for most people, travel being difficult. The synagogue, therefore, became more important in their lives than the Temple as a place to meet and worship at the times of the Temple sacrifices. Synagogues probably became even more prominent after the destruction of the second Temple in 70 CE. Over 50 synagogues of various styles have been excavated in Israel.

B)   The Synagogue as a Community Centre

When do you most feel that you want to get together with people? It may be when you have something to celebrate. You may also prefer to be with someone rather than on your own if you have a particular problem and are unhappy.

Excavated Capernaum synagogue.

From ancient times the Jews have known how to share their joys and their sorrows. One of the Hebrew names for a synagogue expresses the importance of such sharing: **Bet Haknesset** (house of assembly). Other names for a synagogue also indicate its functions. It is called **Bet Hatephilah** (a house of prayer) and **shul**, a Yiddish word based on the German word for 'school'. Much of the time a Jew spends in a synagogue is educational, being instructed, for instance, in Hebrew and the Torah. Shul is the word by which Jews most commonly refer to the synagogue.

People can, of course, study and pray on their own, but sharing such activities with others may bring a sense of solidarity and support. Jews have long stressed the importance of communal prayer. The Talmudic rabbis ruled that some of the most sacred prayers and hymns, for example, the Kaddish, require a minyan: ten adult males. This is rather like

the way in which a certain number, a quorum, is required before an important vote can be taken at, for example, a committee meeting. In most synagogues, this is still so, though in some Reform and Liberal synagogues, women may be included in this number. For all Jews, the synagogue means not the building but the local community or congregation.

Though prayer and study are still the main activities which it seeks to foster, the synagogue serves as a community centre in many other ways. Jewish identity is preserved by various social activities and by services to the community, launched and encouraged by the synagogue. When you visit a synagogue, see if it has a noticeboard or leaflet listing its many activities.

What Jewish symbol tells you that this is a synagogue?

C)   How to Recognise a Synagogue

The exterior of the synagogue pictured above and that pictured on p. 15 have little in common. Indeed, there are few rules about synagogue architecture and so synagogues mirror the style of their periods and cultures. Like the Temple, however, they must have windows, letting light in so that worship is no retreat from life and pouring light out as a sign of God's strength and guidance. Otherwise, the outside of the building is unimportant. A synagogue could simply be a room in a house. What makes a synagogue is what it contains.

If you enter a synagogue nowadays you will know immediately if it is Orthodox, for it will have a separate section, often a gallery, for women. There will be a screen or even a wall between the two areas and separate doors by which to enter. In early synagogues, there was no women's section or gallery and today Progressive Jews see no point in the division. Orthodox Jews follow the Talmudic view that women may be a distraction to men when praying.

An important feature of the synagogue is the **bimah**, a platform from which the Torah is read. It is normally in the middle of the synagogue as Maimonides indicated that it should be, but the Shulchan Aruch states that this was simply to enable everyone to hear and that in a small synagogue the bimah can be anywhere. At the beginning of the nineteenth century, some Reform synagogues placed it directly in front of the Ark.

The Holy Ark, **Aron Hakodesh**, was originally a wooden box covered with gold, in which the two tablets of stone were kept in the Tabernacle erected in the wilderness (see Exodus 25:10–16). The Ark disappeared at the time of the destruction of the first Temple. No-one knows what happened to it. (Have you come across any ideas about this?) In Talmudic times it was called a 'chest' and was portable. From the Middle Ages, the Ark has been a cupboard fixed in the east wall. It contains one or more copies of the Torah and it is the focal point of the synagogue. In front of the Ark, or inside the Ark doors, is a curtain, often beautifully embroidered. Exodus 26:31–3 tells us that in the Tabernacle a curtain hung in front of the Ark.

Placed over the Ark (or 'sanctuary', **heichal**, as Sefardi Jews call it) are often two tablets representing the Ten Commandments and giving the first two words of each commandment, or other texts such as the Talmudic saying, 'Know before whom you stand.'

God's presence and the light of Torah are further symbolised by the **Ner Tamid** (ever-

Model of the Second Temple.

burning light) above the Ark. Most modern synagogues use an electric light, but a few still have the traditional oil lamp, corresponding to the lamp burning continually in the Tabernacle (see Exodus 27:20–1). The Ner Tamid seems to be a relatively recent innovation as there are no references to a continual light in the synagogue before the eighteenth century. Light is, however, an ancient symbol of God's presence. The Temple had a seven-branched candlestick, a **menorah**. This is described in Exodus 25:31–40 and 37:17–24. (Look up these references and then draw a menorah.)

Extension Section

i) Solomon's Temple was destroyed by the Babylonians. Ezra and Nehemiah began another which was completed by Herod. Which nation destroyed this Temple?

ii) On 10 November 1938, 581 synagogues were burned in Nazi Germany. This came to be known as *Kristalnacht*, the 'night of broken glass'. Do you know of any attacks on Jewish places of worship in your lifetime?

iii) The home and the synagogue are the two focal points of Judaism, nurturing and renewing the Jewish way of life. Drawing examples from this chapter and at least one other chapter in Part II of this book, discuss the following quotation:

What the home is to the individual, the synagogue is to the community.

D) Readings

To understand the importance of the synagogue, you need to do more than look at pictures or even have a look round one. You need to be at a service. Everything about the synagogue emphasises the centrality of the Torah and the moment comes when the Torah is not only looked at and handled with reverence but read to the congregation.

When not in use, the Sefer Torah is rolled in a silk or velvet cover and kept in the Aron Hakodesh. On the shield or breastplate are the same Hebrew words as on the tablets above the Ark. Why are these words so important? Note the different style of the Sefer Torah and case (as pictured opposite), favoured by Sefardi Jews.

The Torah is divided into portions, **sidrot**, which are read in turn, so that each year the whole Torah is covered. In rabbinic times in Palestine, the portions were smaller than they are today, and the cycle of readings took three years. This practice was not adopted by the Orthodox, though today non-Orthodox Jews often have a three-year cycle or read only short sections of the weekly **sidra** (singular of sidrot). Traditionally, a particular number of portions of the Torah is read at certain services on Shabbat, festivals, and fasts, and in some synagogues on Monday and Thursday, market days in ancient Israel, when the farmer was able to come into the city and listen to the Torah.

Members of the congregation are called up to read or to recite a blessing before or after

The majesty of the Torah is seen in the decorative crowns, **rimmonim**, which fit over the poles of the Torah rollers. Bells are attached to the crowns. What value do you think hearing the bells (as the Torah scroll is carried round the synagogue) might have for the congregation?

the reading by someone specially trained. This calling up is known as *aliyah* (ascent), and it is an honour and a privilege. Often the man is marking a special occasion, for instance, the completion of a period of mourning a close relative, the Bar Mitzvah of his son, or the Sabbath before his own wedding. Today in Progressive synagogues, women are also granted the privilege of reading. Notice in the photograph below, the **yad** ('hand' or 'pointer'), which helps the reader keep his place as he reads the Hebrew from right to left.

The reader must not run his fingers over the scroll itself. How many other points can you think of which also express the sacredness of the Sefer Torah?

On Shabbat and other days of feasting or fasting, the reading from the **Sefer Torah**, Torah scroll, is followed by a reading from the Prophets. This reading is known as **Haftarah** (conclusion), as it concludes the reading of the Torah. It relates to the particular feast or fast or is in some other way linked to the Torah reading. The practice of reading Haftarah goes back to ancient times. (How many names of the Books of the Prophets can you remember from Chapter 3? Watch out for the connections between the Torah and the Haftarah when you come to study the festivals in Part III.)

E) The Rabbi

As we have seen, any adult male Jew may read from the Torah. He may also lead the prayers and perform any other synagogue rituals. So why have a rabbi?

The Hebrew title **rabbi** means 'my master', and originally it was reserved for teachers of the Mishnah. They were expert in the Torah and decided in cases of Jewish Law, but they did not do this for a living. This was still so in the Middle Ages, when the most famous of them were doctors or merchants. Today rabbis are usually paid by a congregation. They still fulfil the ancient role of teacher of the Torah, giving decisions to meet practical situations. For this, they need considerable knowledge and training. But rabbis also serve as pastoral counsellors (giving comfort and advice), officiants at marriages and funerals, and preachers.

A rabbi and a chazan.

The sermon given by a rabbi, relating faith to the congregation's own world, is a relatively new feature of the morning service. There used to be travelling preachers, some officially appointed, some simply popular because of the stories they told, who expounded biblical or rabbinic texts. In his sermon, a modern rabbi might aim to instruct the people in the teachings of Judaism, often stemming from the weekly readings, to inspire them to live better as Jews, to appeal for funds for worthy causes, or to discuss topical questions in the light of Judaism.

F) Music

Can you think of any particular song or tune that has changed your mood, made you feel happy or sad? Music of varying types can affect us deeply. From ancient times, Jews have known the power of music to create atmosphere and move the heart. In synagogues today, many different melodies are used, some traditional, some more modern, for different parts of the service and for different occasions.

Musical instruments were used in Temple worship, but according to the Talmud and Midrash were no longer allowed once the Second Temple had been destroyed. Nowadays, the organ is often used, though in Orthodox synagogues only on weekdays, for example, at a wedding. Playing the organ would count as work forbidden on Shabbat (see Chapter 15).

To help lead a congregation in its singing, the synagogue often employs a **chazan**, a

Extension Section

i) Herman Adler, Chief Rabbi in Britain from 1891 to 1911, said:

The preacher must feel deep sympathy with every single individual whom he addresses.

Why is this important and how could a rabbi go about ensuring such sympathy?

ii) In Orthodox synagogues, the Torah and Haftarah are read to the congregation in an ancient chant. Signs placed above or below the word tell the reader how to sing the word. The notes are not in the scroll of the Torah or the Book of the Prophets from which he reads in the synagogue, so he has to learn each chant by heart. There are different melodies used for different books of the Bible. Opposite is an example showing the signs (e.g. ⌐ ∴).

Listen to such chanting in a synagogue service or on tape (the JMD tape has examples). What do you think might be a) lost and b) gained by simply speaking the passages as in non-Orthodox synagogues?

iii) A Chasid said: 'The sphere of music is near the sphere of repentance.' What do you think he meant?

iv) What do you think is the point of the old Yiddish maxim: 'Nine rabbis cannot make minyan, but ten shoemakers can'?

Cantillation of the Torah.

cantor. In earlier times the chazan was an administrative official, seeing the needs of the community and attending to them. Now his job is to lead the congregation as it offers its devotions to God. The chazan is usually a highly-trained singer. Many have also composed melodies which have become standard in some synagogues. To enable him to chant the prayers on Shabbat and the festivals, and to assist the rabbi on other important occasions, the chazan undergoes training not only in voice production and technique but also in Bible, Prayer Book, and Halachah.

Questions

A Matter of Fact

1 Where and when did synagogues probably originate? (A)

2 What word do Jews most commonly use for 'synagogue'? (B)

3 From the photographs and information in this chapter, draw a plan of the interior of
  a) an Orthodox synagogue
  b) a Reform synagogue

and label them fully. (C)

4 What are sidrot? (D)

5 What name is given to the reading from the prophets in the synagogue service? (D)

6 To which of their leaders might synagogue members turn for advice? (E)

7 Who leads the chanting in the synagogue services? (F)

Vocabulary

Give the Hebrew words for the following:

1 house of prayer (B)

2 Holy Ark (C)

3 ever-burning light (C)

4 seven-branched candlestick (C)

5 hand or pointer (D)

6 Torah scroll (D)

7 conclusion (D)

8 my master (E)

9 cantor (F)

A Question of Understanding

Try to give at least two religious explanations in answer to each of the following questions.

1 Why might the synagogue be described as the power-house of Judaism? (B)

2 In some synagogues you would find a menorah. But in all synagogues the important symbol of light is the Ner Tamid. Why is it so important? (C)

3 In Jewish worship, no-one is considered to be specially holy or in any sense an intermediary between the community and God. Why then do many congregations appoint a chazan? (F)

Over to You

Answer these questions fully, giving your reasons, and stating arguments both for and against where appropriate.

1 Do you think women should be allowed to read at a synagogue service? Should women be ordained as rabbis as they are in Reform and Liberal Judaism? (see Chapter 9).

2 What is the point of having a sermon? What features would in your opinion make it a good or a bad sermon? Suggest a 'topical question' which a rabbi might consider in a sermon preached next Sabbath.

3 a well-trained voice
a good character and reputation
knowledge of the Prayer Book
acceptability to the congregation

Arrange these suggested qualifications of a chazan in order of importance.

Assignment

Either:

a) After a visit to a synagogue, prepare and write a visitor's guide. Present the guide in an appropriate form and explain to the visitor the use and significance of the various features you have included. Also make a list of the activities of the synagogue you have visited and explain which might appeal most to you if you were Jewish. It might be helpful to see the slides, *The Synagogue* (from the Slide Centre) or *A Synagogue Visit* (from the Board of Deputies), before writing your guide.

Or:

b) i) Members of the congregation are elected to run the synagogue. This is sometimes known as the Board of Management. Find out about the responsibilities of the various members. What are the particular duties of the **gabbai** (warden) and the **shamash** (attendant)? Also find out what you can about the Chief Rabbi in Great Britain. Who is he and what is his role? You could write to a rabbi or the Education Officer at the Board of Deputies.

ii) If you were preparing to write 'A day in the life of a rabbi', what questions would you ask when you went to interview him. (You need not give the answers.)

iii) Imagine you are a Jew who regularly visits the synagogue. In your class is a Jew whose family no longer bothers. What would you say to persuade him or her to give the synagogue another try?

15

Shabbat (Sabbath)

- **Shabbat** means 'to cease', 'to rest'.
- Following the commandment in Exodus and Deuteronomy, Jews set this day apart. They remember that God rested from creation and delivered them from slavery.
- On this day, no creative work is done.
- Shabbat is the last day of the week, beginning at sunset on Friday and ending at nightfall on Saturday.
- On Shabbat, Jews think about God as the creator of everything and of people as God's partners in the world.
- Shabbat is a festival and is celebrated in both the home and the synagogue.

A)   Why Keep Shabbat?

How do you feel when you break up from school? Unless you are unusually keen on school, you are likely to feel relieved and happy. If you take a holiday job, you will still have to get up at a particular time and work, but otherwise you will have more time to yourself and you can choose how you spend the day. Many people look forward to the weekend for similar reasons.

Our need to have a break and to do what we enjoy doing rather than what we have to do may help us understand why Jews keep Shabbat. They believe that Shabbat is God's gift, binding them together as people who have a special relationship with him. It gives them

Sunset over Galilee. Jews wish each other **Shabbat Shalom** (A peaceful Sabbath) or Good **Shabbos** (Yiddish for 'Sabbath').

time to think about what matters most to them as Jews – the family and the Torah.

Shabbat is a day of celebration, aimed at making people feel better physically and spiritually. We see this in the ceremonies of both home and synagogue, all of them meant to bring release from ordinary cares and worries. The Bible gives two reasons for Shabbat. Exodus 20:8–11 says that God made the seventh day holy by resting after making the world. Deuteronomy 5:12–15 reminds the Jews of their slavery in Egypt when they were forced to work. Opportunity to rest is the mark of being free, and Shabbat offers this opportunity. Both reasons for setting this day apart centre on the idea of rest and 'rest' is what the Hebrew word means.

So on this day Jews are to think about what God intends human life to be like. God needs human co-operation to make the world a better place, but on Shabbat God is to be recognised as the only creator. On Shabbat, Jews must stop their creative work and reflect on the powers that God has given, making sure they make the right use of them. They are ultimately answerable to him.

According to the first chapter of Genesis, the day begins and ends at sunset. Orthodox Jews use a Jewish calendar, diary, or newspaper to find out just when Shabbat begins week by week. Because it is not certain to which day the period between sunset and nightfall belongs, Shabbat is observed until nightfall on Saturday. Shabbat, therefore, lasts 25 hours.

Shabbat is binding only on Jews, but other people have borrowed the idea of a day set apart for refraining from work and recharging their spiritual batteries.

B)   What Is Work?

The word 'work' has a bad ring to it. It often suggests something we do not like doing, be it homework or housework. However, to someone who is bored or unemployed, work may be an attractive idea. Sometimes we choose to do things which are hard work, such as rock-climbing or playing tennis, because we enjoy doing them. It is curious how we then regard them not so much as work as leisure.

CALENDAR

Friday, March 1 (Adar 15), **Shushan Purim,** Sabbath begins in London at **5.26**; Manchester **5.31**; Tyneside **5.26**; Glasgow **5.35**.
Saturday, March 2 (Adar 16). Portion of the Law (Torah) כִּי תִשָּׂא Exodus 30: 11 to 34: 35. Portion of Prophets (Haftara) I Kings 18: 1-39 [Sephardim: I Kings 18: 20-39].
Sabbath ends in London at 6.29; Manchester 6.39; Tyneside 6.37; Glasgow 6.47.
Friday, March 8 (Adar 22), Sabbath begins in London at **5.38**; Manchester **5.44**; Tyneside **5.40**; Glasgow **5.50**.

Jewish Chronicle, 1 March 1991.

In the tractate Mishnah Shabbat, the Talmud lists the following activities:

sowing	tying a knot
ploughing	loosening a knot
reaping	sewing
binding sheaves	tearing
threshing	hunting a gazelle
winnowing	slaughtering
selecting	skinning
grinding	tanning
sifting	scraping
kneading	marking out
baking	cutting up the skin
sheep-shearing	writing
bleaching	erasing
dyeing wool	building
combining raw materials	pulling down
spinning	putting out a fire
weaving	lighting a fire
separating threads	striking with a hammer
removing a finished article	carrying anything from a private to a public place (and vice versa)
threading a loom	

Which of these 39 activities would you consider to be work? The Jewish answer is that all of them constitute work, as all of them were needed to build the Tabernacle described in Exodus 35. (Look up this passage to see what the Tabernacle was for.) These then are the activities prohibited on Shabbat. You may think it would be quite easy for a modern-day Jew to avoid these specific activities. But Orthodox Jews would say that anything resembling these is work and therefore forbidden on Shabbat. This would rule out all sorts of activities. Can you think of any?

It is important to recognise two facts. Firstly, it is not the degree of effort involved that makes the work forbidden but whether it is creative as understood in the 39 categories. Thus a Jew could, on Shabbat, carry something heavy in the house or garden, but not do the gardening. Nor could he carry something, however light, from home to the synagogue. Secondly, all Shabbat laws are suspended if there is the least danger to human life, as Jews believe that God wants life and well-being. The Shabbat is meant to be not a burden but a delight.

Orthodox Jews do not drive to the synagogue on Shabbat. Which of the activities listed in the Talmud would they say was involved in using a car? Can you think of any circumstances in which an Orthodox Jew might drive on Shabbat?

The above list of forbidden activities can be divided under seven headings:

- growing and preparing food
- making clothing
- leatherwork and writing
- providing shelter
- creating fire
- completing work
- transporting goods

Look through the 39 activities again and see which of the seven headings each activity comes under.

Extension Section

i) *The Sabbath was made for man, not man for the Sabbath. (A rabbinic saying)*

Far more than Israel has kept the Sabbath, it is the Sabbath that has kept Israel. (Ahad Ha-am)

Explain what you think is meant by either one of these sayings.

ii)   Although specific forms of work are forbidden on Shabbat, work started before Shabbat comes in may be allowed to continue. For example, a fire burning before Shabbat can continue to burn, though no more coal or wood must be added to it. How might Orthodox Jews use this to help them on Shabbat?

iii)   What is the main point of the following passage?

The Sabbath does not mean a mere not working, nor empty idleness. It connotes something positive. It has guided the soul into its mystery so that it is not a day that just interrupts, but a day that renews . . . It is the expression of the direction for life, and not just an instituted day of rest. If it were only that, or if it became that, its essence would be taken from it. It would then be only a hollow shell. (Leo Baeck)

In what ways could the Sabbath become 'a hollow shell'? How might a Jew today prevent this from happening?

C) Shabbat Arrives

In the synagogue, Shabbat is welcomed by the singing of special hymns. The aim is to create an atmosphere of joy and holiness in preparation for the first service of Shabbat, which takes place on the Friday evening.

Most of the hymns sung are from the most ancient Jewish hymn book, the Psalms. Those chosen are Psalms 95–9; 29; and then, in many congregations, Psalms 92 and 93. These psalms express the belief that God is king and that he has begun his rule on earth. Everyone and everything is summoned to worship him as creator of a beautiful world and as a fair judge. (Look, for instance, at Psalm 96:11–13 and Psalm 99.)

Shabbat is then welcomed as a queen or a bride. One of the most popular hymns on this theme was written in the sixteenth century by Rabbi Solomon Halevi Alkabetz. Its English title is 'Come, my friend'. The friend is called to 'Welcome Bride Sabbath, the Queen of the days'.

The Sabbath evening service now begins. At its close is sung a hymn which is called the **Yigdal**. Yigdal is the opening word of the hymn in Hebrew. In English, it begins: 'The living God we praise, exalt, adore!' Based on a summary of Judaism by Maimonides, the Yigdal tries to put into words the foundations of all Jewish belief. Though the different Jewish traditions may differ in the precise interpretation of them, the central beliefs are clear:

- God is the creator – one, spiritual and eternal.
- The teachings of the Prophets are true.
- Moses was the greatest of the Prophets.
- The Torah was revealed to Moses and is unchangeable.
- God knows what human beings do and think.
- He rewards the good and punishes the wicked.
- The Messiah will come and the dead will be resurrected.

Meanwhile, in the home, Shabbat is welcomed by the lighting of two special candles. These candles are symbols of joy, blessing, serenity, and peace. The home is central to the celebration of Shabbat and the Jewish woman has the important duty of performing this welcoming ceremony. At dusk, just before Shabbat begins, she lights the candles, reciting the berachah (blessing) of God as:

King of the universe, who hast hallowed us by the commandments, and commanded us to kindle the Sabbath lights.

Shabbat is welcomed into the home. What atmosphere are the candles intended to create?

The emphasis on the family is expressed in the blessing of the children (to boys: 'God make you as Ephraim and Manasseh'; to girls: 'God make you as Sarah, Rebekah, Rachel and Leah.') and in the reciting of Proverbs 31:10–31 in honour of the Jewish wife.

D) Kiddush

The word **Kiddush** means 'sanctifying' or 'hallowing'. The ceremony of Kiddush sanctifies, makes holy, or sets apart the time of Shabbat and other festivals. If you want a meal to be different, you might put special items on the table and say and do special things to give a sense of occasion. So Kiddush begins the meal and sets a special atmosphere.

The first part of Kiddush is the reciting of Genesis 2:1–3. This speaks of God resting after creating the world. Wine is used to symbolise the sweetness and joy of the day and a blessing is said over two loaves of white bread. These special plaited loaves are called **challot** (singular **challah**). They are a reminder that when the Israelites were in the wilderness after the Exodus, a double portion of manna was given to them on Shabbat (see Exodus 16:4–36). Some people think that this story is also recalled by the white cloth placed over the loaves, symbolising the dew. After the blessing, a piece of the bread is dipped in salt and given to each of those present, who often include guests. After the meal a special grace is recited.

All this reminds those celebrating Shabbat of their dependence on God for all that is good in life. Table songs, stressing joy and togetherness, try to capture this idea.

These words begin the song and come at the end of each verse.

The song, 'This day for Israel', does so particularly well. Here are three of its verses:

> You commanded our fathers who stood at Mount Sinai
> to keep Sabbath and seasons for all of our years,
> to share at our table the choicest of food,
> a Sabbath of rest.

> Treasure for the hearts of a wounded people,
> for souls that have suffered, a soul that is new,
> to sooth away sighs from a soul that is bound,
> a Sabbath of rest.

> You have made this the holy, most blessed of days.
> In six days you finished the work of the worlds,
> this day the saddest find safety and peace,
> a Sabbath of rest. (from *Forms of Prayer*)

Extension Section

i)   Listen to a tape of some table songs (e.g. *Let's Sing Sabbath Songs* or *Shabbat Shalom*, tape and book from JMD, or *The Jewish Sabbath*, tape and booklet from RSGB) or try to learn some of these songs in your class. How do these songs make you feel? Do you think Jewish people feel differently from non-Jewish people about them?

ii)   Listen to a tape of Kiddush for Friday nights at home (e.g. *Let's Sing Sabbath Songs* or JMD tape). Note especially the blessing of God for the wine and Shabbat.

iii)   Read Proverbs 31:10–31. (Part of this passage is set to music on *Let's Sing Sabbath Songs*.) List the main qualities of 'the woman of worth'. What are the qualities you would look for in a 'woman of worth'?

E)   Shabbat Morning

This is when Jews hold the main service of the week. It is very much a family occasion. Synagogue worship on the morning of Shabbat is still the chief bond uniting Jews and keeping them part of a worshipping community. Look back to Chapter 14 and work out what will be the main features of the morning service on Shabbat.

After the service, Kiddush is often made in the hall of the synagogue. It is also said at home before the midday meal.

As the Ark is opened and the scroll taken out, the congregation sings the first line of the Shema. The scroll is carried round the synagogue with great rejoicing. Why do you think this is?

Extension Section

i)   The first verse of a version of the Yigdal, from the Methodist Hymn Book, *Hymns and Psalms*, is printed below. Read it, then say why you think Christians have borrowed this hymn:

Praise to the living God!
All praised be his name,
Who was, and is, and is to be,
For aye the same!
The one eternal God
Ere aught that now appears;
The First, the Last, beyond all thought
His timeless years!

ii)   The Yigdal opens the morning service in the synagogue as well as closing the evening service. What central Jewish belief does it express (see the verse above)? (The Yigdal and the Shema (which expresses the same belief) are both on the JMD tape.)

F)   Shabbat Afternoon

How do you most like to spend Saturday afternoon? A Jew is likely to spend it relaxing. This might include going for a walk or visiting family or friends who live nearby.

There is also an afternoon service in the synagogue. The unusual feature of this service, unlike the weekday afternoon services, is that the Torah is read.

The Kaddish, the Alenu, and the Sabbath Amidah are said at this as at the other two services. The following prayer, recited in the afternoon service, states the ideal of Shabbat. God is blessed for giving his people:

a rest granted in generous love, a true and faithful rest, a rest in peace and tranquillity, in quietude and safety, a perfect rest wherein thou delightest. Let thy children perceive and know that this their rest is from thee, and by their rest may they hallow thy Name.

G)   Havdalah

This is the ceremony conducted in both home and synagogue for marking the end of Shabbat. It is said at any time after nightfall, giving this special day a departing ceremony. Wine and light are used in the ceremony welcoming Shabbat. The same symbols, together with spices, are used to bid it farewell.

Havdalah means 'division', and the ceremony begins with praise of God for dividing

secular	sacred
dark	light
other nations	Israel
six days	Shabbat

There follow two other berachot (blessings), the first over sweet-smelling spices and the second over a lighted candle. The spice-box is passed round, possibly in the hope of sweetening the deeds of the coming week. A similar explanation for the spices is that the memory of Shabbat should linger on into the week in the scent of the spices. A rabbinic saying suggests that on Shabbat people are given an additional soul, bringing them nearer to God. Perhaps then the spices are to refresh the departing soul or to revive the body as it feels weak when the extra soul departs. Which explanation for the spices do you prefer?

Shabbat being over, fire can be kindled and hands are spread out toward the light. This expresses the thought that light is God's gift and is to be used to good purpose. It is also a reminder that the first thing God created was light. With the going out of Shabbat, the 'first day' of creation begins. All five senses of smell, sight, taste, hearing, and touch are used in this ceremony, the physical senses heightening the spiritual.

This lovely ceremony ends by putting out the candle with wine. There are also songs, notably one about Elijah the prophet. Elijah is thought of as a constant companion and as the herald of the Messiah. So in this song Jews ask for help and for the coming of the Messianic Age.

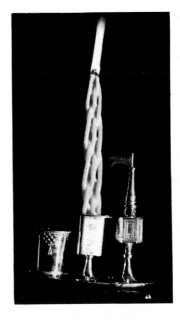

Two or more candles, usually plaited together, are used, rather than a single candle. This could be because the blessing offered at this point praises God for 'lights' rather than 'light'. Another explanation is that two candles are a better symbol of fire than one candle.

Questions

A Matter of Fact

1 Which two biblical passages give the commandment for Shabbat? (A)

2 How long does Shabbat last? (A)

3 What is described in Exodus 35? (B)

4 Who kindles the lights before Shabbat begins? (C)

5 Name one symbol used in the Kiddush. (D)

6 When is the main Shabbat service? (E)

7 Which members of the family would usually attend this service? (E)

8 What is unusual about the afternoon service on Shabbat? (F)

9 In which two places is Havdalah conducted? (G)

10 Arrange these in the order in which they would occur:
   Havdalah
   afternoon service
   kindling the lights
   recreation, such as reading, walking, visiting
   morning service
   evening service.

Vocabulary

Give the Hebrew words for the following:

1 rest (A)

2 sanctifying or hallowing (D)

3 plaited loaves (D)

4 division (G)

A Question of Understanding

Try to give at least two religious explanations in answer to each of the following questions.

1 Why is jogging allowed on Shabbat while dressmaking is not? (B)

2 Why are special hymns sung as Shabbat arrives? (C)

3 According to the song 'This day for Israel', how might Shabbat help people? (D)

4 It has been said that Shabbat is not so much 'time off' as 'time out'. How does Havdalah express this idea? (G)

Over to You

Answer these questions fully, giving your reasons, and stating arguments both for and against where appropriate.

1 Do you think you need one day a week when you drop your usual activities? As a Jew, what do you think you would find most refreshing about Shabbat?

2 Do you think it useful to put religious belief into words? Why do you think Maimonides tried to summarise Jewish beliefs?

3 Do you think smelling the spices at Havdalah might mean more than just seeing them?

4 In rabbinic tradition, the command to 'remember' (Exodus 20:8) indicates the positive aspects of Shabbat, such as reciting the Kiddush, and the command to 'observe' or 'keep' (Deuteronomy 5:12) indicates the negative aspect of refraining from work. Considering both the positive and the negative, do you think Shabbat is a good name for this day?

Assignment

Either:

a) After watching a video (e.g. *Judaism Through the Eyes of Jewish Children* (from RMEP)) or talking to an Orthodox Jew, explain to a friend:

i) the main ways in which an observant Jew would mark Shabbat;

ii) the principles behind these observances;

iii) what you think are the advantages and disadvantages of strict observance of Shabbat.

Or:

b)i) You are preparing to attend a morning service on Shabbat. Describe what you expect to see and hear, indicating why these features are important.

ii) After attending the service, write a letter to the rabbi, thanking him and saying what you gained from it.

16

Minor Festivals and Fasts

- The Jewish Calendar is based on the appearance of the new moon every 29–30 days.
- The most important days set aside annually are the festivals of Passover, Weeks, and Tabernacles, the New Year and the Day of Atonement.
- The Day of Atonement remembers the need of Jews for God's forgiveness. The New Year remembers God's creation of the world. The other major festivals remember God's work in both nature and history.

- The Day of Atonement is also a fast day. Other fast days commemorate the destruction of the Temple. The most important of these is 9 Av.
- There are also minor festivals in Judaism. These include **Chanukah**, **Purim**, and **Tu B'Shevat** (the New Year for Trees).
- Minor festivals and fasts are not subject to the same restrictions as the other festivals and fasts.

A) Anything Special?

We have already come across three special days observed by many Jews, marking events in Israel's history: Yom Hashoah, Yom Haatzmaut, and Yom Yerushalayim. These are observed annually. We have also read about Shabbat, a weekly festival celebrating God's work in creation. As you can see from the chart on p. 127, there are many special days in the Jewish Calendar. All of them, except the Day of Atonement, call to mind God's activity in nature or history or both.

The opening verses of Leviticus 23 tell us about Shabbat. This chapter goes on to institute other 'appointed feasts': **Pesach**

(Passover), **Shavuot** (Weeks), and **Sukkot** (Tabernacles). The first marks the Exodus from Egypt, the second the giving of the Torah on Sinai, and the third the journey through the wilderness to the promised land. These three are called Pilgrim (or Foot) Festivals because, in Temple times, Jews would make a pilgrimage to Jerusalem to offer sacrifices. Though this no longer happens, these festivals are still important and have many celebrations in the home and the synagogue.

Also mentioned in Leviticus 23 are what has come to be called the Jewish New Year, **Rosh Hashanah**, and the Day of Atonement, Yom Kippur. These three days (Rosh Hashanah is observed everywhere in the world for two days) are often called the High Holy Days, which indicates their importance. They are also known as the Days of Awe. (What does this suggest about their mood?)

Another term used of a major festival is **Yom Tov**. Yom Tov is usually characterised by three things:

a)   rejoicing, e.g. ceremonial meals and resting from work;
b)   special prayers and synagogue rituals;
c)   ceremonies and customs related to the subject of the festivals.

ter, we shall look at three minor festivals: Chanukah, Purim, and the New Year for Trees, and five minor fasts (as distinct from a festival, a fast has no rejoicing at all but is entirely sad): the fast of Esther, and four connected with the destruction of the Temple: 10 Tevet, 17 Tammuz, 9 Av, and the Fast of Gedaliah. **Tevet**, **Tammuz**, and **Av** are all names of months in the Jewish Calendar. We need to know how this Calendar works in order to understand the dating of all these special days.

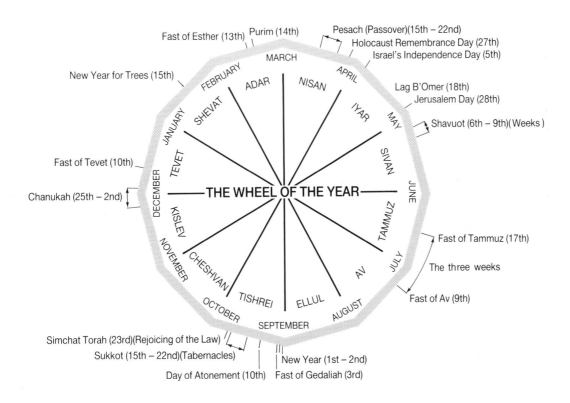

Though festive occasions, they often include solemn moments. Solemnity is the dominant note of the Days of Awe, as Jews think carefully about their relationship with God and with other people. This is especially so on Yom Kippur, also a fast day.

You will have noticed from the chart above that Judaism has many other days, set aside annually, for particular remembrances. These, like Yom Hashoah, Yom Haatzmaut, and Yom Yerushalayim, are not bound by restrictions like the major festivals and fasts and so are called minor festivals and fasts. In this chap-

B)   The Jewish Year

Our calendar, with 12 months of slightly varying length, is a solar calendar, that is, it is based on the movements of the sun. The ancient Israelites also took notice of the sun, as it determined the agricultural seasons of the year. When they worked out their calendar, however, they based it mainly on the movements of the moon. The moon takes approximately $29\frac{1}{2}$ days to orbit the earth. As it gets to the end of its orbit, less and less of it is seen, until it disappears altogether. Then it reappears. It is the *re*appearance of the moon, the new moon, that marks the new month for Jews.

Clearly a month cannot last 29½ days, but each pair of months will add up to 59 days, so the months are taken in pairs, the first having 30 days, and the second 29 days and so on. (There are sometimes slight variations in this.) With this information we can see that there are 354 days in an ordinary Jewish year. But the solar year is 11 days longer. If this were left, the Jewish calendar would fall behind by 11 days each year until the lunar year (that based on the moon) was months behind. This would mean that the festivals would eventually fall at the wrong time of the year. Pesach should be celebrated in the Spring and Sukkot in the Autumn. To avoid celebrating Pesach in the Winter or Sukkot in the Spring, an extra month is put in the calendar every few years. We are used to having a leap year, a year with an extra day, every four years. The Jewish Calendar has a leap year, a year with an extra month, seven times in a cycle of 19 years. The last month of the year, which is called **Adar**, is doubled. Notice where it comes on the chart on page 127.

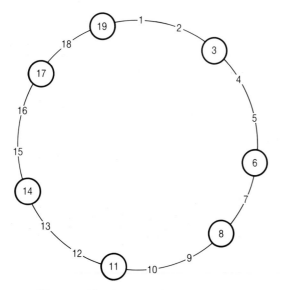

In every 19-year cycle, these are the years which are leap years.

Jewish festivals and fasts occur at set dates in this Calendar. For example, Pesach lasts from 15 to 22 of the month called **Nisan**. The months of the Jewish Year are numbered from Nisan because it occurs in the Spring, a time of new beginnings. Note, however, that the Jewish New Year Festival, Rosh Hashanah, actually comes in the Autumn. The dates to which 15–22 Nisan correspond in the non-Jewish calendar will vary slightly from year to year. For instance, in 1992 Pesach falls on 18 April, in 1993 on 6 April, and in 1994 on 27 March.

C) Rosh Chodesh (The New Moon)

Even though the new moon is marked in most diaries, few non-Jews pay much attention to it. In ancient Israel, however, the appearance of the new moon was a matter of importance. People watched out for it in order to know when the next month started and when, therefore, to celebrate their festivals. The new moon would be expected on the day after the 29th. The supreme rabbinical court in Jerusalem would wait until two reliable witnesses had testified that they had actually seen the new moon. For varying reasons, such as weather conditions, the new moon would not necessarily appear on the 30th day and so no witnesses could say that they had seen it. In this case, the rabbinical court automatically announced the *following* day as **Rosh Chodesh** (the new moon).

This caused a problem for Jews outside Israel. How would they know whether the court had announced the day after the 29th Rosh Chodesh or had waited for the next day? It could take the messengers from Jerusalem some time to reach them. So to be quite sure that they were observing the festivals on the right date, these Jews automatically observed each festival for an extra day. The one exception is the Day of Atonement which, because of the hardship of fasting for two days, lasts only one day.

Orthodox Jews outside Israel still follow this practice. They regard it as a means of expressing the special holiness of the land of Israel, where they adhere to the exact dates laid down in the Bible. Reform Jews, in whatever country, do not observe the extra days, since they believe that, from the historical point of view, they are no longer required. When the supreme rabbinical court no longer existed to announce the new moon, a permanent calendar was worked out. This is still used.

The day of the new moon is mentioned in the Torah alongside Shabbat and other festivals. In early times, it was treated as a festive day when people did only essential work. Over the centuries, different ideas developed about just what work was allowed on the day. Today the new moon is little different from any other day.

The day itself is called Rosh Chodesh, literally 'head of the month'. The time of the forthcoming new moon is solemnly announced in the synagogue on the previous Shabbat, as the new moon was announced in the ancient rabbinical court. After the Torah reading, the congregation prays that the new month will be one of 'life and peace, gladness and joy, deliverance and consolation for the House of Israel'. On the actual day, the account of the ancient sacrifices of Rosh Chodesh is read from the Torah. Also part of **Hallel** is recited. **Hallel** is the Hebrew for 'praise' and the word is used to mean Psalms 113–18. These are especially joyful psalms and are, therefore, sung during most festivals.

D)   Chanukah

The spirit and purpose of this festival are summed up in its name. **Chanukah** is the Hebrew for 'dedication' and the festival commemorates the dedication (setting apart for sacred purposes) of the Temple, or rather, the *re*dedication of the Temple after it had been desecrated (made impure) by opponents of the Jewish faith in the second century BCE (see Chapter 1). The story of the rededication of the Temple, and of the events which led up to it, is told in 1 and 2 Maccabees. (Read 1 Maccabees 1–4 for the main story.) The climax came when, on 25 Kislev 165 BCE, Judah and his men entered the defiled Temple and tore down the desecrated altar. They built a new altar and relit the great menorah. After the original purifying and rededicating ceremonies, it was agreed that there should be an annual celebration of this event (1 Maccabees 4:59).

Besides being the Festival of Dedication, Chanukah is also the 'Feast of Lights'. It gets this name from the Talmud, which tells of a miracle in the Temple when Judah and his men rededicated it. When they entered the Temple, they found just one jar of oil that had not been defiled. With this they lit the menorah. This amount of oil would normally last only one day, but miraculously it lasted eight days, giving time for fresh, pure oil to be prepared. Traditionally, this is why Chanukah is an eight-day celebration.

Food fried in oil is often eaten at Chanukah. (What is the oil meant to be a reminder of?) This is a recipe for *latkes* (potato pancakes).

The Talmud says that, in order to celebrate this miracle, a lamp should be lit on each of the eight days of Chanukah. These eight lights have become the main symbol of the festival. In fact, there are nine lamps or candles as one candle is used to light each of the eight special candles, which must not be used for any practical purpose. The lighting-candle is called the **shamash** (servant), and it is placed in the middle of the Chanukah menorah, often called a **chanukiah**. On the first night of Chanukah the first candle (furthest right on the chanukiah) is lit. On the second night, another candle is added. The servant candle lights the new candle and then the one on its right and so on, until by the last night all the lights are burning. Placing the candles from right to left but lighting them from left to right gives equal importance to both sides of the chanukiah, indicating that God's presence is everywhere. The Talmud says that the lights are to burn where people can see them and so a chanukiah is often to be seen in the windows of Jewish homes at Chanukah.

Lighting the Chanukah candles.

think of Chanukah as the Jewish Christmas, because children are given presents, it is a Festival of Light, and it falls in December. However, it is important to remember that what Chanukah means for Jews has no connection with the meaning of Christmas for Christians.

Extension Section

i) A traditional children's game at Chanukah is played with a **dreidle** (spinning top). Each of the top's four sides has on it a Hebrew letter. Together the letters stand for the Hebrew phrase: 'A great miracle took place there.' What miracle is this? What word games could be played with a dreidle?

ii) Design a poster which you think captures the essence of the festival. You could first look at Chanukah posters from JEB.

iii) Listen to some of the songs of Chanukah on the JMD tape or *Enjoy Chanukah at Home* (from RMEP). Listen also to *Enjoy Purim at Home* (from RMEP) or *Let's Sing Purim Songs* (from JMD).

E) Purim

Another minor festival which remembers a difficult period in Jewish history and which urges trust in God is **Purim**. Like Chanukah, this festival is not commanded in the Torah but stems from the decision of the rabbis to commemorate an historical event. In the case of Purim, the story on which the festival is based is found in the Bible. It comes in the Book of Esther. The book is not long and you should read it right through for the whole story. Its main points are as follows:

The candle-lighting takes place when all the family is together. There are special songs and presents are given. Non-Jews sometimes

• In the fifth century BCE, Jews living in Persia were ruled by King Ahasuerus (thought to be Xerxes I).

- Ahasuerus married a girl called Esther, who concealed the fact that she was Jewish.
- Esther's only relative, Mordecai, uncovered a plot to kill the Jews and told Esther.
- This plot came from Ahasuerus' Prime Minister, Haman, who hated the Jews. Mordecai (who worked for the king) refused, because of his Jewish faith, to bow down to Haman. Haman, therefore, persuaded the king that his Jewish subjects were not loyal.
- Haman's plot seriously backfired when Ahasuerus was informed of it by none other than his own wife, Esther. Impressed by his wife's risking her own safety by admitting her Jewishness, he executed not the Jews but Haman himself. Haman had superstitiously drawn lots (for which the Book of Esther uses the word **purim**) to decide on what day to slaughter the Jews. This day, 14 Adar, became then the day of his own execution.

Though a minor festival, Purim has come to occupy a major place in Jewish hearts. It has a carnival atmosphere. Children in particular join in the fun of it all. At school, they often dress up and enact a play based on the story of Esther. They also boo, stamp, and wave **greggers** (rather like football rattles) every time Haman's name comes up in the reading in the synagogue. Reading the whole of Esther in public is one of the four mitzvot of Purim. It is read not from a book but from a scroll. Because the Hebrew for 'scroll' is **megillah**, Esther is often called simply 'the Megillah'. The Megillah is read both in the evening and the following morning.

Esther 9:22 speaks of the contrast between sorrow and gladness, mourning and holiday. To try to capture this contrast, Jews observe a fast on the day before Purim. They are remembering the fast of Esther before she went to plead with her husband to spare his Jewish subjects (Esther 4:16). The other three mitzvot of Purim itself are: festivity and rejoicing (a good meal is usually part of the day); gifts to the poor; and gifts to each other (Esther 9:19,22).

Amidst all the jollification, Purim has a serious theme. The theme is the need for courage, trust, and honesty, when standing up for what is right. The festival is intended to provide hope for Jews, especially those living in difficult conditions. The hope rests on a belief that it is best to trust in God, and that goodness and truth will triumph.

Because the word 'God' does not appear in the Megillah, artists have felt free to illuminate the scroll.

F) Tu B'Shevat (The New Year for Trees)

Tree-planting in Israel.

In modern life, we speak of the calendar year (beginning in January), the financial year (beginning in April), and the academic year (beginning in September). Ancient Israel also had more than one New Year, according to what aspect of its life was being measured. The agricultural New Year was considered to begin on 15 Shevat. Look back at the chart on p. 127 to see when this falls. Farmers in ancient Israel had an obligation to set aside, each year, a proportion of their crops for the priests and the poor. There needed to be a date from which these contributions (tithes) were counted, and this was fixed as 15 Shevat. The Talmud suggests that the reason for this choice of date was that it marked the end of the rainy season in Israel. The sap of the trees became active again, bringing new life, and so a new crop of fruit, to the trees.

In Israel, the New Year for Trees is marked by tree-planting. Jews living in other parts of the world often contribute money to such tree-planting projects. They also express their ties with Israel by eating fruit particularly associated with Israel, such as pomegranates and olives. It is a tradition to try to eat 15 kinds of fruit. Can you think of 15 different kinds of fruit that grow in Israel?

G) Fasts

An important part of celebrating for Jews is eating. When wanting to do the opposite of celebrating, Jews stop eating and fast. The Day of Atonement is the most important fast day, during which Jews express sorrow for wrongdoing (see Chapter 20). Other fast days lament the loss of the Temple. Psalm 137:5–6 gives the reason for the continued mourning for the Temple:

If I forget you, O Jerusalem,
let my right hand wither!
Let my tongue cleave to the roof of my mouth,
if I do not remember you,
if I do not set Jerusalem
above my highest joy!

Some Jews do not think it right to emphasise the Temple and pray for its restoration (see Chapter 5). Others, however, believe that the Temple was such a vital sign of God's presence with his people that it must remain a focus for Judaism.

The fasts lamenting the loss of the Temple are 10 Tevet, 17 Tammuz, 9 Av. A related fast is 3 Tishrei, the Fast of Gedaliah. After they had destroyed the Temple and deported many Jews in 586 BCE, the Babylonians appointed Gedaliah as governor over the people remaining in Judah. But rivals murdered Gedaliah, shattering hopes of any continuing Jewish community in Judah. 10 Tevet marks the beginning of the Babylonian siege of Jerusalem. 17 Tammuz is the date when, in 70 CE, the Romans breached the walls of Jerusalem, leading to the destruction of the second Temple.

The three weeks following 17 Tammuz are the saddest time of the Jewish Year, with mourning customs (e.g. not listening to

The Temple in ruins.

Jews in Babylon.

music) intensified as 9 Av approaches. 9 Av, in Hebrew **Tishah B'Av**, is the most important fast after the Day of Atonement (only these two fasts last 25 hours). On this date in 586 BCE, the Babylonians destroyed the first Temple and, in 70 CE, the Romans destroyed the second Temple. Other tragedies in Jewish history also occurred on Tishah B'Av, notably the fall of Bar Kochba's fortress in 135 CE, the expulsion of the Jews from Britain in 1290 CE, and the expulsion of the Jews from Spain in 1492 CE.

Tishah B'Av is marked by an intense atmosphere of sadness in the synagogue. The curtain is removed from the Ark and the covers from the reading desk. Lights are low and the biblical Book of Lamentations, lamenting the destruction of Jerusalem, is chanted mournfully. At the morning service, prayers are said quietly without the adornments of tallit and tephilin.

Amidst the sadness, there is hope for the future and, in the seven weeks following Tishah B'Av, each Shabbat service includes messages of consolation and promise, beginning with Isaiah 40. Read the opening of this passage and notice which words are designed to bring comfort to the exiles in Babylon.

Questions

A Matter of Fact

Copy out this chart, filling in the gaps (e.g. in the second column of the first line, the missing word is 'Passover'). It may help you to look at the chart on p. 127.

Jewish dates	Festival or fast	Ordinary month	Jewish dates	Festival or fast	Ordinary month
15–22 Nisan		March–April		Day of Atonement	Sept–Oct
27 Nisan		April–May	15–22 Tishrei		Sept–Oct
28 Iyar	Jerusalem Day			Chanukah	December
6–7 Sivan	Weeks	May–June	10 Tevet	Fast of Tevet	
17 Tammuz	Fast of Tammuz		15 Shevet		Jan–Feb
9 Av	Fast of Av			Fast of Esther	Feb–March
3 Tishrei		September	14 Adar		Feb–March

Vocabulary

Give the Hebrew words for the following:

1 new moon (literally 'head of the month') (C)

2 praise (C)

3 dedication (D)

4 scroll (E)

A Question of Understanding

Try to give at least two religious explanations in answer to each of the following questions.

1 Why does Judaism set days aside? (A)

2 Why are Chanukah, Purim, and the New Year for Trees called 'minor festivals'? (B)

3 Why do Orthodox Jews outside Israel observe the festivals for an extra day? (C)

4 Why is Chanukah called the Feast of Lights? (D)

5 Why do Jews fast on Tishah B'Av? (G)

Over to You

Answer these questions fully, giving your reasons, and stating arguments both for and against where appropriate.

1 The Haftarah reading (that is, the reading from the Prophets) on Chanukah includes the words: 'Not by might, nor by power, but by my Spirit, says the Lord of hosts.' (Zechariah 4:6). How far do you think these words sum up the point of Chanukah?

2 Though God is not mentioned in the Book of Esther, he is thought to be active, making sure that goodness and truth win through. What circumstances can you think of when Jews might find it hard to believe that goodness and truth prevail?

3 Look up Deuteronomy 20:19–20. How important do you consider the concerns of this passage to modern-day Jews?

Assignment

a) Write a short scene between two of the major characters of the Book of Esther (either Haman and Mordecai; Esther and Ahasuerus; or Esther and Mordecai).

b) Write a paragraph explaining why your characters act as they do.

c) What do you think about the outcome of the story of the Book of Esther for:

i) Esther;

ii) Haman;

iii) Ahasuerus?

17

Pesach (Passover)

- Pesach (Passover) is a very important festival. It celebrates the beginnings of the Jewish people, when God delivered them from slavery in Egypt.
- The celebrations of Pesach aim to recreate for every Jew this experience of being set free.
- As at the time of the original Exodus, only unleavened bread is eaten.
- Pesach falls in the Spring, on the dates 15–22 Nisan.

- It celebrates God's control of both history and nature.
- The highlight of the festival is the opening meal, the Seder.
- This meal is surrounded by symbols and stories of the Exodus.
- Pesach expresses the sense of belonging to a people, chosen by God and depending on him.

A)   Getting Ready

Imagine you are getting ready for a special occasion – a birthday party, for instance. If you are involved in cleaning the house and making the food for the party, you will be very busy beforehand. The importance of an occasion may be measured by the time and effort we put into getting ready for it. If this is true, then the festival of Pesach must be very important for Jews. It is the first pilgrim festival of the year and it lasts seven days (eight days outside Israel). The first and last days of the festival are holy days, when no work, apart from the preparation of food, can be done. The middle days are ordinary days, when only important work can be done. The preparations, however, take much longer than seven days and require great effort. The whole family helps turn the house upside down. Though many people go in for spring-cleaning, that of Jews before Pesach is extraordinarily thorough. They are making sure that the house has absolutely no leaven in it.

B)   Matzah (Unleavened Bread)

This removing of all trace of leaven is in response to Exodus 12:17–19. This passage tells us that Pesach is the Feast of Unleavened Bread, in Hebrew **matzah** (plural **matzot**). Matzah is bread made from flour kept specially dry. It is baked within 18 minutes of coming into contact with water. This means that it does not rise. Bread made of any of the five grains (wheat, rye, oats, spelt (a sort of wheat), or barley), which has been in contact with water for 18 minutes before baking, is leavened. The Hebrew for anything leavened is **chametz** (literally 'sour' or 'fermented'). Matzah is the only grain product Jews can eat at Pesach. This is baked under supervision at a Jewish bakery. Indeed, the preparation of all Pesach foods comes under special supervision to guarantee no contact with chametz. Food so prepared has a special seal on it: Kasher for Pesach.

Making matzah. The strict view is that the cereal must be constantly supervised from cutting, milling, sifting, transporting, kneading, and baking.

The command to remove all chametz from the home is followed so completely that many families have special kitchen utensils, crockery, and cutlery for the festival. These items are used only at Pesach and are stored away for the rest of the year. Food containing leaven may be held by a non-Jew during Pesach and taken back afterwards. What is important is that a Jew must not have chametz on his premises at this time.

The busiest time is on the eve of Pesach. The search for chametz has to be done thoroughly. The children hide pieces of bread (usually 10) and the father has to find them. This adds to the excitement for the children. More importantly it demonstrates the thoroughness of the search. Clearly, if any piece has not been found, the search will need to be more thorough. But why go to all these lengths to avoid leaven? To understand this

we must go right back to the origins of the festival.

C) How Pesach Began

Unleavened bread, together with other special foods, was eaten by the Children of Israel just before they escaped from slavery in Egypt. There was not time to wait for the bread to rise (Exodus 12:34). To recreate the physical conditions of this experience and so relive the Exodus, Jews avoid all leaven (Exodus 12:17–20). On the first day of the festival (for Orthodox Jews outside Israel on the first two days), Jews specifically eat unleavened bread, matzah, following the command of Exodus 12:18. It is a way of entering physically into the experience of their ancestors in being enslaved and then freed.

On the morning of Pesach, all remaining chametz is burnt.

There is also a spiritual significance attached to leaven. Because it makes bread rise, leaven has come to symbolise the tendency in human beings to become proud and self-reliant. Not eating chametz and eating matzah is a reminder of the Jews' dependence on God. With the physical spring-cleaning goes a cleaning out of what is bad in their lives.

It is possible, of course, to go through the motions, not thinking about their meaning. Many non-Jews do precisely this at Christmas time. To try to avoid this, the rabbi reminds his congregation, in the synagogue on the Shabbat before Pesach, of the significance of all the rituals.

D) The Freedom Festival

Pesach, like other Jewish festivals, is linked with nature. It falls in the Spring, on 15–22 Nisan. In the early Spring, the crop-farmers of ancient Israel would celebrate the barley harvest. These agricultural celebrations were, at some point, combined with pastoral and historical celebrations. In Egypt on the night of the first Passover, every Israelite family was commanded to offer and eat a lamb (Exodus 12:3–6). The Torah later commanded the Israelites to sacrifice a lamb every year to recall that offered in Egypt (Deuteronomy 16:2). This was called the Paschal (of the Passover) lamb. Whilst God's control of nature is remembered in this Springtime festival, it is the historical event of the first Passover that Pesach celebrates most of all. The focus is on God's control of history, in particular his liberating the Israelites from Egypt.

We read in Chapter 1 about the Exodus, the 'going out' from Egypt. Egypt had been a good place to be in the time of Jacob's son, Joseph. By the time of Moses, however, the Pharaoh feared the growing number of Israelites. He exploited them, using them as slaves (Exodus 1:8–14).

The Book of Exodus tells about the plagues God sent on the Egyptians, trying to persuade Pharaoh to let the Israelites go. Pharaoh resisted for a long time. The final deadly plague was the killing of the Egyptian first-born. Exodus 12 describes how the Israelites were to mark the doorposts of their houses with blood

from the lamb, so that God would know that they were not Egyptians. He would pass over them and not kill their first-born. The Hebrew word, Pesach means 'to pass over', and so the festival takes its name from God's passing over the homes of the Israelites. This plague finally did persuade Pharaoh to release the Israelites, but before they had got very far he changed his mind, perhaps regretting the loss of his slave-labour. We can read in Exodus 14 the story of how the Israelites got across the Sea of Reeds, while the pursuing Egyptians drowned. The Israelites were then free.

The Ten Commandments open with a reference to the Exodus: 'I am the Lord your God who brought you out of the land of Egypt, out of the house of bondage.'

Pesach is then the celebration of freedom. Without the events commemorated by this festival, there would be no Jewish people. In every Kiddush, on Shabbat and other festivals, Jews speak 'in remembrance of the Exodus from Egypt'. But it is Pesach which more than anything celebrates this birth of a nation. It is, therefore, the birthday of the Jewish people.

Extension Section

i)   The day before Pesach is a fast for first-born sons. This is based on the sparing of the first-born Israelites during the tenth plague. The stress is on God's mercy in sparing them, rather than on gloating over the death of the Egyptian first-born. As you read about the Seder, notice this emphasis again. In practice, the fast is not usually undertaken. The fulfilling of the mitzvah calls for a celebration, a festive meal. The day before Pesach, the first-born fulfils the mitzvah of attending an 'ending'. This is where a group complete the learning of a tractate of the Talmud. The obligation to celebrate this with a festive meal takes precedence over the fast. What point can you see to present Jewish practice?

ii)   Deuteronomy 16:1–8 speaks of the 'bread of affliction'. What other periods of affliction besides that in Egypt might Jews call to mind at Pesach?

iii)   Look up this passage and Leviticus 23:5–6, 10–11 and list the ways in which the Israelites are to celebrate Pesach.

E)   The Seder

The best thing about a birthday is usually the party. This is true of Pesach. The highlight of the festival is a special celebratory meal held on the first night. Orthodox Jews outside Israel have another such meal on the second night. To this are invited relatives and other guests, especially people who would otherwise be on their own. (It is rather difficult to hold a party for one.) Sometimes this celebration is like a family 'get together' with accompanying rituals playing only a small part. Many Jews, however, are committed to re-creating the Exodus experience for everyone present. To help them do this the meal follows

a set order. The Hebrew word for 'order' is **seder**, which is then the name given to this celebration.

The mother says the blessing for the candles and kindles the lights, welcoming this festival just as she welcomes Shabbat. The father, and possibly other members of the family, attend the evening service in the synagogue. The prayers for the service are found in the special Prayer Book for the festivals. (Do you remember what the evening service and the Festival Prayer Book are called? If not, look back at Chapter 13.) On the father's return, the Seder begins.

1. *Recite the Kiddush* – blessings over the wine to consecrate the Festival.
2. *Wash the hands* – prior to partaking of the green herbs.
3. *Partake of the green herbs.*
4. *Divide the Matzah* – so that the Afikomen may be put away.
5. *Read the Haggadah.*
6. *Wash the hands* for the meal proper.
7/8. *Recite the two blessings over the Matzah.*
9. *Recite the blessing over Bitter Herbs.*
10. *Eat the Hillel sandwich.*
11. *Serve the Meal.*
12. *Eat the Afikomen.*
13. *Say the Grace after meals.*
14. *Conclude the Hallel Psalms.*
15. *Pray that God will accept your Seder service with favour.*

The order.

You will see from the list above that those attending a Seder are in for a long night. There are many features to the occasion which help keep people's interest. Everybody likes a good story and the Seder revolves round the story of the Exodus. This is set out in a special book called a **Haggadah**. This is the Hebrew word for 'telling'. The Haggadah tells the story of the slavery and freedom of the Jewish people. It may include stories of more recent Jewish experience, but its basis is the account of the Exodus in the Bible and the Mishnah. At an ordinary birthday party only one person's existence is celebrated. At the Seder, every Jew celebrates his or her existence as part of the people of God. It is remarked in the Seder that: 'Every Jew should regard himself as if he had personally come out of Egypt.' Everyone present is given a copy of the Haggadah and may take it in turn to read from it. Another feature which helps everyone feel involved is that the story is told in the form of questions and answers. This is the best way of learning. Only when we are asking questions are we really interested in the answers.

The **Haggadot** (plural of Haggadah) usually have the Hebrew text accompanied by a translation in the language of those celebrating the Seder.

F)   Tonight's the Night

The effort that has gone into the preparation and the atmosphere of the Seder raises one obvious question: 'Why is this night different from all other nights?' In the course of the evening, this question is answered. It is answered not just with words, but with things to see and taste. If you look back at the 15 steps of the Seder on p. 138, you will see that besides eating matzah everybody eats not only the usual green herbs but also bitter herbs. Another symbol is a cushion placed beside the person conducting the Seder. In ancient times free people would recline to eat. The cushion symbolises the comfort of being free to eat in a relaxed position.

With the children lies the future of the Jewish people, and it is appropriate that it is the youngest child present who asks the questions. The general question about the difference of 'this night' leads into four specific

questions about the evening's rituals:

a) 'Why on this night do we eat unleavened bread?'
b) 'Why on this night do we eat bitter herbs?'
c) 'Why on this night do we dip our herbs?'
d) 'Why on this night do we recline?'

The one leading the Seder (usually the father) gives the answers to these questions as he points to the various symbols. We have already seen that unleavened bread is linked with both slavery and freedom. On the Seder table will be three matzot, standing for the three groups in ancient Israel: the priests, the Levites, and the ordinary Jews. The fourth step in the Seder is to take out the middle matzah and put it away. (It is often hidden for the children to find later. The fun of this may help them stay awake.) It is the last thing to be eaten at the Seder. This matzah is called the *Afikomen* (see steps 4 and 12), which is probably a Greek word meaning 'dessert', the last taste of the meal. It is fitting that this should be matzah, as unleavened bread is the central symbol of Pesach.

The herbs are other important symbols, reminding everyone of what it is that is being commemorated. The most usual green herb is parsley or long lettuce, the leaves symbolising

You can buy packets of matzah in the supermarket. Matzot are wafers, round, square, or oval-shaped. They are always flat. Why is this?

freedom and the bitter stalk slavery. Horse-radish is often one of the bitter herbs. Its taste is particularly bitter and forms a powerful reminder of the misery of slavery. The green herbs are dipped in salt water, a symbol of both the tears of the slaves before they were freed and the sea they crossed to freedom. Another symbol combining both slavery and freedom is the **charoset**. This mixture of fruit, nuts, spices, and wine is seen to resemble the mortar with which the slaves had to make bricks. When eaten, charoset gives the sweet taste of freedom. The bitter herbs are dipped in it.

These items of food are usually placed on a special Seder dish. With them are two items which are symbols to look at but not to eat. One is an egg, hard-boiled, then roasted. This is a reminder of the sacrifices offered in the Temple. Another reminder of sacrifice is a lamb bone. This stands for the Paschal lamb, the lamb slaughtered at Pesach.

Not only food, but also drink plays an important symbolic role. Red wine is used, the red perhaps symbolising the blood of slavery or the lamb's blood used to mark the Israelites' houses at the first Passover. Everyone has to drink four cups of wine (or grape juice) during the course of the Seder. The reason given in the Talmud is that the four cups stand for the four promises of Exodus 6:6–7. Here four different verbs are used as God promises Moses that he will rescue his people. He will 'bring out, deliver, redeem,

Step 10 is to eat a sandwich made of two pieces of matzah, filled with bitter herbs and charoset. This is a reminder of Hillel, who ate matzah, bitter herbs, and some of the Paschal lamb at the same time.

take'. It is worth noting that Moses is only once mentioned in the Haggadah, and that in passing. All the emphasis is on God.

A fifth promise is given in Exodus 6:8 and this is symbolised by another cup. In Talmudic times, people disagreed about whether a fifth cup of wine should be drunk. A compromise was reached by pouring out a fifth cup but not drinking it. When the rabbis had a question that could not be resolved, they would leave it to be answered by the prophet Elijah when he returned. Elijah is expected to herald the Messianic Age when all disputes will be resolved and true freedom and peace will reign. So this cup, standing on the table in Elijah's name, came to be called Elijah's cup. There also arose the custom of opening the door to encourage Elijah's arrival.

The wine is used to make a further point during the Seder. When each of the ten plagues is mentioned, each person spills a drop of wine to express sorrow at the suffering of the Egyptians. Pesach celebrates the Israelites' deliverance, not other people's suffering. For this reason also, part of the Hallel (the psalms of praise sung at most festivals) is left out. This attitude to enemies cannot be easy, especially for Jews whose own relatives have suffered persecution. It should be remembered that there are still countries where Jews experience oppression. This is why the Seder ends with the words:

The redemption is not yet complete . . .
Peace, shalom . . .
Next year in Jerusalem,
Next year may all be free.

Extension Section

A video, *Pesach*, is available from JMD. Some famous Seder songs, including 'The Four Questions', are on a United Synagogue tape (from JMD), *Educational Selections for the Seder Service*. There is a *Seder Handbook* by Clive Lawton (from the Board of Deputies). This includes the popular song, 'One Little Goat', as does the JMD tape. The song tells how a cat eats the goat, a dog eats the cat, a stick beats the dog, fire burns the stick, water put out the fire, a cow drinks the water, a butcher slaughters the cow, the angel of death slays the butcher, and God kills the angel of death. This may not sound a very cheerful song with which to end a Seder. It is usually taken to be an allegory of Jewish history. What do you think the song means and why is it appropriate for Pesach?

Questions

A Matter of Fact

1 What grain product do Jews eat at Pesach? (B)

2 In what season of the year does Pesach fall? (D)

3 What persuaded Pharaoh to release his slaves? (D)

4 Which sea did the Jews cross after escaping from Egypt? (D)

5 At what time of day does the Seder begin? (E)

6 What symbolises freedom to eat in comfort? (F)

7 What is the Afikomen? (F)

8 What does the lamb bone symbolise? (F)

9 What four promises are recorded in Exodus 6:6–7? (F)

Vocabulary

Give the Hebrew words for the following:

1 unleavened bread (B)

2 leavened bread (B)

3 pass over (C)

4 order (E)

5 telling (E)

A Question of Understanding

Try to give at least two religious explanations in answer to each of the following questions.

1 Why is chametz not eaten at Pesach? (C)

2 Why may those at a Seder read in turn from the Haggadah? (E)

3 Why are the green herbs dipped in salt water? (F)

4 Why is the fifth cup known as Elijah's cup? (F)

Over to You

Answer these questions fully, giving your reasons, and stating arguments both for and against where appropriate.

1 What do you think this festival teaches about freedom?

2 Proverbs 24 tells the Jews: 'Do not rejoice when your enemy falls.' Why should Jews remember this at Pesach?

Do you think this is good advice generally?

3 It is sometimes suggested that to experience a Seder you need to attend one in a Jewish home, rather than reconstructing one in the classroom. What do you think about this?

Assignment

a) What do children learn from their parents during the Seder?

b) Why is it important that these things are passed on?

c) As a Jew, what would you most want to pass on to your children and how would you go about it?

18

Shavuot (Weeks)

- Shavuot is the Feast of Weeks. It falls seven weeks after Pesach.
- Shavuot completes Pesach by celebrating God's gift of freedom. At Pesach God's people gain physical freedom; at Shavuot spiritual freedom.
- Freedom comes in the form of the Torah, given to Moses on Mount Sinai.
- Shavuot is a one-day Summer festival (two days outside Israel), coming at the time of the wheat harvest.
- Flowers and fruit act as reminders of this agricultural link.
- All the synagogue readings at Shavuot focus on the theme of God's revelation.
- God reveals himself as holy, loving, compassionate, true, and just. To be obedient, his people must also show these qualities.

A) Counting the Days

If you are looking forward to something exciting and important, you may well count the days. You may count the days to seeing someone special or to a holiday. Whatever it is you want to happen cannot come too quickly. On the second day of Pesach, Jews begin counting the days to the Festival of Shavuot. Shavuot commemorates what Jews believe is the most important event in human history, the giving of God's Law. Whilst Pesach gave the Jews their physical freedom, it was at Shavuot that they gained their spiritual freedom by accepting the Law.

This counting of the days from Pesach to Shavuot is called counting the **Omer**, though it is actually counting *from* the Omer. An Omer was a measurement of barley. The Torah commands that 'from the morrow after the Sabbath' (which is taken to mean the second day of Pesach) a sheaf of barley should be brought to the Temple in Jerusalem (Leviticus 23:15). There is out of gratitude for the barley harvest. This offering of barley must be made every day until the next crop, wheat, is harvested. Then an offering of wheat must be made (Leviticus 23:16). The wheat offering will begin seven weeks after the barley harvest. The wheat harvest, therefore, takes the name Shavuot (weeks). Shavuot is the Feast of Weeks. Not only the weeks but the days must be counted. These total 49. The next day, the 50th after Pesach, is Shavuot, and that is why the festival is sometimes called *Pentecost*, the Greek for 50. Nowadays Shavuot falls on a fixed date, 6 Sivan and, outside Israel, also 7 Sivan. But the days of the Omer period are still counted, to capture the sense of waiting for the Law.

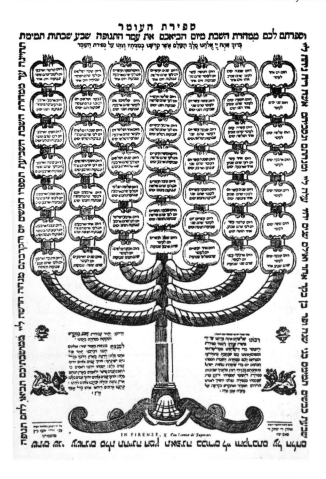

This eighteenth-century wall calendar is one of the many aids devised to help count the Omer.

Chapter 1). The fasting, which had marked the sadness of the plague and the Bar Kochba Revolt, was lifted. This date, the 33rd of the Omer, has, therefore, become a minor festival. The first 32 days remember a bad period in Israel's history, and the 33rd acknowledges God's intervention to help the nation survive. Mourning turns to celebration. There is often a surge of hair-cuts and weddings on this day. The Hebrew words for the 33rd day of the Omer are **Lag B'Omer**.

C)   The Wheat Harvest

Flowers have become a symbol of the fragrance which the Torah brings into Jewish life.

B)   Lag B'Omer

Since the period of the Omer is one of anticipation, it may seem odd that the first 32 days of it are regarded as a sad period by Orthodox Jews. This includes some of the features linked with mourning the dead, such as not cutting the hair or celebrating weddings (see Chapters 11 and 20). The origins of this practice of mourning are obscure, but one explanation is that many of the disciples of Rabbi Akiva died from a plague during this period.

On the 33rd day of the Omer, apparently, the epidemic ended. Also on this date there was a victory in the Bar Kochba Revolt (see

The Torah does not tell us the exact date when Moses was given the Law on Mount Sinai. On the basis of Exodus 19, however, it has been calculated to have been the third month, that is, Sivan. Since the sixth day of Sivan is Shavuot, the two events, the beginning of the wheat festival and the revelation on Sinai, became one festival. The original emphasis was probably on the agricultural aspects of the festival. For Jews today, the essence of Shavuot is their receiving of God's Law.

Nonetheless, this second pilgrim festival, like the first, Pesach, still includes some echoes of a harvest festival. These are not special rituals (like eating unleavened bread at Pesach) so much as customs that developed over the centuries. One of them is to decorate the synagogue with flowers and plants, representing the flowering of Mount Sinai when the Torah was given.

Another custom is to eat dairy dishes, especially cheesecake. Various explanations have been given for this. One is that until the laws about meat were given, Jews ate only milk dishes so that they would not get it wrong. Another is that milk is a good symbol of the Torah, as it nourishes young and old. A further thought is that eating milk products is a reminder that God brought the Jews out of Egypt into 'a land flowing with milk and honey' (Deuteronomy 26:9).

Deuteronomy 26 speaks of the importance of gratitude for the land and its produce. The Israelites are to remember their humble and harsh beginnings (verse 5). They are to offer to God the first fruits (thought of as the best) of the harvest (verses 1–3,10). There is no longer a Temple in which to offer first fruits, but the harvest should not be taken for granted. 'The Feast of First Fruits' is, in fact, another name for Shavuot. Shavuot has, however, no special rituals linked to a theme (such as freedom at Pesach and trust at Sukkot), for the theme of Shavuot, the giving of the Torah, is too big to be represented. The Torah is *the* theme of Judaism and as such embraces all others.

D)   Freedom from and Freedom for

There was for some time a television advertisement showing a man just released from prison. He is looking very lost. Then he sees his wife who is waiting for him and his face lights up. He has someone to be released for. Simply to be let out, whether from prison or simply from school, is only a gift if there are things you want to do.

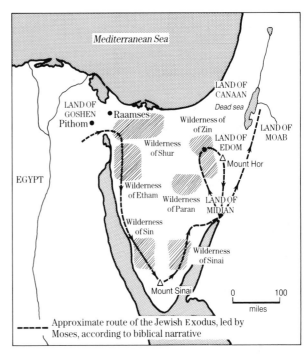

All three pilgrimage festivals commemorate the Exodus. Pesach is linked particularly to the coming out of Egypt and Sukkot to the journey into Canaan. What links Shavuot to Mount Sinai?

The rabbis refer to Shavuot as 'the concluding festival' to Pesach. This expresses the thought that the deliverance from slavery remembered at Pesach was not an end in itself. God says to Moses when assuring him that he is sending him to deliver his people, 'When you have brought forth the people out of Egypt, you shall serve God upon this mountain.' (Exodus 3:12). What the people are being given is not freedom to do nothing, but freedom to serve God. Maimonides says that liberty without law is a doubtful blessing. (What do you think he means by this?)

The link between freedom from slavery and freedom for service is expressed at many points during Shavuot. Firstly, many people stay up throughout the night Shavuot begins, studying the Torah. They may study one particular topic or read from an anthology of written and oral law called 'The Arrangement for the Night of Shavuot'. The second night may also celebrate the privilege of the Torah.

Often the Book of Psalms is read. The Psalms are a reminder of King David, since the tradition is that he composed them.

Secondly, the readings in the synagogue focus particularly on God's revelation. Central to the service on the first day of Shavuot is the solemn reading of the Ten Commandments from Exodus 20:1–17. On the second day, the Torah passage is Deuteronomy 15:19–16:16. Other readings are:

Ezekiel 1 – the prophet's vision of God;
Habakkuk 3 – God's power in revelation;
Ruth – the story of a Moabite woman who becomes a loyal Jew. (You could read this short book.)

E)   Receiving the Torah

Shavuot celebrates the giving of the Torah by God on a particular day. Every day, however, a Jew needs to receive the Torah and obey it. This is what makes him or her a member of the covenant people. Pesach speaks of God setting all Jews free, not just in the past, but in the present. So Shavuot completes the freedom of Pesach for any Jew who 'stands here with us this day' (Deuteronomy 29:15). If someone offers you a gift, it is not much use to you unless you accept it. So each Jew needs to accept the spiritual freedom given by the Torah.

We have seen in Chapter 3 that God gives his people particular mitzvot (obligations) by which to express their obedience. We have seen in many chapters specific mitzvot: laws about what to eat and when to pray, for example. Underlying all these are certain beliefs about God and about how he wants his people to live. These fundamental ideas are to do with how people behave. These central ethical points come in the Ten Commandments, but they run throughout the Bible. They are also the underlying principles of the Talmud. They can be summed up as holiness, love, compassion, truth, and justice.

A Rembrandt painting of Moses with the Ten Commandments. Where in the synagogue would you see two stone tablets?

Extension Section

> Stern Lawgiver! yet thou dost wear
> The Godhead's most benignant grace;
> Nor know we anything so fair
> As is the smile upon thy face;
> Flowers laugh before thee on their beds;
> And fragrance in thy footing treads.

(from William Wordsworth, 'Ode to Duty')

What connections can you see between the ideas in this poem and the festival of Shavuot?

F)   Holiness

Holiness means being set apart. God is holy in being set apart from the material world and all its limitations. Yet God is believed to be present in the world, available to his people in signs of his presence, such as holy places (for example, the Ark), holy days when secular concerns are put aside (for example, Shabbat), and holy books (for example, the Talmud). All these are aids to holiness, enabling a person to be close to God even while living fully in the material world. For not only God but his people are to be set apart. God says to them: 'You shall be holy; for I the Lord your God am holy.' (Leviticus 19:2). This holiness is available to all Jews as they observe God's laws. They are made holy, sanctified, as they fulfil the mitzvot. So before performing any mitzvah, it is essential to recite the berachah (blessing):

Blessed art thou, O Lord our God, King of the Universe, who hast hallowed us by thy commandments.

G) Love

The Jew is commanded to love God (Deuteronomy 6:4) and also his neighbour as himself (Leviticus 19:18). The context of Leviticus 19:18 makes plain that it is not a command to feel an emotion, such as liking, for everyone. This is clearly an impossibility. Rather it is a command to act in a certain way, not to take revenge or bear a grudge against someone who has wronged him. Rather he must behave towards others (whether he likes

When someone asked Rabbi Hillel to teach him the entire Torah whilst standing on one leg, he gave the Golden Rule.

them or not) as he would like them to behave towards himself. The Babylonian Talmud records Rabbi Hillel's summary of the entire Torah as 'That which is hateful unto thee, do not do unto thy neighbour.' This has become known as the Golden Rule.

Love of neighbour is commanded because of the worth and dignity of every human being. Judaism believes in the sanctity of human life and in personal responsibility. Every Jew, therefore, has the responsibility to behave in a way that expresses respect. He must respect both himself and others.

H) Compassion

We all know how important it is to have someone who will treat us kindly and sympathetically. Especially if something has gone wrong, through either our own fault or other people's, we want more than respect. We want compassion or mercy. Compassion is one of the highest values for Judaism. The Bible and Jewish prayers frequently speak of the mercy of God. To be God-like, Jews are, therefore, called upon to be merciful.

This means to feel with others (the literal meaning of the word 'compassion') in their troubles. Mercy is, however, not just a feeling but an activity. It may help us if people sympathise with us. It helps us even more if they actually do something. So Jews are called upon not only to feel but also to show mercy. They are to be particularly compassionate towards those who are in a vulnerable position, with no-one to protect them. So, again and again, the Bible singles out for kindly treatment the stranger, the widow, and the orphan (e.g. Exodus 22:21–3).

Closely linked with compassion is charity, the practice of compassion. This may take the form of money, or it may be giving assistance or encouragement to someone in difficulties. Visiting someone who is unwell is an important act of charity, or benevolence, and the

Who is helping whom?

Shulchan Aruch devotes a whole section to rules for such visiting. You may find it odd that there should be rules about such things, but perhaps we need such guidelines. It is all too easy, when trying to help someone, to make matters worse. Staying too long with someone who feels tired or visiting too frequently is the sort of thing the Shulchan Aruch discourages. The emphasis has not to be on your goodness in visiting but on the tact and sensitivity needed by the person who is ill.

I) Truth

In action and in speech, Judaism stresses the need for truth. A Jew is to practise compassion not because he wants credit for it but because he believes in the value of every human being. For the same reason, he is to treat his neighbour with the generosity which he would like shown to him, not pretending to like him. The rabbinic expression for a hypocrite is 'one whose inside is not like his outside'. So the Jewish ideal is to make the inside and the outside the same. The aim is genuinely to want the good for other people, being particularly careful not to damage their reputation (e.g. Leviticus 19:16). This sort of honesty with yourself, with others, and with God is very

demanding, but, according to Jewish writings, this is what God requires.

J) Justice

Justice could be said to be truth in action. It is fair play. In Jewish writings, God is described as just in his dealings with people. So Jews are required to be just. This is not in contrast to loving people or showing compassion. The same chapter in the Bible which speaks of loving your neighbour (Leviticus 19:18), and of showing compassion for the vulnerable (Leviticus 19:9), also speaks of judging (that is, practising justice towards) your neighbour (Leviticus 19:15). The idea is that God is both just and merciful with people, so Jews must be both just and merciful also.

Extension Section

Below is an extract from Rosemary Friedman, *To Live in Peace* (Piatkus, 1987). Sarah is nearing the end of a long process of instruction in the Jewish faith before her conversion. Read the extract and then say what Sarah finds so attractive about Judaism.

> *She had, she supposed, regarded herself if anything until meeting Josh, as a humanist, but now she saw her humanism as a set only of personal ideals (restatements, in fact, of Jewish ideals) which had no mode of transmission from one generation to the next and absolutely no system for producing decent people. Her husband's heritage – with its emphasis on right conduct and the sanctity of human life – which she had at first believed to consist of no more than a few arbitrary dietary laws, ritual and defined prayer and a sense of affinity with others, turned out to her amazement to take nothing for granted – there were blessings for all life's experiences – and to possess the most extensive system of legislative good known to mankind. Goodness had both to be defined and*

formulated (it was as difficult to become a good person as it was to become a good tight-rope walker) and this Judaism had done. Violence and oppression were repugnant to the teaching which embraced the whole domain of life, and paid due regard to the human condition, its difficulties and dilemmas. There were entire texts governing speech alone (speaking evil about someone was a serious sin and one who humiliated his fellow man in public was regarded as if he had shed blood) and the laws of ethics governed not only business relationships, treatment of the elderly, the weak, the poor, but in every area of conduct with titbits from which, at unexpected moments, Sarah would regale Josh.

'Did you know that according to the Talmud a Jew is not allowed to raise the hopes of a shopkeeper by asking the price of an item which he knows he's not going to buy?' or 'Listen to this: it's forbidden to turn back a poor man empty handed, even if one gives as little as a dried fig!'

In reply to Josh's scepticism, that he didn't think such injunctions of earth shattering importance, Sarah informed him that while each particular law might not seem that significant, added together they represented unique consideration for fellow human beings.

Questions

A Matter of Fact

1 What crop is harvested in Israel at Shavuot? (A)

2 In what Hebrew month does this festival occur? (A)

3 What does Pentecost mean? (A)

4 What is the main event celebrated at Shavuot? (C)

5 What, according to Maimonides, might be a doubtful blessing? (D)

6 What are the main ethical principles of Judaism? (E)

7 State one place in the Torah which says God's people must be holy. (F)

8 What is the Golden Rule? (G)

Vocabulary

Give the Hebrew words for the following:

1 measurement of barley (A)

2 weeks (A)

A Question of Understanding

Try to give at least two religious explanations in answer to each of the following questions.

1 Why is Lag B'Omer a festival? (B)

2 Why are dairy products eaten at Shavuot? (C)

3 Why is Shavuot sometimes called 'The Feast of First Fruits'? (C)

4 Why should a Jew exercise compassion? (H)

5 Why would it be hypocritical to celebrate Shavuot while spreading rumours about someone? (I)

Over to You

Answer these questions fully, giving your reasons, and stating arguments both for and against where appropriate.

1 What situations can you think of in which you would find it difficult to 'love your neighbour as yourself'? What reasons might a Jew give for making the effort?

2 Do you think it is possible to be just and merciful at the same time?

3 Why do you think non-Jews tend to know less about Shavuot than about the other two pilgrimage festivals?

Assignment

a) Read Leviticus 23:15–21 and Deuteronomy 26:1–11. Describe or illustrate what an ancient Israelite would do to celebrate Shavuot.

b) Why is it appropriate that each of these passages is followed by a verse instructing concern for the underprivileged?

c) Give examples of how a Jew nowadays might fulfil these obligations towards others. Do you think that everyone should fulfil them?

19

Sukkot (Tabernacles) and Simchat Torah (Rejoicing of the Law)

- Sukkot ('Tabernacles' or 'Booths') is the third pilgrimage festival of the year. It takes place at the conclusion of the fruit harvest in Israel.
- Sukkot celebrates God's protection of the Israelites during their 40-year journey from Egypt through the wilderness.
- Jews fulfil the mitzvah to 'dwell in booths' by sitting in a sukkah, a temporary shelter. This reminds them of their dependence on God.

- Four species of plant are held during Sukkot. These are a reminder of the harvest and also of the variety of people making up the Jewish community.
- Eight days after the beginning of Sukkot (nine days outside Israel) comes the festival of **Simchat Torah** (The Rejoicing of the Law). This celebrates the cycle of Torah readings in the synagogue.

A) Who Is in Control?

Human beings are complex and intelligent creatures. They can claim to have considerable control over their lives, with sophisticated machinery and technology. It may be, however, that modern developments, such as computers and life-support machines, have their dangers. In particular, they may give an exaggerated sense of control. It is true that, in times of difficulty, we may sometimes feel out of control. Generally, however, we tend to think everything depends on us. From the point of view of someone who believes in God, this way of thinking is a mistake, for it is not human beings but God who is in control, and we depend on him.

The Jewish Festival of Sukkot is a deliberate reminder of this dependence and of the need

to trust not in ourselves but in God. Sukkot is the Hebrew for 'huts', 'booths' or 'tabernacles', and the festival takes its name from the period when the ancient Israelites had no permanent homes but only temporary shelters. This was during their long journey through the desert after the Exodus from Egypt to the land of Canaan. To recreate these conditions, Jews are commanded to 'dwell in booths for seven days' (Leviticus 23:42). So the Festival of Sukkot is observed for seven days (eight days by Orthodox Jews outside Israel) as a re-enactment of this original dependence on God. In this way, Sukkot, like other festivals, is not just commemorating past events. It makes the events happen again, now.

Since Sukkot, like the other two pilgrimage festivals, is also a harvest festival (Leviticus 23:39), the Sukkot (booths) could also represent the shelters of the farmers gathering in the harvest, who lived on the job. Certainly God's provision of the harvest is recalled at Sukkot, though the main emphasis of the festival is historical rather than agricultural. Sukkot is the final harvest of the year and takes place from 15 to 22 Tishrei, in the Autumn. Like Pesach, the first and the last days of the festival are holy days, on which all work except the preparation of food is prohibited.

Building a sukkah.

B) Back to Nature

Sometimes people try to get away from the sophistications of modern, urban society by growing their own food and generally living simply. Many people, while not permanently leaving the comforts of their homes, choose to spend some time camping where they can be more in touch with nature. Sukkot is a religious version of this 'back to nature' idea. God is seen as the creator and the one on whom everything depends. The psalmist speaks of God hiding me 'in his sukkah; in the shelter of his tabernacle' in 'the day of trouble'. By this he means that God will give protection and spiritual strength when all other security is gone. So the **sukkah** (tabernacle, hut, booth) becomes a symbol of trust in God. We have seen in Leviticus the mitzvah to live seven days in sukkot (plural of sukkah). An Orthodox Jew will still take this literally by building a sukkah.

A sukkah must have certain characteristics. It must have at least three walls, made of material that can withstand the wind. Even more importantly it must have a particular kind of roof. The roof must be made of plants that cannot be used for food. These plants must be in their natural state (boards of wood cannot be used) and detached from the ground (the branches of a growing tree cannot be used). It must be possible to see the sky through it and it must not be so dense that a heavy rain cannot come through. Nor must it

have an additional covering, for example, an overhanging balcony. The flimsiness of the sukkah is designed to encourage Jews to put their trust in the creator and not in the size and strength of their houses.

Synagogues often have a room with a sliding roof which can be drawn back. In place of the roof is positioned a covering, made according to the requirements for the roof of a sukkah. This room then becomes a sukkah. The rabbis speak of adorning the mitzvot. So a sukkah, whether in a home or synagogue, is made as attractive as possible, with hanging fruit, flowers, paper chains, and coloured lights.

Jews will often build their own sukkah at home. The mitzvah may also be fulfilled by making Kiddush in a synagogue sukkah.

The mitzvah is not to build a sukkah but to live in it. Some Jews do precisely that, even sleeping in the sukkah for the seven or eight days. However, in countries like Britain, where the climate in late September, or early October can be quite cold, most Jews would simply eat in the sukkah. Even this mitzvah does not apply to someone who is ill, or if it is raining. The Talmud is critical of someone who tries to prove his piety by staying in the sukkah at times not required by the Torah. Nonetheless, some effort has to be made. This is why the festival is celebrated not in the Spring, when the Exodus occurred, but in the Autumn, when sitting in a sukkah is more likely to entail some discomfort through cold.

C)   It Takes All Sorts

The second most distinctive ritual of Sukkot is holding in the hand four plants. The mitzvah for this, as for the sukkah, comes in Leviticus 23. In verse 40, we read:

And you shall take on the first day the fruit of goodly trees, branches of palm trees, and boughs of leafy trees, and willows of the brook; and you shall rejoice before the Lord your God seven days.

This festival concludes the harvests in Israel, and so these plants are symbols of God's provision. The 'fruit of goodly trees' is taken to be the **etrog,** a citrus fruit, which looks rather like a lemon but tastes and smells quite different. The 'branches of palm trees' are called the **lulav,** and the 'boughs of leafy trees' are represented by myrtle. These, together with willows, constitute the 'four species', the **Arba Minim**. Why these four particular species were originally chosen is not altogether clear, but they are understood by the rabbis to be the biblical requirement.

Many Jews think that there is a deeper symbolism attached to the Arba Minim. They think that the four plants stand, in some way, for different sorts of people. One suggestion is that the etrog stands for the heart, that is,

Jews gather in great numbers at the Western Wall in Jerusalem during Sukkot. Do you remember from Chapter 6 why this is such a special place for Jews?

someone who is kindly and compassionate; the lulav stands for the backbone, that is, someone who is brave and assertive; the myrtle stands for the eye, that is, someone who is capable of seeing good in others; and the willow stands for the mouth, that is, someone who speaks with knowledge and understanding of the Torah.

A similar way of interpreting the four species, as indicating different types of character, is to take taste as standing for the Torah and scent as standing for good works. On this interpretation, the etrog, having both taste and scent, represents someone who knows the Torah and practises it; the fruit of the lulav, having taste but no scent, represents someone learned in the Torah but who does no good deeds; the myrtle, having scent but no taste, represents someone who does good deeds but does not know the Torah; the willow, having neither scent nor taste, represents someone who is both ignorant and selfish. This interpretation is the most popular of the many suggested. Its point, like that of the interpretation above, is that it takes all sorts to make a world. No-one must be left out of the Jewish community. Each person, with his or her strengths and weaknesses, combines with others to form God's people. In terms of the world at large, this reflects a generous yet realistic view of human nature.

The Arba Minim are arranged in a particular way, with three myrtle twigs and two willows tied to the lulav. They are held in the right hand and a blessing is recited concerning taking the lulav. (As the largest of the four, this represents the whole group.) The etrog is held in the other hand. This happens in the synagogue on each day of Sukkot (except Shabbat). Many communities not only hold but also wave the lulav during the recital of the festive psalms, the Hallel. This waving is done in all directions, symbolising that God is everywhere.

Each etrog is carefully examined to see that it is as near perfect as possible.

D) The Obligation to Rejoice

Many people think that religion is very solemn, but in Judaism there is also an obligation to rejoice. We see this duty in the festival meal which follows a Brit, a Pidyon Haben, a Bar Mitzvah, a wedding, and the completion of a Talmudic tractate. We also see it in the observance of Shabbat and all three pilgrimage festivals. The element of rejoicing is particularly strong in the Pilgrimage Festival of Sukkot. Indeed, Sukkot is called 'The Season of our Rejoicing'. The people are commanded to rejoice at Sukkot (Leviticus 23:40) and this they do.

In Temple times, there was, during Sukkot, a festive procession to and from the spring that supplied the water for the Temple. Water was poured out on the altar as a great offering. We who live in a country where we are seldom without water may find it hard to understand this ancient Israelite ceremony. But the end of Sukkot marked the beginnings of the rain, rain which was vital for any future harvest in such a hot country. In celebration of water, there would be dancing to flutes, harps, and cymbals. The exuberance of the water-offering is reflected in the Mishnah, which says:

> He who has not witnessed the joy of the water-drawing has never in his life experienced real joy.

The seventh day of Sukkot now has a special name, **Hoshanah Rabbah** (the Great Hosannah). The Hebrew **Hoshanah** means 'Save us', and on this day many prayers beginning with this word are recited. They are said by people, carrying the lulav and etrog, processing round the bimah seven times. On this day, when God's deliverance is prayed for, there is the sense of God's judgement, and so there are some features of Hoshanah Rabbah which resemble those of the Day of Atonement (see Chapter 20).

Extension Section

i)   Watch the first part of the video *Jewish Festivals in a Jewish School* (from RMEP). What reasons would you give for the popularity of the Festival of Sukkot with Jewish children?

ii)   This part of the video is entitled 'Jacob's Day', remembering a tradition that on each day of Sukkot a special guest is invited. Jacob is the guest on the third day. Then come Joseph (one of Jacob's 12 sons), Moses, Aaron (Moses' brother), and David. Who are the guests on the first two days?

iii)   Watch the second part of the video, showing an assembly for Sukkot. Do you think such an assembly should also be held in a non-Jewish school? Give reasons for your answer.

Simchat Torah in Israel.

F)   The Rejoicing of the Law

We have seen that the Festival of Shavuot commemorates the giving of the Torah and that the whole festival of Sukkot is characterised by rejoicing. Why then is there a special day for the rejoicing of the Torah?

There is a Midrash about King Solomon celebrating when he finished reading the Torah. The Talmud, therefore, set the practice of reading the final portion of the Torah on a particular day and of celebrating the event.

E)   The Eighth Day of Assembly

Leviticus 23:39 commands that 'on the eighth day shall be a solemn rest'. As the conclusion of the festival, there is then observed an 'eighth day of assembly', **Shemini Atzeret**. Although it comes straight after Sukkot, Shemini Atzeret is a separate festival and so, like all festivals, it begins with Kiddush and ends with Havdalah (see Chapter 15). A central feature of the musaf (additional service) on Shemini Atzeret is the prayer for rain.

Outside Israel, Shemini Atzeret is observed for two days. The second of these two days came, sometime after the eleventh century CE, to be known as **Simchat Torah** (Rejoicing of the Law). In Israel, Shemini Atzeret and Simchat Torah are celebrated on the same day.

A synagogue on Simchat Torah.

This day now is the second day of Shemini Atzeret (the first and only day of Shemini Atzeret inside Israel). Sometime after the twelfth century CE, the practice of reading the first chapter of the Torah on this day was introduced. So there came to be a day on which the Torah reading was completed with Deuteronomy 33:1–34:12 and then begun again with Genesis 1:1–2:3.

This day is called Simchat Torah, the Rejoicing of the Law, because it celebrates the joy of having God's Law by which to live. On this day, the synagogue becomes an exceptionally lively place. All the Torah scrolls are taken out of the Ark and carried round the bimah seven times, with everyone joining in the procession. These seven circuits are often taken to represent Joshua's march round Jericho described in Joshua 6. Any formality disappears and, as people process, there is singing, dancing, and clapping. Many people are called up to read from the Torah. The greatest honour, however, goes to the one who reads the final portion of Deuteronomy and to the one who reads the first portion of Genesis. They are called 'bridegrooms'. They represent the Jewish congregation joined to the Torah as a bridegroom to a bride. There is sometimes a tallit over the heads of the readers, like the chupah at a wedding. Everything is designed to express great joy.

Extension Section

Read the following extract (i) from Rosemary Friedman's *Proofs of Affection* (Futura, 1985) and then say what it is about the Simchat Torah ceremonies that Rachel dislikes. Next read the extract (ii) from Chaim Potok's *In the Beginning* (Penguin, 1975). What contrasting points of view of Simchat Torah emerge? Which extract do you think best captures this festival?

(i)

At a sign from Rabbi Magnus the choirmaster in the curtained gallery above the Ark flipped his tuning fork and the choir struck up. One by one, with their precious burdens, the scroll-bearers stepped down into the main body of the synagogue. Like the Pied Piper of Hamlin they were joined on their way by the children with their flags, who emerged from the pews, propelled by encouraging pushes from their fathers. Swaying from side to side the ragged procession made its way down the aisle. The first circuit had begun.

Looking down from the gallery upon the disarray, listening to the discord, with its undertones of chatter and intermittent cries of small children, Rachel felt more disenchanted with the scene than usual. Next to her she was aware that her mother, smiling, was following every step, every movement of her father with proud eyes. It seemed a lifetime ago that she had herself been one of those small children. Dressed in her uncomfortable best, she had made the circuits with Josh, holding tightly to his hand and waiting eagerly for the end of the morning and the sweets. Josh, she remembered, had, for the benefit of the ladies distributing them, invented a small brother, in some years afflicted with measles and in others with mumps, according to his imagination, and invariably had came away with double rations.

The Rejoicing of the Law. According to Solly it was among the first Laws of the world and throughout the ages the greatest of legislators had borrowed freely from it; it was essentially just, free and humane. The ancient and tribal rites being performed beneath her seemed to denigrate, by their undignified disorder, anything that the religion might have to offer. She felt no pride in the shambles, the cacophony, the alienated eternity of every minute.

(ii)

The little synagogue was crowded and tumultuous with joy. I remember the white-bearded Torah reader dancing with one of the heavy scrolls as if he had miraculously shed his years. My father and uncle danced for what seemed to me to an interminable length of time, circling about one another with their Torah scrolls, advancing upon one another, backing off, singing. Saul and Alex and I danced too. I relinquished my Torah to someone in the crowd, then stood around watching the dancing. It grew warm inside the small room and I went through the crowd and out the rear door to the back porch. I stood in the darkness and let the air cool my face. I could feel the floor of the porch vibrating to the dancing inside the synagogue. It was a winy fall night, the air clean, the sky vast and filled with stars. The noise of the singing and dancing came clearly through the open windows of the synagogue. An old cycle ending; a new cycle beginning. Tomorrow morning Moses would die, and the old man would read the words recounting his death; a few minutes later he would read the first chapter and the beginning three verses of the second chapter of Genesis. Death and birth without separation. Endings leading to beginnings. And then, on Shabbat, he would read all of the first portion of the Book of Genesis: the Creation, Adam and Eve, the Garden of Eden, Cain and Abel. And the following Shabbat he would read the story of Noah and the Flood. And then Abraham and Sarah and the Covenant and Isaac and the sacrifice and Rebecca and Jacob and Esau and Joseph and . . .

The noise inside the synagogue poured out into the night, an undulating, swelling and receding and thinning and growing sound. The joy of dancing with the Torah, holding it close to you, the words of God to Moses at Sinai. I wondered if gentiles ever danced with their Bible. 'Hey, Tony. Do you ever dance with your Bible?'

Questions

A Matter of Fact

1. What is designed to remind Jews of their dependence upon God? (A)

2. At what season does Sukkot take place? (A)

3. To which country were the Israelites heading from Egypt? (A)

4. From which passage in the Bible do Jews take the mitzvah for the lulav? (C)

5. What is an etrog? (C)

6. What is sometimes called 'The Season of our Rejoicing?' (D)

7. What two names are given to the eighth day of Sukkot in Israel? (E)

8. What two portions of the Torah are read on Simchat Torah? (F)

9. Who are called 'bridegrooms' on Simchat Torah? (G)

Vocabulary

Give the Hebrew words for the following:

1. hut, booth, tabernacle (B)

2. four species (C)

3. save us (D)

4. Eighth Day of Assembly (E)

5. The Rejoicing of the Law (F)

A Question of Understanding

Try to give at least two religious explanations in answer to each of the following questions.

1   Why do Jews think it is important to remember that God 'made the people of Israel dwell in booths' (Leviticus 23:43)? (A)

2   Why may a sukkah not be built under a balcony? (B)

3   How might the Arba Minim be said to offer a realistic view of human society? (C)

Over to You

Answer these questions fully, giving your reasons, and stating arguments both for and against where appropriate.

1   Why do you think some people assume religion is something solemn? What would you select from what you have learned of Judaism to convince them otherwise?

2   Do you think that it is right to rejoice when things may be going badly for you or for people you know? How do you think a Jew would be likely to answer this question?

Assignment

a)   Describe the two main rituals of Sukkot. (You may also illustrate them.)

b)   Think about the point of these rituals and write a short poem entitled 'Harvest for the World'.

c)   In 1989, some Jews who had finally got permission to leave Russia were stranded in Italy. They were awaiting visas to enter America. One of them, when interviewed on television, said that he had spent all his life in camps: first a concentration camp, next a labour camp, and then a refugee camp. How do you think he might have felt about the festival of Sukkot?

20

The Days of Awe

- The most important days in the Jewish Calendar are the Days of Awe. These stress the need for awe or reverence of God.
- On these days, Rosh Hashanah (the New Year) and Yom Kippur (the Day of Atonement), Jews reflect on their responsibilities.
- Admitting that they have done wrong, Jews believe that they need to repent, that is, turn back to God.
- The shofar (ram's horn) is sounded to stimulate this repentance.
- New Year customs express the importance of getting rid of the bad and increasing the good in the year ahead.

- Yom Kippur is the holiest day of the Jewish year.
- On this day, Jews ignore physical needs, such as eating, to help them to concentrate on spiritual needs, notably forgiveness.
- They spend much time in the synagogue, where they confess their sins to God.
- The ceremonies of Yom Kippur go back to the Torah. The readings describe the Temple ritual of atonement and God's willingness to forgive those who are genuinely sorry.

A) What's New?

On 1 January, many people wish each other 'A Happy New Year'. We may well wonder, however, just what is new about it. The day may not feel very different from 31 December. It is, after all, just a date, a way of marking the years. Sometimes we try to make the New Year different by making New Year resolutions, for example, to work harder. Whether we keep these resolutions usually depends on how serious we are about them.

So far as Jews are concerned, the New Year begins on 1 Tishrei. Though they count Nisan as the first month of the year, the time when the Exodus took place, they regard Tishrei as beginning a new calendar year. Leviticus 23:24 speaks of 'a day of solemn rest, a memorial proclaimed with blast of trumpets' in 'the seventh month, on the first day of the month'. Counting Nisan as the first month, this brings us to Tishrei. It is, however, not the Bible but the Talmud that calls this day the New Year. The rabbis believed that the world was created on this day and so called it Rosh Hashanah, literally the 'Head of the Year'.

Rosh Hashanah is then, by Jewish reckoning, the birthday of the world. Attention is, therefore, directed to God as creator. More particularly, Rosh Hashanah is celebrated as the birthday of the human race. So it is relationships, of people with God and with each other, that come under scrutiny at this festival. New Year resolutions are not considered an optional extra for Jews. Rather they are required by a God who makes ethical demands on his people.

B)   A New Start

Jews believe that God gives human beings free will, that is, we are free to choose how we live. God says:

> See, I have set before you this day life and good, death and evil . . . choose life.
> (Deuteronomy 30:15,19)

But Jews also believe that choosing the good is quite a struggle. It can at times be a real battle as we try to do what is right. Sometimes this battle is lost and we are left feeling disappointed and unhappy with ourselves. Then is the time, Jews believe, to confess what we have done wrong and to ask for God's forgiveness.

This involves repentance. The Hebrew for repentance is **teshuvah** which literally means 'returning'. The returning is to God and his will. Human nature being what it is, this returning often takes great effort.

You perhaps know the series of jokes about changing light bulbs. One of these jokes makes an important point. It goes: 'How many psychotherapists does it take to change a light bulb?' The answer is: 'Only one, but the light bulb has really got to want to change.' Teshuvah, repentance, means really wanting to change. It must involve an inner honesty. You know that if someone apologises to you, it only means something if you know he or she means it. If not, then there is no point in saying sorry. In the same way, Jews believe, it is no good asking for God's forgiveness if you do not really regret what you have done.

C)   The Sound of Repentance

Jews believe that it is possible to have a change of heart at any time, as God is always willing to accept genuine repentance. Nonetheless, they think that, as the New Year approaches, they should make a special effort to take stock of how they think, speak, and act.

Every morning (except Shabbat) in the month leading up to Rosh Hashanah, a shofar (ram's horn) is sounded. This is meant to arouse soul-searching and repentance. For a few days at the end of the month of Ellul, special prayers of penitence, that is, prayers expressing sorrow, are said early in the morning.

Blowing the shofar.

The Torah speaks in various places of blowing trumpets on the first day of the seventh month (e.g. Leviticus 23:24; Numbers 29:1). There are many suggestions as to why the shofar should have been chosen as the instrument to summon repentance. In the Bible, it represents God as the ruler of history who reveals himself at Sinai (Exodus 19:16) and will gather all nations on judgement day (Isaiah 27:13). Perhaps the explanation lies simply in the sort of sound produced by the shofar. It has a primitive quality to it, exciting and stirring. Maimonides suggested that it may alert those who are spiritually asleep.

On Rosh Hashanah itself, the blowing of the shofar is the central feature of the morning service in the synagogue. There are very specific instructions about just how and when it is to be blown. The main thing to notice is that there are three different types of blast: a single, long note; three shorter notes; and nine very short notes. Each type of blast has a different significance; for instance, the long note calls for attention and a march in a new direction. In general, however, the sound of the shofar suggests the crying of the penitent. This is not just remorse, that is, feeling bad about wrongs committed, but also the desire to be reunited with God. It is rather like the longing to make up with someone you care about and yet have hurt.

D) Customs of Rosh Hashanah

In addition to the mitzvot to hear the shofar and to refrain from work, Rosh Hashanah has a number of customs. These combine the joy and solemnity of the festival by celebrating the arrival of a new year with its opportunities, while remembering the need to cast off the old with its mistakes.

In the home, Rosh Hashanah is welcomed, like every festival, with Kiddush. Afterwards, it is customary to eat food containing honey, such as cake, biscuits, or apples dipped in honey. The hope is expressed that the new year will be a sweet one. Whether it is or not will, of course, depend not just on circumstances, but on how each individual behaves. The hope that good deeds will abound in the coming year is also expressed as this meal by eating fish, which are found in shoals, or pomegranates, which have numerous seeds.

The customary greeting on the eve of Rosh Hashanah is 'May you be inscribed for a good year.' The idea is that God has a Book of Life in which he records the quality of people's lives. What he records and what the new year will bring depends on the past year and on what resolve for improvement takes place in people between Rosh Hashanah and Yom Kippur. The Book of Life is said to be sealed on Yom Kippur. These days are truly days of awe, as they encourage a reverence for God and what he asks of people.

'May you be inscribed for a good year.' The greeting in the card often also wishes well over the fast. Which fast is this?

Tashlich (casting away).

After the afternoon service in the synagogue on the first day (unless this falls on Shabbat, then on the second day), Rosh Hashanah is often marked by the custom of **Tashlich**. Tashlich means 'casting away'. Some Jews feel that it helps to make a physical demonstration of casting away all that is bad about their lives. They do this by going to a stream, river, or sea and reciting a verse from the prophet Micah about God casting 'all their sins into the depths of the sea' (Micah 7:19). Look up this passage and notice the stress on God's forgiveness in the previous verse.

E)   The Ten Days of Returning

Rosh Hashanah marks not the end of a period of repentance but the beginning. The holiest day in the Jewish Year, Yom Kippur, is yet to come. The ten days from Rosh Hashanah to Yom Kippur are called the Ten Days of Returning or Penitence (Teshuvah). Before Yom Kippur, people are given time to examine themselves, so that on that day their confession will be full and heartfelt.

These Ten Days include the Fast of Gedaliah (see Chapter 16) and **Shabbat Shuvah**, the 'Sabbath of Returning'. On Shabbat Shuvah, Hosea 14 is read. Read this chapter and suggest why it is particularly appropriate to the occasion.

F)   Final Preparations

On the eve of Yom Kippur, final preparations are made for the day itself. Some families give special donations to charity. We have seen in Chapter 18 that a concern for the poor is part of Judaism. Giving money to the poor on this occasion has, however, an additional significance. In the time of the Temple, there was a ceremony in which the people's sins were thought to be carried away. At the heart of this ceremony was a goat, driven out of Jerusalem into the wilderness. The goat was thought to carry the sins of the people. After the destruction of the Temple, the custom developed of slaughtering a chicken instead and giving it to the poor for the festive meal held before Yom Kippur. Some very Orthodox Jews still do this, but most give not a chicken but money instead. The ancient idea is remembered as people recognise that they have done wrong and need to make amends.

THE GOAT SHALL BEAR ALL THEIR INIQUITIES UPON HIM TO A SOLITARY LAND.

Some men go to the mikveh (see Chapter 10) on the eve of Yom Kippur, as a sign of spiritual cleansing. In preparation for the evening prayers, many men put on a white kittel over their clothes. Sometimes women and girls also wear garments with white in them. White predominates in the synagogue throughout the Ten Days from Rosh Hashanah. This is seen in the dress of the rabbi and cantor and in the curtains of the Ark. White symbolises purity and festivity.

One mark of a festival is a special meal. This is held on the eve of Yom Kippur since Yom Kippur itself is a fast day and so cannot include any food or drink. It may seem odd to fast on a festival, but the point of the fast is not to punish yourself by making yourself miserable. The aim is to take your mind off physical needs and concentrate on the spiritual.

Linked to this aim are the ideas that fasting can express sincerity in the desire for forgiveness: it can encourage self-discipline, much needed if the New Year resolutions are to be kept; and it can encourage compassion. Fasting is not then an end in itself but a way of fulfilling the purpose of Yom Kippur. The Talmud also forbids sexual intercourse, anointing (washing), and the wearing of leather shoes (a sign of comfort) on Yom Kippur. This is in fulfilment of Leviticus 23:27 which reads:

On the tenth day of this seventh month is the day of atonement . . . and you shall afflict yourselves.

G) Atonement through Confession

This passage in Leviticus gives the authority and the name for Yom Kippur. Yom is the Hebrew for 'Day' and Kippur the Hebrew for 'Atonement'. In the Talmud, the Day of Atonement is called *The* Day. By this the rabbis mean that it is the most important day in the Jewish Year. It is what the entire High Holy Day period has been leading up to. It is the day when people seek to be at one with God by confessing their sins.

In order to make this confession, Jews gather in the synagogue. Before the evening service begins, a special prayer is chanted. This is called **Kol Nidrei**, which means 'All our vows'. This prayer calls upon God to cancel all vows which have not been fulfilled. Judaism is very clear that God cannot forgive you any sin against someone else if you have not tried to put things right yourself. This prayer cannot then be used to cancel commitments which Jews have simply failed to fulfil. The vows that are cancelled are ones that they could not be expected to keep. The clearest example of such vows comes from the time of the Spanish Inquisition, when Jews were required to swear allegiance to the Christian Church to avoid persecution. The Kol Nidrei prayer enabled such Jews still to worship God without feeling that they had denied him. The ancient tune used for this prayer is sad and

haunting and so calls to mind the difficulties which Jews have often faced in keeping their religion.

The opening of Kol Nidrei. Judah the Pious said: *'Chant your supplications to God in a melody that makes the heart weep, and your praises of Him in one that will make it sing. Thus you will be filled with love and joy for Him that seeth the heart.'*

Once the confession begins, no allowance is made. Attention is firmly fixed on the responsibility of each Jew as a member of the Jewish people to keep certain ethical demands. *The Authorised Daily Prayer Book* contains two prayers of confession. Both, like most Jewish prayers, use the plural, 'we', throughout. The shorter one begins:

We are guilt-laden: we have been faithless, we have robbed, and we have spoken basely.

The longer confession lists 44 sins, such as violence, deliberate lying, and tale-bearing. It is not that every person present will have committed all 44 sins. Rather, no one is singled out as specially sinful. Each person can, during the confession, ask forgiveness for his particular sins, while remembering that he shares the sorrow and, sometimes the consequences, of other people's sins.

H) 'The Day' in the Synagogue

Yom Kippur continues in the synagogue the morning after the Kol Nidrei service with the shacharit and then the musaf, the additional service for festivals (see Chapter 14). The Torah reading is Leviticus 16 which, as we have seen, gives the command for keeping Yom Kippur. It also gives the details of the ancient Temple ritual involving the goat carrying the people's sins. The ritual is dramatic and vivid. Even though there is today no Temple, the musaf takes the congregation through the ancient ceremonies of Yom Kippur as outlined in the Talmud. The aim of the service, as of old, is to release people from feeling guilty for the past so that they can feel free to start again.

Many people make a special effort to attend synagogue on Yom Kippur, often staying for most of the day. During the minchah (afternoon service), Leviticus 18 is read and then the Book of Jonah. If you read Jonah you will see how the book emphasises the need for repentance, the dominant theme of the Days of Awe.

Extension Section

i)   Read the whole of Ezekiel 18 and then indicate which of the following points is made by the chapter:

a)   Committing adultery offends God.
b)   Worshipping other gods (idols) is not an important sin.
c)   We suffer for what others have done.
d)   It is never too late to repent.
e)   God wants to get his own back on people.
f)   Bad children always have bad parents.
g)   Whether or not we lead a good life is up to us.
h)   God is fair in his judgements.

Which of the above points, not made by Ezekiel, do you think may also be true?

ii)   During the morning service on Yom Kippur, Isaiah 57:14–58:14 is read. Read this passage and indicate which part makes the point that fasting must be accompanied by justice and kindness.

There is at the end of Yom Kippur a further service. This service, held only on this occasion, is called **Neilah**. This means 'the closing'. In ancient times, prayer would be offered as the Temple gates closed. The Neilah service has grown from this and the thought is now of the closing of the heavenly gates, the gates of God's judgement. The gates, open for repentance, are symbolised by the door of the Ark being open throughout the Neilah service. Words recited during the service challenge the congregation with the whole point of Yom Kippur:

Have I any pleasure in the death of the wicked, says the Lord God, and not rather that he should turn from his way, and live?

(Ezekiel 18:23)

I)   Final Marks of Yom Kippur

A single blast of the shofar announces the end of the 25-hour fast. At home, Havdalah is performed and the fast broken. Some people break the fast by beginning to build a sukkah. Sukkot is the next festival after Yom Kippur. By this immediate preparation to keep the mitzvah of Sukkot, Jews are expressing the essence of their faith: God has given them mitzvot by which to live.

Questions

A Matter of Fact

1   From which biblical passage do Jews take the command for 'a memorial proclaimed with blast of trumpets'? (A)

2   What special prayers are said in the month of Ellul? (C)

3 What is the customary greeting on Rosh Hashanah? (D)

4 What is the Book of Life? (D)

5 How many different sorts of sound are made by the shofar? (D)

6 What sweet substance is often eaten on Rosh Hashanah? (D)

7 What might men do as a sign of cleansing? (F)

8 What do the rabbis call 'The Day'? (G)

9 When is the Kol Nidrei prayer recited? (G)

10 What are the opening words of the shorter prayer of confession on Yom Kippur? (G)

Vocabulary

Give the Hebrew words for the following:

1 The New Year (literally the 'Head of the Year') (A)

2 returning (B)

3 ram's horn (C)

4 casting away (D)

5 Sabbath of Returning (E)

6 Atonement (G)

7 All our vows (G)

8 the closing (H)

A Question of Understanding

Try to give at least two religious explanations in answer to each of the following questions.

1 Why is the shofar sounded on Rosh Hashanah? (C)

2 Why might Jews go to a stream, river, or sea on the afternoon of Rosh Hashanah? (D)

3 Why might a contribution be made to charity on the eve of Yom Kippur? (F)

4 Though your sins are like scarlet;
they shall be as white as snow;
though they are red like crimson,
they shall become like wool.   (Isaiah 1:18)

How is this symbolised in the synagogue on Yom Kippur? (F)

5 Why is food not eaten on the festival of Yom Kippur? (F)

6 Why is the Ark left open throughout the Neilah service? (H)

Over to You

Answer these questions fully, giving your reasons, and stating arguments both for and against where appropriate.

1 Why do you think Rosh Hashanah and Yom Kippur are called the High Holy Days? Do you think that it is better or worse to attend synagogue only on these days than never at all?

2 Do you think that all sins are equally serious? Does it matter, for instance, how many people are affected and what your intentions were?

3 'It doesn't matter what you do. God always forgives.' What reply might someone who takes Yom Kippur seriously give to this?

4 'Judaism can be understood only as it is lived.' How far do you think this is true?

Assignment

Design a greeting card for Rosh Hashanah. Design it carefully so that:

a) it shows what happens during the festival;

b) it suggests the meaning behind it;

c) it expresses typical Jewish feelings about the festival.

Useful Addresses

Anglo–Israel Association,
9 Bentinck Street, London W1M 5RP

Board of Deputies of British Jews (Education Officer, Central Jewish Lecture and Information Committee, the Jewish Museum, and JMC Workshop),
Woburn House, Upper Woburn Place, London WC1H 0EP

Centre for the Study of Judaism and Jewish–Christian Relations,
Selly Oak Colleges, Bristol Road, Birmingham B29 6LQ

Council of Christians and Jews,
1 Dennington Park Road, London NW6 1AX

CTVC Films/Video Library,
Beeson's Yard, Bury Lane, Rickmansworth, Herts WD3 1DS

Holocaust Educational Trust,
BCM Box 7892, London WC1N 3XX

(JEB) Jewish Education Bureau,
8 Westcombe Avenue, Leeds LS8 2BS
and Sacred Trinity Centre, Chapel Street, Salford M3 7AJ

(JMD) Jewish Music Distribution,
PO Box 2268, Hendon, London NW4 3UW

Jewish National Fund Education Department,
Harold Poster House, Kingsbury Circle, London NW9 9SP

Manchester Jewish Museum,
190 Cheetham Hill Road, Manchester M8 8LW

(RMEP) Religious and Moral Education Press,
Hennock Road, Exeter, Devon EX2 8RP

Slide Centre,
Ilton, Ilminster, Somerset TA19 9HS

Spiro Institute for the Study of Jewish History and Culture,
Westfield College, Kidderpore Avenue, London NW3 7ST

Sternberg Centre (RSGB, Centre for Jewish Education and London Museum of Jewish Life), Manor House, 80 East End Road, London N3 2SY

Stylus,
21 Commercial Way, Abbey Road Industrial Park, Park Royal, London NW10 7XE

(ULPS) Union of Liberal and Progressive Synagogues,
12 Clipstone Street, London W1P 7DG

Yakar Educational Foundation,
2 Egerton Gardens, London NW4 4BA

Hebrew Word List

Most of the words in this list are Hebrew (a few are Aramaic or Yiddish), the language of Jewish written works and the official language of Israel. Variations of spelling occur in many of these words. This is because the Hebrew alphabet has had to be transliterated into our own. Where a word involves 'Ch', this should be pronounced rather like the 'ch' in the Scottish word 'loch'. (You will often see these words spelt with 'h' in place of 'ch', e.g. **Hasid** instead of **Chasid**). Notice also that to make a Hebrew word plural, you do not add 's', but the ending 'im', e.g. **kibbutz**, **kibbutzim** or 'ot', e.g. **mitzvah**, **mitzvot**. The meaning of the word in Judaism is what is most important and this is given first. The literal translation is then given where this is particularly helpful in understanding the meaning.

Adar   12th month of Jewish Calendar.
Adonai   Lord.
Aggadah   narrative portions of Talmud and Midrash; story, telling.
Agunah   (Aramaic) a woman's state of being considered married when her husband has disappeared; anchored.
Alenu   concluding prayer of synagogue service; It is upon us.
Aliyah   going up to read Torah, emigration to Israel; going up.
Amidah   an important Jewish prayer; standing.
Arba Minim   The Four Species used at Festival of Tabernacles (e.g. willow).
Aron Hakodesh   part of synagogue containing Torah scrolls; Holy Ark.
Ashkenaz   Germany.

Askenazim   Western Jews.
Av   5th month of Jewish Calendar.

Bar Mitzvah   boy who has reached adulthood (13 years); son of the commandment.
Bat Chayil   ceremony for girl of 12 years; daughter of worth.
Bat Mitzvah   girl who has reached adulthood (12 years); daughter of the commandment.
Berachah (plural **Berachot**)   blessing.
Baruch Atah   Blessed art Thou.
Bet Din   Rabbinical court; house of law.
Bet Haknesset   synagogue; house of assembly.
Bet Hatephilah   synagogue; house of prayer.
Bimah   platform in synagogue from where Torah read.
Brit Milah   covenant of circumcision.

Capel   (Yiddish) skull-cap.
Challah (plural **Challot**)   special loaf used on Sabbaths and festivals.
Chametz   anything leavened, especially bread; soured.
Chanukah   8 day festival; dedication.
Chanukiah   Chanukah Menorah, nine-branched candlestick.
Charoset   mixture of apples, wine, cinnamon, nuts eaten during the Passover meal.
Chasid (plural **Chasidim**)   a member of the Chasidic movement; pious.
Chazan   cantor, person who leads the prayers in the synagogue.
Chevra Kaddisha   (Aramaic), burial society; sacred society.
Chukim   statutes, laws for which no reason is given.
Chupah   marriage canopy.
Cohen   descendant of priestly family; priest.

Dreidle (Yiddish) spinning top.

Ellul 6th month of Jewish Calendar.
Eretz Yisrael the land of Israel.
Etrog citron.

Gabbai synagogue warden.
Gaon (plural **Gaonim**) head of Babylonian academy; excellency.
Gemara (Aramaic) combined with Mishnah to form Talmud; completion.
Genizah storage place for disused scrolls and books.
Get Divorce contract.
Greggers (Yiddish) rattles.

Haftarah synagogue reading from the Prophets; conclusion.
Haggadah (plural **Haggadot**) book read during the Passover meal; telling.
Halachah Jewish Law; way, going.
Hallel Psalms 113–118; praise.
Haskalah Jewish Enlightenment Movement.
Havdalah ceremony at end of Sabbath and festivals; division.
Heichal Sefardi name for Holy Ark; sanctuary.
Hoshanah Hosanna; save us.
Hoshanah Rabbah The Great Hosanna.

Iyar 2nd month of Jewish Calendar.

Kabbalah Jewish mysticism.
Kaddish prayer said by mourner; sanctified.
Kavanah direction, devotion.
Kasher permitted food; right, fit.
Kashrut food laws.
Kedoshim Jewish martyrs; holy ones.
Ketubah marriage contract.
Ketuvim Writings (3rd section of Hebrew Bible).
Kibbutz (plural **Kibbutzim**) communal settlement in Israel; a gathering together.
Kiddush blessing recited over wine; sanctifying, hallowing.
Kiddushin marriage; sanctification.
Kiddush Hashem martyrdom; sanctifying the name of God.
Kippah skull-cap.
Kislev 9th month of Jewish Calendar.
Kittel plain white garment worn by Jewish men on Day of Atonement.
Kol Nidrei prayer on eve of Day of Atonement; All our vows.

Lag B'omer 33rd day of counting the Omer.
Lulav palm branch.

Maariv evening service.
Machsor festival prayer book; cycle.
Magen David six-pointed star; shield of David.
Mappah comments on Shulchan Aruch; tablecloth.
Mashiach Messiah; anointed.
Masorah tradition.
Matzah (plural **Matzot**) unleavened bread.
Megillah (plural **Megillot**) biblical book of Esther; scroll.
Menorah seven-branched candlestick.
Mezuzah (plural **mezuzot**) parchment scroll fixed to right hand doorpost; doorpost.
Midrash (plural **Midrashim**) interpretation, a book of interpretation; searching, rooting out.
Midrash Rabbah the Great Midrash, the title of a particular book of Midrash.
Mikveh (plural **Mikvaot**) immersion pool; a gathering (of water).
Minchah afternoon service.
Minyan 10 adult (over 13 years) males (number required for saying certain prayers).
Mishnah the Oral Law; repetition, learning.
Mishneh Torah Law Code by Maimonides.
Mishpatim laws for which reason is clear; judgements.
Mitnagdim opponents of Chasidic movement.
Mitzvah (plural **mitzvot**) obligation, commandment.
Mohel one who performs circumcision.
Musaf the additional service.

Neilah concluding service on Day of Atonement; closing.
Ner Tamid light kept burning in synagogue; continual light.
Neviim Prophets (2nd section of Hebrew Bible).
Niddah woman who is menstruating; separated.
Nisan 1st month of Jewish Calendar.

Omer measurement of barley.

Parev (or **Parve**) food neither milk nor meat; neutral.
Pesach Passover.
Pidyon Haben redemption of the son (first-born).
Purim festival of Esther; lots.

Rabbi (Chasidic **Rebbe**) spiritual leader of Jewish community; my master.

Rimmonim silver ornaments used to decorate Torah scroll.

Rosh Chodesh New Moon; head of the month.

Rosh Hashanah Jewish New Year; head of the year.

Sandek person who holds baby at circumcision; representative.

Seder Passover meal; order (of service).

Sefarad Spain.

Sefardim oriental Jews.

Sefer Torah Torah scroll; Book of the Torah.

Shabbat (Yiddish **Shabbos**) Sabbath; rest.

Shabbat Shalom a Sabbath greeting; Peaceful Sabbath.

Shabbat Shuvah Sabbath during the Ten Days of Repentance; Sabbath of Returning.

Shacharit morning service.

Shalom hello, goodbye; peace.

Shamash synagogue attendant, candle for lighting Chanukah lights; servant.

Shavuot festival of Pentecost; Weeks.

Shechitah the Jewish method of slaughtering animals.

Shema Jewish prayer declaring oneness of God; Hear.

Sheloshim the 30 day period after funeral; 30.

Shemini Atzeret 8th day of assembly, festival after Sukkot.

Shevat 11th month of Jewish Calendar.

Shiva the seven day period after funeral; seven.

Shoah Holocaust; whirlwind.

Shochet slaughterer of animals.

Shofar ram's horn.

Shtetls (Yiddish) small towns.

Shul (Yiddish) synagogue.

Shulchan Aruch Law Code by Joseph Caro; Prepared Table.

Sidra (plural **Sidrot**) portion of Torah read in synagogue.

Siddur prayer book; order (of prayer).

Simchat Torah Rejoicing of the Law.

Sofer scribe.

Sukkah (plural **Sukkot**) hut, booth, tabernacle.

Sukkot Festival of Tabernacles.

Tallit prayer shawl.

Tallit Katan (commonly called **tzizit**) small tallit.

Talmud collection of Jewish law and story, combining Mishnah and Gemara; learning.

Tammuz 4th month of Jewish Calendar.

Tanna (plural **Tannaim**) teacher of 1st/2nd century CE.

Tannach (also **Tenakh**) Hebrew Bible.

Targum Aramaic translation of the Bible.

Tashlich prayer said at Jewish New Year; casting away.

Tephilah prayer.

Tephilin leather boxes containing biblical passages worn during morning prayers (phylacteries).

Teshuvah repentance; returning.

Tevet 10th month of Jewish Calendar.

Tishah B'Av 9th of Av, fast day.

Tishrei 7th month of Jewish Calendar.

Torah 1st section of Hebrew Bible, whole Bible, entire Jewish Law; teaching, direction.

Tosefta collection of rabbinic teachings similar to the Mishnah; addition.

Trefah forbidden food; torn.

Tu B'Shevat 15th Shevat, New Year for Trees.

Tzizit tassels at each corner of tallit, tallit katan; fringes.

Yad pointer for Torah scroll; hand.

Yad Vashem monument.

Yarmulkah skull-cap.

Yarzheit (Yiddish) anniversary of a death; year's time.

Yeshivah (plural **Yeshivot**) college for study of Talmud.

Yigdal hymn expressing main Jewish beliefs.

Yom Haatzmaut Israel's Independence Day.

Yom Hashoah Holocaust Remembrance Day.

Yom Kippur Day of Atonement.

Yom Tov major festival.

Yom Yerushalayim Jerusalem Day.

Zaddik (plural **zaddikim**) Chasidic leader; righteous one.

Index